# GAME DESIGN

## ESSENTIALS

# GAME DESIGN
## *ESSENTIALS*

Briar Lee Mitchell

WILEY

John Wiley & Sons, Inc.

Acquisitions Editor: Mariann Barsolo
Development Editor: Sara Barry
Technical Editor: James Haldy
Production Editor: Christine O'Connor
Copy Editor: Tiffany Taylor
Editorial Manager: Pete Gaughan
Production Manager: Tim Tate
Vice President and Executive Group Publisher: Richard Swadley
Vice President and Publisher: Neil Edde
Book Designer: Happenstance Type-O-Rama
Compositor: Craig Johnson, Happenstance Type-O-Rama
Proofreaders: Louise Watson and Scott Klemp, Word One New York
Indexer: Robert Swanson
Project Coordinator, Cover: Katherine Crocker
Cover Designer: Ryan Sneed

Copyright © 2012 by John Wiley & Sons, Inc., Indianapolis, Indiana
Published simultaneously in Canada
ISBN: 978-1-118-15927-9  (pbk.)
ISBN: 978-1-118-22609-4 (ebk.)
ISBN: 978-1-118-23933-9 (ebk.)
ISBN: 978-1-118-26407-2 (ebk.)

For general information on our other products and services or to obtain technical support, please contact our Customer Care Department within the U.S. at (877) 762-2974, outside the U.S. at (317) 572-3993 or fax (317) 572-4002.

Wiley publishes in a variety of print and electronic formats and by print-on-demand. Some material included with standard print versions of this book may not be included in e-books or in print-on-demand. If this book refers to media such as a CD or DVD that is not included in the version you purchased, you may download this material at http://booksupport.wiley.com. For more information about Wiley products, visit www.wiley.com.

Library of Congress Control Number: 2011945558

10 9 8 7 6 5 4 3 2 1

# Dear Reader,

Thank you for choosing *Game Design Essentials.* This book is part of a family of premium-quality Sybex books, all of which are written by outstanding authors who combine practical experience with a gift for teaching.

Sybex was founded in 1976. More than 30 years later, we're still committed to producing consistently exceptional books. With each of our titles, we're working hard to set a new standard for the industry. From the paper we print on, to the authors we work with, our goal is to bring you the best books available.

I hope you see all that reflected in these pages. I'd be very interested to hear your comments and get your feedback on how we're doing. Feel free to let me know what you think about this or any other Sybex book by sending me an email at nedde@wiley.com. If you think you've found a technical error in this book, please visit http://sybex.custhelp.com. Customer feedback is critical to our efforts at Sybex.

Best regards,

Neil Edde
Vice President and Publisher
Sybex, an Imprint of Wiley

*for Richard and Adam*

# ACKNOWLEDGMENTS

*I would like to* express my sincere gratitude to the professional team at Sybex (an imprint of Wiley) for all their hard work. Writing a book is a huge undertaking, but I was not alone and had an amazing group of people who helped shepherd it to you.

Thank you to the terrific team who worked with me: Mariann Barsolo, Sara Barry, Pete Gaughan, Jim Haldy, Christine O'Connor, and Tiffany Taylor. Their professionalism and skills were instrumental in producing this book, and I'm grateful for their enthusiasm and support.

My partners in Star Mountain Studios, Richard and Adam (who truly lives in the secret cow level), are my friends and fellow game makers. They were a constant source of information and guidance with the research and writing of this book. I so enjoy making games with them, and I look forward to making many more. My friend Jack Keely, an amazing illustrator and author, has been a tremendous supporter of this endeavor as well, always there at the right time with the right comment or cartoon to keep things fun and focused.

A special thank you to my parents, Gerry and Steph—according to them, I can do no wrong.

# ABOUT THE AUTHOR

*Briar Lee Mitchell, MA,* runs Star Mountain Studios, www.starmountainstudios
.com, a successful gaming company, with her partners, Richard Sternberg and
Adam Ryan. They produced an online video game with Joe Perry of Aerosmith,
*Genie Joe and the Axeman*, and *Apparitions* with Jason Hawes and Grant Wilson,
the Ghost Hunters and founders of The Atlantic Paranormal Society (TAPS).

Briar is also on the faculty at the Art Institute, teaching game art, animation,
and VFX techniques for TV, film, and games.

Briar began work as an illustrator in 1977 and has degrees from the University
of Toledo (Ohio, BA in art) and the University of California, San Francisco (MA in
medical and biological illustration).

She worked in conjunction with Lucasfilm on the very first interactive videodisc
for the Smithsonian, titled *The Life and Times of Albert Einstein*. The videodisc
and a portrait she painted of Albert Einstein are still at the Smithsonian.

Briar joined the Society of Illustrators of Los Angeles (SILA) in 1992 and
served as president for two years. Through her association with SILA, she
became a member of the Air Force Art Program; she traveled around the world
with the Air Force to document its work in paintings that have been inducted
into the National Archives in Washington, DC. Her travels have taken her to

Asia, the South Pacific, New Zealand, and as far away as McMurdo Station at the South Pole along with noted director/producer James Cameron.

You can view Briar's work for environments at www.paisleyshark.com and her medical/forensic work at www.medicalart-briarlee.com. You can contact Briar at briarlee@aol.com.

In the photo with Briar is Bardy, an amazing Labrador who is her partner in K9 Search and Rescue.

# CONTENTS AT A GLANCE

# Contents

**CHAPTER 5**     **Detailed Development of Visuals**     **111**

**CHAPTER 6**     **Navigation and Interfaces**     **139**

## APPENDIX A    Answers to Review Questions    249

## APPENDIX B    Education, Training, and Working in Games    255

# INTRODUCTION

*We have played games* for thousands of years, to learn how to improve military skills, increase math and business abilities, learn new talents, sharpen old ones, and just have fun. Games are an integral part of being human, and there seems to be a game to fit each of our many different interests. Games have evolved right along with humans, and their development has been influenced strongly by culture and technology.

The gaming experience changed remarkably with the introduction of video games in the 1960s and 1970s, when intrepid inventors built them and made them available for everyone to enjoy. As technology has bloomed and the Internet has radically changed everyone's life, the growth of games, with their inventive use of this technology, continues to enthrall gamers in ever-increasing numbers.

Faster animation, more detailed graphics, and advanced sophistication in sound contribute to creating gameplay that is intriguing, compelling, and addictive. Consumers are spending more money and time on games, whether on a console, their home computer, or a mobile device or phone. There is no abatement in the desire to play, which means opportunities for those of us who love both playing and creating games.

Game makers have evolved to embrace the constantly improving technology to bring us more sophisticated and compelling games to play. Their efforts appear seamless to the gamer, but the work behind the scenes requires a huge array of skills and teamwork.

I hope this book will be an inspiration to those of you on the starting line of finding your way into the intriguing world of making games.

## Who Should Read This Book

This book is for people who are interested in computer games and what goes into making them, folks who might want to segue into this field, and students in game art.

## What You Will Learn

You'll gain a great understanding of how games are made and the importance of gameplay style. You'll get practical advice on creating characters, props, environments, and interfaces. The book also provides practice working with visuals, audio, navigation, and interfaces. Throughout, you'll learn to keep gameplay at the forefront, which is what any successful game maker does.

In addition to learning about making games, you'll learn a great deal about the industry. When you finish this book, you'll know more about the roles and pipelines involved in the production of games and be able to refine your own ideas about what you want to do in the industry.

If you have an interest in making games or working in the industry and you just aren't sure where to start, there is a lot of information here to help you understand how games are made, who does what during production, and methods for distributing and marketing games.

## Reader Requirements

If you have an interest in computer games, enjoy playing them, and might like to make them, those are all the requirements you need.

# What Is Covered in This Book

*Game Design Essentials* is written to help people who have an interest in creating games and may wish to segue into this field, and for students already in school. The book's web page is located at www.sybex.com/go/gamedesignessentials, where you can download files mentioned in the book and additional documents.

**Chapter 1: Game Design Origins**   In order to understand how games are designed and created today, you'll examine their historical origins. This chapter includes a look at some of the earliest games known to man and how their design and gameplay are apparent in modern productions.

**Chapter 2: Gameplay Styles**   This chapter examines what gameplay styles are and how important they are to a successful product. Too often, new game makers focus on the look of the game, when in fact the most important component of a successful game is gameplay. You'll study elements that make up good gameplay and review the major categories of gameplay style.

**Chapter 3: Core Game Design Concepts**   This chapter walks through the first steps of writing a game and takes you from concept to script to Game Design Document to pitch. You'll learn how to prepare the synopsis, establish the goals, and write a logline. Chapter 3 covers essential information about describing the look and functionality of characters, props, and environments and about creating lore.

**Chapter 4: Visual Design**   This chapter covers the basics of how to begin designing characters, props, environments, and interfaces from concept to finished art. Information provided includes methods for working on original work, how to find inspiration, and the impact gameplay style and demographics have on designing visuals for a game.

**Chapter 5: Detailed Development of Visuals**   Chapter 4 discussed some of the initial visuals created for a game. This chapter provides more detailed descriptions for creating 3D models, color, texture, and lighting. In addition, the chapter provides an overview of design graphics.

**Chapter 6: Navigation and Interfaces**   Navigation, when referencing game design, deals with how the player can move through a game. This includes adjusting visuals and sound, where to find interactive elements in the game, and how to move about the world being created. An interface is what allows a gamer to interact with the game. This chapter examines some of the types of interfaces typical to games, including diegetic and non-diegetic.

**Chapter 7: Designing Levels and the Game Design Document**   The levels reviewed in this chapter have to do with where the player is in the game world, and what they experience while they are there. You'll learn how to plot out a physical area for a game and then understand how game makers plan events. The Game Design Document (GDD) is a written tome that game makers create, which contains everything related to the game from initial log line to the full, finished list of assets that have been or need to be created for the project.

**Chapter 8: Sound**   Sound for games helps to define the mood for the project and can telegraph changes in the gameplay. The chapter explains how musical scores are created and describes the methods audio designers use to create sound effects.

**Chapter 9: Job Descriptions, Game Tracking, and Legal Issues**   This chapter reviews a variety of jobs and their duties, along with how they relate to large versus small productions. In addition, game pipelines and how they work with regard to tracking a production are discussed. The chapter also covers legal issues related to game production and game marketing, such as trademarks, copyright, and standards.

**Chapter 10: Distribution and Marketing**   Game sales have increased tremendously over the past few years, surpassing even the feature film industry. As methods for playing games through the Internet, home computer systems, and so on have increased, so have the methods for marketing games. This chapter looks at some of those unique methods, such as in-game advertising and advergames.

**Appendix A**    This appendix contains the answers to the review questions from each chapter.

**Appendix B**    This appendix is about getting started in the field. It provides information on education, internships, entry-level positions, and a wealth of resources for networking and staying current. The appendix also provides detailed information about preparing a flatbook, a reel, and other materials you may need as you apply for jobs and internships.

**Appendix C**    This appendix contains an excerpt from the Game Design Document (GDD) for *Red Harvest* from Bedlam Games. This excerpt shows you the kind of information and the level of detail found in a GDD.

# CHAPTER 1

# Game Design Origins

*In order to understand* how game design has evolved, let's take a look back at their origins, to get some insight into how games today are planned and executed. Looking beyond your own knowledge base is the core of learning, and that is what this book is aimed at doing—helping you learn how games are designed and made.

There is no doubt that human beings enjoy games. According to Hudson Square Research, game-sale revenue surpassed that of films in the United States in 2005 and became a global phenomenon in 2008, exceeding film sales. Game revenue in 2011 reached $48.9 billion. You can read more at `http://www.videogamesblogger.com/2008/04/09/global-videogame-sales-surpass-movie-industry-in-2008.htm`. Literally thousands of games have been developed and played for millennia, with the oldest known one, *The Royal Game of Ur* (2500 BC), chronicling the start of it all in recorded history. We play games for fun, we play them to learn, and we play them to be competitive.

In this chapter, we'll take a look at how gaming evolved and how many of the core principles are still applicable in today's games.

▶ **What is a game?**

▶ **History: going way back**

▶ **Going electronic**

▶ **And now we are digital**

## What Is a Game?

If we define a *game* as an activity that brings pleasure, that definition is too broad. Many things can bring pleasure, like reading, cooking, or engaging in conversation with a good friend. However, if you combine an activity with a challenge and a set of rules, then you have the basics of what makes a game. The challenge is to reach the end goal—to win—using the game components and the rules for using them.

Some games require elaborate playing pieces and richly constructed environments, either virtual or practical; however, some games can be played verbally or by thinking through the demands of the game to achieve the win. Rhyming games, for example, don't need tangible elements. When I was a child, taking long road trips with my family, my mother sought to distract us from getting bored and unruly by having us play the *I Spy* game. The rules were simple: watch the other cars on the road and try to "spy" as many different license plates as possible, or color or make of car, or just convertibles or motorcycles, and so on.

One of my favorite games that can be played without pieces, *The Six Degrees of Kevin Bacon*, is a trivia game based on the philosophical concept of six degrees of separation. This concept, proposed by Frigyes Karinthy, holds that everyone is linked to everyone one else in the world through a chain of no more than six people. In February 1994, during an interview with *Premiere Magazine*, Bacon commented that he had worked with everyone in Hollywood. The movie *Six Degrees of Separation*, based on Karinthy's premise and the play written by John Guare, debuted around the same time, prompting people to associate Bacon with that phenomenon.

Games can be played individually, one on one, or in groups. Our fascination with games has grown to be a global phenomenon extending beyond traditional board and card games to small and efficient handheld units, personal computers, powerful home-entertainment systems, and the Internet, where millions of gamers can log in with high-speed connections to play everything from simple games of solitaire to massive multiple-player competitions in real time. Figure 1.1 shows one type of competition where gamers come from all over the world to compete with one another in online games that are broadcast on enormous Jumbotrons to fans who come just to watch them play. What is fascinating about this image is that the majority of people at the event are so intrigued with the gameplay that they come just to watch others battle it out. Gaming has become so large in some instances that, as you see in the picture, it has become a spectator sport.

Games are designed to entertain, to teach, and to spark the spirit of competition. As far as entertaining games go, several top sellers vie for the crown of being the most popular, including *Mario Bros., Halo, The Legend of Zelda, Grand Theft Auto,* and *Metroid Prime.* The reigning champ for entertaining games, according to GamePro, is *Windows Solitaire*—the single-player version. This casual game has been played by millions of people.

One remarkable example of an educational game is *Oregon Trail*, dreamed up over 40 years ago by three student teachers in Minnesota. Don Rawitsch, Bill Heinemann, and Paul Dillenberger created the landmark game that traces the 2,000-mile path traveled by pioneers in the old West from Independence, Missouri to Willamette Valley, Oregon.

**FIGURE 1.1** World Cyber Games

For many players, *Oregon Trail* was their introduction to the world of digital games, and it still holds the record for the most sales for an educational game. Fans of the game watched it grow from a small game designed to help students learn history in the Minnesota school system to a game played on multiple platforms today including Windows, iPhone, iPod Touch, and Facebook. Players travel the route, and along the way they must keep track of their resources and deal with many hazards such as bad weather, rough terrain, and poor health. The last of these spawned one of the most popular catch phrases of the game: "You have died of dysentery."

Prestige or financial gain can be associated with how well you do at playing games. People who play online games where scores are tracked compete not only at playing the game but also with each other to see who can achieve the highest score. Gamblers playing games of chance like poker, roulette, and craps can achieve both notoriety and tremendous financial gain—or, in some cases, devastating losses.

In order to understand how and why games came about, it's critical to grasp some of their core principles, such as rules, chance, and the elements used to design them. Understanding some of this background will also shed light on the broad range of game types. Simply trotting out names of games and a brief description of the products won't help you understand why certain games or trends in gaming developed the way they did.

## Why Are There Rules?

To say that a game has *rules* is another way of saying there is a structure to adhere to in order to understand how the player can compete and win. The term *rules* sounds stifling, but in the world of gaming, it's the very framework that allows the player to master the gameplay.

This isn't to say that every single game has rules; however, some people would argue that having rules is one of the definitions of what a game is. Other gamers prefer to design and/or play more freeform games that don't rely on rules. All games must have some sort of *game mechanic* in order to be created, so if you eliminate that as a definition of rules, then technically there are games without rules, and there are games that can be played differently from the intended set of goals laid out by the developers.

Game mechanics are basically the building blocks of the game design. For example, in *World of Warcraft*, mana for spells is a game mechanic. The game uses the concept of mana to define how many spells a player can cast. Combine that with the game mechanic of "spirit" to define how fast a player replenishes their mana. Mechanics and rules are pretty closely entwined. Mechanics tend to be more subtle, behind-the-scenes rules, though they can also be pretty large and noticeable, like games that are turn-based—a turn is a game mechanic to control the amount of action a player can do in a given situation. Games without rules are primarily *sandbox games*, where you're typically given a world and some direction and then set free to do as you will. To allow you to act freely, a lot of variety in game mechanics is built into these games. A term for that is *emergent gameplay*: basically, making the world interactive enough that the player can do things the designers hadn't originally intended.

Designer Will Wright creates games that fall into this sandbox category. Take a look at his creation, *The Sims*, which is essentially an ecology god game. You're given all the tools to affect the makeup of a planet, and you watch how it evolves and what sorts of life forms thrive. Everything in the world, from the buildings to the weather to the beings that inhabit it, is decided on by the player.

Will Wright commented on the way he played *Grand Theft Auto: San Andreas*, explaining that he didn't play the game as the designers intended, which would have involved stealing cars and doing missions to build a criminal empire. He instead played as though his character was a homeless guy wandering around the city and trying to survive.

**FIGURE 1.2** This screenshot from the sandbox game *The Sims 2* shows elements designed and placed by the player into the game world.

You can basically do the same in a game like *Fable* or *Fallout 3*. Rather than play the main story quest lines and go out and fight, you can focus on being a businessperson, traveling from town to town buying and selling. The same emergent gameplay can be found in Blizzard's *World of Warcraft*. There are people who solely play the auction house in the game, buying and selling rare items, instead of following quest lines. That wasn't the intended reason for putting the auction house in the world, but people made it into a game.

Simulators tend to be all mechanic with no given goals. This puts them into a more freeform type of gameplay. There are still game mechanic–related "rules," such as only being able to build things with the items that are provided and only being able to build in a designated area.

Another good example of a game that is entirely mechanic is *Minecraft*. Although you need to do some basic things to survive, the huge appeal is constructing whatever you want, like a cow cannon or a complete replica of the Enterprise. Entire servers of people are working together to build stuff without any direction from the developers.

There are also experimental games like *Night Journey,* which is a freeform game conceived by artist and MacArthur fellow Bill Viola. The game is designed to allow players the opportunity to explore the beautiful worlds based on Viola's art, in an effort to gain enlightenment. This freeform game has been developed at the USC Interactive Media Division.

Games with rules generally come with instructions for how to play. Often, when a player is faced with a long list of rules to learn, they're put off. They don't want to have to read so much just to learn how to have fun. This is similar to the phenomenon of people who buy an expensive piece of equipment and then toss away the manual. They want to turn it on and grasp how to use it just by working with the functions offered by the system; they don't want to have to read and study how to use it.

Game designers often count on the ability of players to intuitively understand how to play their games. For example, some gamers look at a game board, see how it's laid out, and grasp right away how to play. Game designers like to count on the intuition of players, because often, the more instruction provided up front, the less fun tends to be had. In other words, when you design a game, keep in mind that struggling with learning and following a lot of instructions tends to be frustrating.

## GAMES AND INTUITION

Game designers rely on players' intuition to understand how to play games. Intuition associated with games can also come in the form of games that help you improve your intuition, such as trying to guess what is hidden on the game board. For example, the games at The Boundary Institute site, www .gotpsi.org, try to determine whether humans can improve their psychic abilities by playing certain types of games. The site's free online games let you test your psychic ability, and many believe that the more you practice at this form of guessing, the more heightened your psychic abilities become.

Of course, you need to be clear with the instructions; but many designers have learned how to deal with players' intuitive ability by allowing the gamer to turn off tutorials so they can learn how to play the game just by jumping in and then sinking or swimming.

Rules define how to win. They can resolve dilemmas when players come to loggerheads and explain how to break a tie. An interesting phenomenon is associated with games that have rules (which is most of them): if there are rules, then there are ways to break them. In other words, ways to cheat!

# Cheaters?

Cheating in gaming can take two similar but different paths. If you're playing to win, and you don't care about following all the rules, then you can break them and cheat to get what you want. However, cheating can also be a way to get a leg up in the game. For example, if you've been playing a game to get to the next level but can't quite get there, learning a *cheat*, such as how to make your weapon more powerful for a short amount of time—long enough to kill that boss—is another way to bend the rules and advance through the game.

These latter types of cheats, although in the truest sense they let you gain an unfair advantage in the game, can actually add to the fun of the gameplay. A favorite one is the *God Mode* cheat in *Quake*. Using the keyboard, the player types in ~**God**. That allows the player to walk about in the game, invincible. They can be attacked repeatedly without suffering damage or dying and, therefore, finish the level—or they can go look out the window, which they couldn't do before because too many bad guys were in the way.

God Mode started with the company id Software, which programmed it into their *Commander Keen* game, and it has become synonymous with similar abilities in dozens of other games. It allows players to finish certain parts of the game that they might not have been able to complete otherwise and to move around environments that before would have been too hazardous to pass through. Testers often use it to move past certain parts of the game so they can try areas they want to get information about.

In Raven Software's *Jedi Knight II*, a God Mode is built right into the apparent gameplay and doesn't require a coded cheat to access it. In the final boss fight, a beam of energy shines in the center of the room. Players can run through the beam and gain God Mode for a minute.

Other games, like id Software's *Descent*, can detect when God Modes are turned on and reduce the shields that protect the player in the game. Some players enjoy this challenge and access the God Mode for its short duration just to be able to attempt the level with a handicap. The bragging rights associated with winning that way are important to these players.

Many gamers who have already played through a game and wish to replay but scoot through certain, perhaps boring, parts of the game (like fast-forwarding a recorded TV program or movie to get to the good parts) may use cheats to advance to the "more fun" areas of play.

Many websites offer cheat codes, or *walkthroughs*, which can explain how to understand and then master the strategy part of the game. Simply type into any online browser the name of the game followed by *cheat, cheats, cheat codes*, or *walkthroughs* to find them. Walkthroughs may be written instructions or videos showing actual gameplay.

These same walkthroughs can also guide players to find Easter eggs. An *Easter egg* is a wacky device first dreamed up at Atari by designer Warren Robinett. In the game *Adventure* (credited as being the first action/adventure game, released in 1979), a player might stumble upon a hidden message in the game, which was actually Warren's name. Although Easter eggs don't necessarily help a player win a game, finding them tends to be a unique achievement for many players. Entire websites, such as www.eeggs.com, are devoted to talking about them.

Occasionally, an Easter egg can help a player find a hidden area in the game to play a secret level or find a hidden stash of goodies. Not finding the Easter egg won't prevent a player from winning a game, but the Easter eggs are fun and add to the excitement of the gameplay.

Easter eggs may be written messages or jokes, access to a hidden level or power ups, or media events like songs or movies that play if the gamer stumbles across the correct area where they're hidden. For example, in Sony's game *Call of Duty: Black Ops*, after you load the game and go to the Mission S.O.G. (Special Operations Group), the main character, Hudson, enters a tent and a song is playing. The song is "Fortunate Son" by Creedence Clearwater Revival. The same song plays in the movie *Forrest Gump* when Forrest and Bubba first arrive in Vietnam.

> ▶
>
> **Virtual Easter eggs are hidden in games by designers and contain messages or jokes. Finding them usually doesn't aid gameplay like a cheat, but it's boast-worthy.**

## Chance

When we think of *chance* with reference to games, usually what comes to mind are games associated with gambling, like poker or roulette. Chance, however, has a much larger role in all gaming. If you play through a game and have the same exact outcome every time, then the challenge for playing it is missing. Game designers work at making their games not only enticing, fun, and playable, but also replayable, by having that outcome be less predictable.

The ability to factor chance into game design can make or break a game. *Jewel Quest*, which was introduced into the world of gaming online, is extremely successful (in terms of the vast number of people who have played and are still playing it) because of the fast pace of the game and the unpredictable nature of what gems appear.

Figure 1.3 shows a screenshot from the game *Bejeweled*, where you see this fast-paced matching feature first popularized by *Jewel Quest*. The goal is to swap two gems that are side by side to make a match of three or more identical ones.

The result, when three or more jewels line up, is a fun, loud animation (the reward) and a void on the playing field created when the matched gems disappear. The unpredictable aspect of the game really comes into play when new gems drop into that void for you to play with.

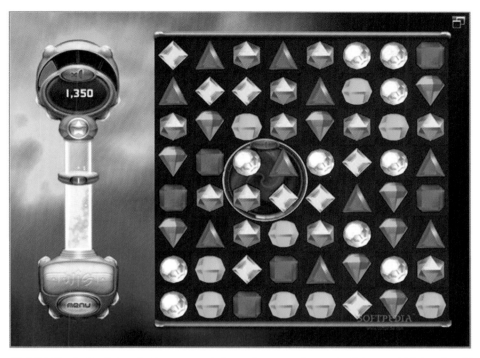

**FIGURE 1.3** *Bejeweled* is a game of chance because players don't know which jewels will come up next.

## CHANCE AND FAST-PACED GAMEPLAY

*Tetris* is an excellent example of how chance can make a game more playable and exciting. While the player frantically turns and turns and turns game pieces being dropped into the playing field, the level of excitement rises because the player doesn't know what shape will be dropped next. The pieces tend to drop rather quickly, so playing against time increases players' adrenaline as they rush to make a match and clear enough space for the new tiles to drop into. If they aren't able to clear the already fallen tiles in time, the game is lost.

Some players feel that games that rely on chance aren't games at all, but rather mindless time wasters. For many, a game needs rules and a goal to be a game, which excludes sandbox/simulators or games that rely on the roll of something like dice to advance through the play. *Candy Land* and *Snakes and Ladders* by that definition wouldn't be games because winning doesn't rely on skill or logic. Designers need to be aware of these gray areas and understand that, because of how vast the world of making games has become and how it continues to grow and expand, the concept of what a game is and how it must be played will evolve as well.

# History: Going Way Back

Humans have enjoyed playing games for as long as our history has been recorded. Early Egyptians played games like *Senet* for leisure. It was so popular, in fact, that four copies of the game crafted from ebony and ivory were found in King Tut's tomb. The game is a battle between good and evil, in which the evil forces try to keep the good from reaching the highly prized Kingdom of Osiris by blocking holes in the game board with their pegs. Figure 1.4 shows an image painted on a tomb wall of Nefertari playing *Senet*. The game took on such an important role in Egyptian society that during the New Kingdom (between the sixteenth and eleventh centuries BC) it was viewed as having religious and magical properties.

**F I G U R E  1 . 4**  *Senet* shows that games have long been important to human society.

# Leisure Games

*The Royal Game of Ur,* considered the oldest known game (circa 3100–2500 BC), was discovered in a tomb in the city of Ur, Sumer (modern day Iraq), along with instructions on how to play it.

*Moksha Patamu,* created in India during the second century BC, is considered a precursor to the modern game *Snakes and Ladders,* sometimes called *Chutes and Ladders.* The game was designed to teach children about good and evil. If the player landed on a good square, they could continue to move up in the game. Landing on a snake, though—essentially an evil square—caused the player to plummet back toward the bottom. The British learned about the game during their Empire days (British colonial rule 1858–1947) in India and introduced it to the Western world in the 1890s.

Figure 1.5 shows an image of a *Snakes and Ladders* game from the 1890s. The game appealed to the Victorians, who were drawn to the moral values that the game sought to teach. The good squares idealized virtues like penitence, thrift, and industry, and when landed on elevated the player higher up in the game to even more desirable virtues like grace, fulfillment, and success. By the toss of the dice, though, a player could land on an evil square like indolence, indulgence, or disobedience, and slide down to even more undesirable forms of evil like poverty, illness, and disgrace.

Board games in the United States first appeared in the 1800s and brought with them the moral teachings that were so popular in England at that time. Many, such as *The Mansion of Happiness,* were based on the same pursuit of high moral values as espoused in *Snakes and Ladders.* George Fox created *The Mansion of Happiness* in England in 1800. This board game was designed to teach moral values by allowing the player to advance forward on the board, into the Mansion (eternal happiness), if they landed on squares that contained imagery and text related to good deeds such as kindness and working hard. Players who landed on the bad squares, which exemplified vices like sloth, greed, or cruelty, moved backward. The game was published in the United States after George S. Parker & Co. (Parker Brothers) bought the rights to it in 1894.

Figure 1.6 shows what this 66-space spiral-track game looked like. The game mechanics were influenced by the rigid Puritanical tenets, which held that a virtuous life filled with virtuous deeds was the way to happiness; therefore dice were prohibited from being used with the game. Instead, a spinner or teetotum was used to help the player advance through the board.

A *teetotum* is like a dreidel. This spinning top can have four or more sides, with numbers, dots, or combinations of letters that indicate how far a player can move.

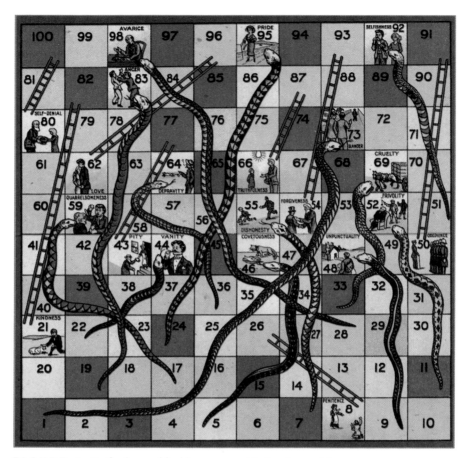

**FIGURE 1.5** *Snakes and Ladders* was used to teach moral lessons.

It's interesting to note that, although it was a game that children were encouraged to play to reinforce their understanding of virtuous behavior, most were forbidden to play it on the Sabbath.

The first recognized board game produced in America was *Travellers' Tour Through the United States,* published in 1822. Although the original designer and artist aren't known, the publisher was F. & R. Lockwood. It was also a roll-and-move game using a teetotum. Unlike other boards games like *The Mansion of Happiness* that were British imports and based on moral values, this game allowed players to roll and then advance across a map of the United States—at the time this game was published, the furthest-west states were Missouri and Louisiana.

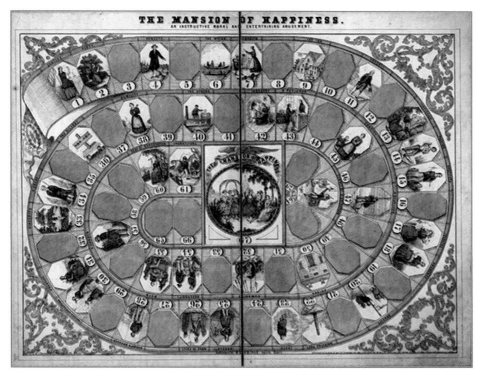

**FIGURE 1.6** Like *Snakes and Ladders*, *The Mansion of Happiness* taught moral values.

The cities on the map weren't named; instead, they were numbered. The goal was to correctly name the city indicated by the number. If you didn't, you lost a turn. In the advanced version of the game, the player had to provide the population of the city as well.

Milton Bradley, a lithographer based in Springfield, Massachusetts, had been seeking improved methods of printing before he segued into the games business. As production methods improved for printing and mass production, the games industry enjoyed a surge in popularity and distribution. Costs went down and availability to the public increased as more efficient means of producing games became accessible.

In 1860, Bradley founded his game company, named for himself. He specialized in creating small, portable games that soldiers fighting in the Civil War could carry with them and play in their down time. These games were backgammon, chess, checkers, dominoes, and a game of his own invention, *The Checkered Game of Life*. The portability of these games allowed more and more people to enjoy them and furthered the development of games in the United States.

The Milton Bradley Company was acquired by Hasbro in 1984 and later produced *Simon*, shown in Figure 1.7. The game, based on the simple children's game *Simon Says*, was one of the first electronic games on the market. The popularity of the game—a craze, actually—swept the country.

**FIGURE 1.7**  Simon was an early popular electronic game.

As the numbers and types of games increased, the need to build into them teaching mechanisms like an emphasis on good morals decreased. Games were becoming a staple to help enjoy leisure time, either individually or in groups, especially family time together.

> Today's average age range of gamers, 12–55, covers about half the population of the United States. Game production will continue growing to meet the demands of that significant market.

## Playing at War

Many cultures developed games as a way to train armies for war. In China, during the Ming Dynasty (1368–1644) and Qing Dynasty (1644–1911), the games *Cuju* and *Daqiu* (strike ball) were developed as sports requiring physical skills along with wushu (martial art), wrestling, hunting, and archery. Of course, leisurely pastimes were sought by the general population; elaborate sets of backgammon were also created, crafted from jade (Qing Dynasty), but games that taught fighting skills were extremely popular.

The origins of jousting can be traced back to gladiator combat during early Roman times and was played by the Mongols, who enjoyed tests involving games on horseback. Jousting grew to its most popular form during the age of chivalry in the Middle Ages. The word *joust* is derived from the Roman word *juxtare*, meaning "to meet together." These games were a favorite spectator sport and allowed knights an opportunity to improve their fighting skills.

## GO (WEIQI)

The very popular game *Go*, or *weiqi* in Chinese, dates back nearly 2,000 years. This game has a simple design but is actually quite difficult to play because of the cunning varieties of tactics that can be used. It was a favorite of Mao Tse-Tung, who insisted his generals master the game to become better military strategists.

Many board games like *Stratego* and *Kriegspiel* (German for "war game") had scenarios involving armies or kingdoms battling one another for land or other riches. The military was the first to implement computer games or, more to the point, computer simulations, to help teach and train personnel. Unlike the scenarios of board games, simulations endeavor to immerse the player in an actual situation.

Although placing someone into a real battle is the best way for them to learn how to fight, the risks are enormous. Simulations help train soldiers without putting their lives in peril. A simulation allows soldiers to practice repeatedly what to do in certain situations to better prepare them for the real thing. A soldier has a better chance of reacting appropriately and quickly enough to survive an actual fight if he has practiced with a simulation.

The military use of simulations has expanded to include flight training, tank and other large vehicle operations, predicting weather patterns, and combat. Figure 1.8 shows a screenshot of a modern use of this type of simulation in *Close Combat: First to Fight*: in the figure, Marines are clearing an area. Players use the same kinds of weapons and tactics they would use in an actual encounter.

The first military simulation, the Tactical Warfare Simulation Evaluation and Analysis, appeared in 1979 at Camp Pendleton and used 35mm slides depicting training scenarios.

**FIGURE 1.8** *First to Fight* is a military simulation game.

Computer simulations are still widely used by all branches of the military and have been embraced by the corporate sector for training employees and by schools to aid in the classroom. Many industries regularly use simulations to help train employees including pilots, engineers who operate critical elements of nuclear facilities, and bio-technicians who routinely work with hazardous materials, to name a few.

# Going Electronic

The first electronic game creation is credited to Thomas T. Goldsmith, Jr., and Estle Ray Mann, who made an interactive missile simulator based on the look of radar displays from World War II. The gameplay was completely analog and used a cathode ray tube (CRT) beam that allowed the player to position a dot on the screen indicating where their missile would strike.

An electronic version of *Tic-Tac-Toe*, built by A. S. Douglas as part of his Ph.D. on Human-Computer Interaction at the University of Cambridge, debuted in 1952. The game was programmed for an EDSAC vacuum-tube computer, which used a CRT display.

In 1958, during the time that Dwight D. Eisenhower was president of the United States, William Higinbotham created *Tennis for Two,* which was played on an oscilloscope at the Brookhaven National Laboratory in Upton, New York.

A milestone in this early form of electronic gaming occurred at the Festival of Britain in 1951, where Ferranti debuted its computer, the Nimrod. The computer was designed solely to play the game *NIM*, where the goal was to collect all, or lose all, from three piles of tokens depending on the game mode selected. The name of the game came from the German word *nimm* meaning "take." NIM was a game of mathematical strategy, and some have linked it to the ancient game of *Jianshizi* or "picking stones," from China. The mathematical component to the gameplay made it ideal to adapt to the binary mathematical abilities of the early computers. Figure 1.9 shows a diagrammatic drawing of how the Nimrod was designed with rows of blinking lights

In addition to being designed to play the game, the Nimrod also let the viewing public see what a computer could be capable of. A smaller version of it currently resides at the Computerspielemuseum in Berlin, Germany.

**The Nimrod is sometimes referred to as a BT game—"before transistors."**

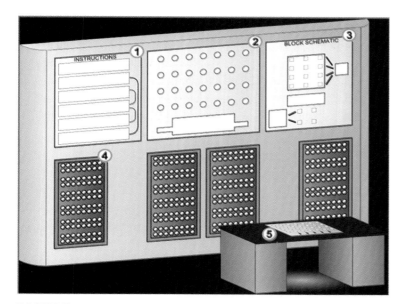

**FIGURE 1.9** Nimrod

## The Brown Box

▶

Originally called TV Game Unit #7, the Odyssey earned the nickname "The Brown Box" from the wood-grain simulated self-adhesive vinyl used to make the prototype look more attractive.

Say hello to the Odyssey by Magnavox, which debuted in 1972. For the first time, consumers could play video games in their own homes. Ralph Baer and his associates at Sanders Associates came up with the concept and patented the idea (1967–68). The Odyssey was an analog system that the player could attach directly to their TV set in order to play games.

Some of the games that the Odyssey could play were *Pong, Checkers,* and sports games. A lightgun attachment allowed the player to target shoot, and an additional attachment provided amusement with a golf putting game.

One of the problems associated with the Odyssey was an ill-conceived marketing campaign that erroneously led consumers to believe it would only run on a Magnavox television. The Odyssey performed quite well; however, because it didn't have any audio, all the games were silent.

## And Now We Are Digital

▶

*Video* refers to a raster display device, which is the way the first electronic games were viewed. The term is used erroneously to describe digital games today.

Exactly who created the first digital game remains a bit of a mystery. Some early developers were interested in making games, whereas others strove to create art, and still others used game-like technologies to explore scientific principles. Because all this work was going on simultaneously, the identity of the person who created the first digital game is frequently disputed.

*Spacewar!,* often credited as being the first game designed for computer use (although preceded in development by *OXO* in 1952 and *Tennis for Two* in 1958), was created at the Massachusetts Institute of Technology by designers Steve Russell, Martin Graetz, and Wayne Wiitanen. The game was played with two spaceships, called the needle and the wedge, that navigated through star fields and could fire a limited number of missiles. The goal of this two-player game was to shoot each other's ships down and avoid colliding with stars.

The hugely successful game was ported to additional platforms and soon inspired other designers to explore this innovative digital world as a canvas to create new games. As technology increased and games became more sophisticated, gameplay styles evolved to include adventure games, board games, platform games, card games, role-playing games, and shooters, to name a few. *Spacewar!* is highly credited for its inspiration to later designers.

Figure 1.10 shows an excellent image of how the game appeared to players, including the CRT device used to display the game. The first version of the game took about 200 man-hours to write. The Digital Equipment Corporation (DEC) PDP-1 system used for the game allowed multiple users to share the computer at the same time.

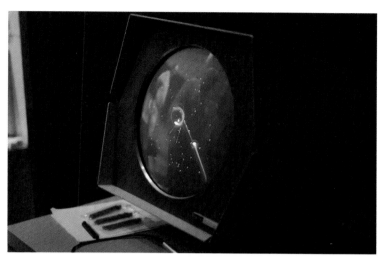

**FIGURE 1.10** *Spacewar!* was one of the earliest games designed for computers.

Steve Russell was inspired to create *Spacewar!* after reading the *Lensman* series by E. E. Smith, where the hero was chased across the galaxy by villains and had to invent new ways to outwit his pursuers during the journey. Game designers take note: often, excellent gameplay can come from inspirations such as novels, comics, movies, stories from the news (current and historical), and personal experiences.

Methods for creating digital games are as varied as the types of coding used to write them, the game engines designed and built to play them, the vast number of gameplay styles with which the gamer can engage with them, and the many playing systems available to run them. Some of the most popular digital games today are *The Sims,* developed by Maxis; Blizzard's *World of Warcraft*; *Angry Birds,* developed as a mobile-phone game by Rovio Mobile; and Nintendo's *Super Mario Bros.* These modern games draw on some of the earlier design concepts of the shooter from *Spacewar! Mario Bros.* also involves puzzles and strategy first encountered in *Senet.*

The *Mario Bros.* games became such a successful franchise in part because of the motivational gameplay. As players move through the playing fields, they can randomly hit question-mark graphics and capture extra coins. Whether they catch the question marks or not doesn't help or hinder their ability to win a level, but the addictive quality of wanting to capture them motivates players to keep going after them.

*Spacewar!* is considered the first shooter game. *Shooter* is a type of gameplay style where the goal is to shoot down or kill an opponent.

## Put Another Quarter In!

In 1971, the United States was still three years away from exiting the Vietnam War, CBS debuted its hit TV show *All in the Family,* Apollo 15 completed the fourth manned mission to the moon, and Bill Pitts and Hugh Tuck created *Galaxy Game,* the first coin-operated video game, at Stanford University.

Bill and Hugh made the game on a 16-bit minicomputer called a DEC PDP-11 and it was later adapted to a coin-operated console using a DEC PDP-11/20 with vector displays. Only one unit was made, which was installed at Stanford's Tresidder Union; however, it was modified to accommodate up to eight consoles, allowing gamers to play against each other. The game was patterned after *Spacewar!*

Figure 1.11 shows a photograph of *Galaxy Game,* which was restored in 1997 and acquired by the Computer History Museum in Mountain View, California. In 2010, it was loaned to Google and resides at the company's headquarters campus—Googleplex—also in Mountain View.

*Arcade game* **is another term for a coin-operated game.**

▶

Two months after *Galaxy Game* debuted, the first commercial video arcade game was released by Nolan Bushnell and Ted Dabney; it was also based on *Spacewar!* The game, called *Computer Space,* was an interesting first attempt at producing and marketing arcade games; however, even with $3 million in sales, it was a failure.

**FIGURE  1.11**  *Galaxy Game,* the first coin-operated video game

The phenomenon of arcade and video games blasted into a worldwide frenzy shortly thereafter, with coin-operated boxes showing up in arcades (environments built just for those games along with pinball, ball toss, and so on) as well as convenience stores, hotel lobbies, restaurants, bowling alleys, shopping malls, theatres, laundromats, and airports. Early types of arcade games, where the player deposited money to play, were pinball games (dating back to the 1930s), batting or hoop-toss games, and shooting galleries.

Prior to the arcade video games, Sega created the first electromechanical game, called *Periscope*. The game had pieces of plastic used to simulate waves, and the player aimed a light gun at approaching submarines in an attempt to sink them. The game cost 25 cents to play and set the standard for that pricing. Arcade games for years after priced most of their gameplay at that amount.

One of the earliest arcade games, *Pong*, was created by Nolan Bushnell and based on the 1958 game *Tennis for Two*. This arcade game debuted in arcades in 1972; however, it grew in popularity when a home version was released by Atari during the Christmas season in 1975. (Atari was founded by Nolan Bushnell and Ted Dabney.) This simple game came preloaded into a console that could be hooked up to a television set; players rotated a dial on the console, which moved a paddle back and forth on the TV screen, to hit the ball back and forth.

The game was extremely simple and became boring fairly quickly, but it was one of the first interactive games that two players could play at home. *Pong*'s success led the way to further development with home gaming systems and games.

## Game Boy and More

The Mattel Corporation released the first handheld, portable electronic device in 1977, called *Auto Race*. A handheld device has speakers, display monitor, and game-control elements combined into one unit. This unique new gaming system allowed more gamers to explore and play games and prompted more interest in developing newer and faster gaming systems.

Nintendo further advanced handheld systems with its highly popular Game Boy, which was released in 1989. Game Boy remains highly popular even today with newer hybrids like the Nintendo DS, DSi, and Nintendo 3DS models.

Following the release and popularity of the Odyssey and Atari, home systems also have grown. Now they allow hugely interactive games that are fast paced, run in real time, and support massive graphics and lengthy gameplay in the privacy of players' homes. Some of these systems include Sony PlayStation, Microsoft Xbox, Nintendo GameCube, Wii, and the XaviXPORT.

Technology is providing amazing methods for playing games. Innovative storylines and interactivity continue to draw more and more players into virtual worlds for everything from casual fun with card or matching games to massive role-playing environs where the gameplay can go on for years.

This brief look back at the history of games and who made them is just a taste of how and why the phenomenon of gaming has brought us to where we are. Game designers now draw on a rich legacy, from the cultural phenomenon of the *Royal Game of Ur*, to the impact of moral values during the development of the board games in the 1800s, to the "Oh wow!" factor of computer games and their stunning graphics and interactivity today.

Innovative designers continue in this long tradition by pairing technology with the understanding of why people like to play games. The variety of games will continue to develop and grow as technology improves and players continue to make demands on the industry for bigger and better games.

## THE ESSENTIALS AND BEYOND

Games and gaming have existed for thousands of years, driven by the human need to enjoy leisure time, to advance fighting skills without losing actual lives, to improve cognitive or even psychic skills, and to push the limits of our desire to be competitive. Innovative storylines, gameplay styles, graphics, and playing systems have developed as more technical improvements continue to thrill gamers; however, all games have their roots in historical examples.

### ADDITIONAL EXERCISE

Take a look at the game *Senet*. You can find a version on the book's website (www .sybex.com/go/gamedesignessentials) that can be printed and played with dice and markers, like tiddlywinks, or you can play the Shockwave version from the British Museum online here: www.ancientegypt.co.uk/life/activity/main.html. Play through the game a couple of times with the original rules; then break the game board apart and try using the same number of squares but in a different configuration, such as a spiral, or create gaps that you can only jump if you make a specific roll of the dice. The game was originally designed for two players; however, attempt to expand that by allowing a third player to join in. By taking a simple concept and then pushing the limits of the game or introducing new variables, you can see how new games can be built based on a workable existing game.

*(Continues)*

## THE ESSENTIALS AND BEYOND *(Continued)*

### REVIEW QUESTIONS

1. What is the name of the first game recorded by human history?

   A. *Snakes and Ladders*          C. *The Royal Game of Ur*

   B. *Senet*          D. *The Mansion of Happiness*

2. True or false: The first arcade video game was created at the University of California, Los Angeles.

3. Which game is often credited as being the first digital one?

   A. *NIM*          C. *Pong*

   B. *Spacewar!*          D. *Tic-Tac-Toe*

4. Although most board games today are played as a form of leisurely pastime, early forms of these games were designed to what?

   A. Teach how to farm better          C. Teach moral values

   B. Instruct players on proper etiquette in social settings          D. Help players improve their psychic abilities

5. True or false: The Odyssey gaming system is digital.

6. What was the first board game published in the United States?

   A. *Travellers' Tour Through the United States*          C. *Twister*

   B. *The Mansion of Happiness*          D. *Candy Land*

# CHAPTER 2

# Gameplay Styles

*Gamers tend to be* loyal fans of particular gameplay styles. Some prefer shooters, others like intricate story-based games, and still others love to beat the clock with timed action or strategy games.

Game designers understand that players tend to keep playing the same types of games, so they do a great deal of market research to find which gameplay styles are the most popular or profitable. In addition, knowing which games don't do as well, and studying those, can provide valuable insights before you invest time and money into designing your own games.

In this chapter, you'll explore different gameplay styles and some of the elements common to them. I encourage you to try as many play styles as you can to experience them for yourself. In addition, we'll take a look at the Entertainment Software Rating Board (ESRB) and how game companies voluntarily allow this organization to review and categorize their products based on the content of the game.

We looked at the history of games to provide insight into how and why certain games developed the way they did. With the introduction of digital technology and literally millions of gamers with a vast array of likes and dislikes, appreciating gameplay styles is an important aspect of understanding effective design.

▶ **What defines a gameplay style?**

▶ **Clustering gameplay types**

▶ **Playing for fun and to learn**

▶ **Entertainment Software Rating Board**

## What Defines a Gameplay Style?

This concept is a bit elusive; however, the core understanding of what a gameplay style is becomes easier if you think of it this way: games that have similar challenges with similar methods for winning or besting the challenge tend to be classified the same way. Games can also be classified by the kinds of people who like to play them. Using that method for categorizing a game is known as understanding the *demographic* for the product.

In a game, the player usually has a goal that he or she is attempting to achieve. To reach the goal, players make decisions during gameplay that affect the outcome. The player may need to slay an enemy or collect items or repeat a certain action until a specific score is reached in order to move to the next level or achieve the final goal—winning the game!

We'll examine the following categories in greater detail. Although they don't include all styles, large numbers of gamers play them:

- ▶ Role-playing games
- ▶ Action games
- ▶ Adventure games
- ▶ Action-adventure games
- ▶ Shooters
- ▶ Simulations
- ▶ Strategy games

## Role-Playing Games

A role-playing game (RPG) is an extremely popular style whose attributes can be found in other games, including adventure and action-adventure. An RPG's unique qualities lie in allowing a gamer to assume the role of a character (such as a wizard, warrior, or knight) in the game, which is usually set within an illusory world that is highly influenced by the narrative (story) that drives the game.

### ONLINE RESOURCES FOR RPG FANS

Fans of RPGs can exchange information about them at www.rpg.net. Most of the commercial RPGs, including *Final Fantasy*, *World of Warcraft*, and *EverQuest*, have official sites with fan forums where players can swap tips, movies showing gameplay, screenshots, art, and strategies for playing the games.

The origins of the style can be found in tabletop games where players use trading cards or carefully written descriptions and storylines and then discuss how their characters react in different situations. *Dungeons & Dragons,* created by Gary Gygax and Dave Arneson, was released in 1974 by Tactical Studies Rules, Inc. This highly popular game, often known simply as *D&D,* is an excellent example of one of these tabletop games. One player is the Dungeon Master, who assumes the role of the storyteller and adjudicator.

Live-action games of the RPG type are also quite popular and are known as *live action role play (LARP)*. Devoted gamers refer to themselves as LARPers; they write and then play out elaborate storylines while dressing as characters and interacting with each other.

Gamers still gather to play tabletop games, especially *D&D*. Information about when and where they gather, along with storylines, can be found at the Wizards of the Coast website, www.wizards.com.

## Action Games

Action games challenge players through physical challenges, testing their hand-eye coordination and reaction time. Action games include shooters, discussed later, along with fighting games and platform games.

An early, successful action game was an arcade amusement called *Space Invaders,* designed by Tomohiro Nishikado and released in 1978. During gameplay, the player manipulated a laser cannon that moved from side to side across the bottom of the screen. The goal was to shoot as many aliens as possible as they descended toward the bottom in rows. If the player succeeded in shooting all the aliens during this timed game, he won. However, if any alien touched the ground, the game ended instantly and the aliens were declared the victors. The popularity of this game is one of the reasons shooters tend to be thought of as their own category.

Figure 2.1 shows what the alien creatures from *Space Invaders* looked like. They were extremely simple, made from just a few pixels; because of the game's limited memory, that was all the designers had to work with.

Platform games like *Donkey Kong* show the playing field from the side. The gamer navigates an avatar through a series of obstacles—for example, jumping from platform to platform—while evading hazards.

*Pixels* (those tiny squares you see when you zoom in on an image) are the smallest units of data in a game. Different color combinations are used to create graphics.

**F I G U R E  2 . 1**  The block-like appearance of the *Space Invaders* aliens is due to the small number of pixels used to make them.

> *Resolution* refers to how many pixels are used to make up the entire screen you're viewing.

> The blocky *Space Invader* images became iconic and were often used in films and TV shows to represent any creature or alien in a computer game.

> Action games often feature levels with distinctive looks and are often designed with obstacles that can be negotiated at high speeds— again, requiring excellent hand-eye coordination.

In earlier games, resolution was very low because that was all the technology at the time could support. *Space Invaders* used a black-and-white raster display (the grid of pixels) and ran at a resolution of 224×260 pixels. By today's standards, that is a small display; modern console games are typically 1280×720 or 1920×1080 and use millions of colors.

Because there were so few games for early designers to study when making new ones, their inspiration tended to come from a variety of sources. Nishikado was inspired by the video game *Breakout* and the movies *The War of the Worlds* and *Star Wars* when he designed the look for the characters. We'll talk more about inspiration in Chapter 4, "Visual Design."

Although action games can include first-person playing approaches, for the most part they tend to allow gamers to navigate levels using an avatar and a third-person point of view (POV). This avatar, the protagonist, is then maneuvered through various levels to do any or all of the following:

▶ Overcome obstacles

▶ Collect items (things needed like a key to enter the next level or power ups)

▶ Defeat bad guys and bosses

▶ Solve puzzles

Figure 2.2 shows a graphic from the game *Call of Duty 4, Modern Warfare*, a highly popular game from Activision. During gameplay, gamers go on military-type missions and race through flying bullets, explosions, and various forms of combat while shooting, jumping, dodging, and sometimes dying. For the most part, action games require skill and excellent hand-eye coordination to maneuver the avatar through these physical challenges.

The design of these games includes not only the avatar's abilities (physical capabilities such as jumping, wielding a weapon, and so on) but also unique environments for the levels. Levels tend to have very different looks. A gamer may successfully navigate his or her avatar through a level that looks like a jungle to move on to the next level, which may be the meteor-pelted surface of the moon or a seafloor on a distant planet. This type of eye candy provides a visual stimulus to gamers who are highly focused on the fast-paced skills required to maneuver their avatars through the perilous environments.

**FIGURE 2.2** In *Call of Duty 4, Modern Warfare*, you can see how accurate the game is with explosions, realistically geared players, and plenty of action.

# Adventure Games

Adventure games tend to allow players to move at their own pace through the various parts of the world, solving puzzles, unearthing treasures, and experiencing the story as it unfolds. Because of this slower pace, players can really study the environments, so the worlds are often more elaborate, richly illustrated, and quite often filled with things to explore, click, and open.

This form of gameplay originated in the 1970s with designer Will Crowther in his *Colossal Cave Adventure,* also known as *ADVENT* or *Adventure. Colossal Cave Adventure* was based in part on the layout of Mammoth Cave in Kentucky. Although the game was partially an exploration of a real place, there was an element of fantasy, with elves and wizards roaming the twisty mazes that cut through caves.

In Figure 2.3, you can see a sample from this text-based game. Text-based games are also known as *interactive fiction* because instead of using a mouse or other control device to navigate, players type in commands.

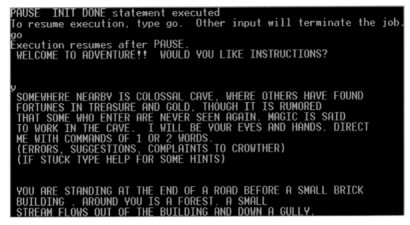

```
PAUSE  INIT DONE statement executed
To resume execution, type go.  Other input will terminate the job.
go
Execution resumes after PAUSE.
 WELCOME TO ADVENTURE!!  WOULD YOU LIKE INSTRUCTIONS?


y
 SOMEWHERE NEARBY IS COLOSSAL CAVE, WHERE OTHERS HAVE FOUND
 FORTUNES IN TREASURE AND GOLD, THOUGH IT IS RUMORED
 THAT SOME WHO ENTER ARE NEVER SEEN AGAIN. MAGIC IS SAID
 TO WORK IN THE CAVE.   I WILL BE YOUR EYES AND HANDS. DIRECT
 ME WITH COMMANDS OF 1 OR 2 WORDS.
 (ERRORS, SUGGESTIONS, COMPLAINTS TO CROWTHER)
 (IF STUCK TYPE HELP FOR SOME HINTS)


 YOU ARE STANDING AT THE END OF A ROAD BEFORE A SMALL BRICK
 BUILDING . AROUND YOU IS A FOREST. A SMALL
 STREAM FLOWS OUT OF THE BUILDING AND DOWN A GULLY.
```

**FIGURE 2.3** *Colossal Cave Adventure* is an example of a text-based game.

*Maniac Mansion*, the first video game released by Lucasfilm Games, utilized an engine called SCUMM that allowed players to point and click instead of having to type so many commands.

The film *Big* opened with a boy playing a game that had the look and feel of *Maniac Mansion* combined with *Colossal Cave Adventure*.

The opening text provided instructions on how to interact with the computer using commands of one or two words. In order to move around in the game, the player typed in commands such as **Enter** if the game told them they were near a door, or compass directions (**north**, **south**, and so on) to navigate to new areas of the game. Many early players sketched out a map on paper to track their travels as they dialogued with the computer.

Contrast the text in Figure 2.3 with the richly illustrated *Myst III, Exile* in Figure 2.4.

**FIGURE 2.4** *Myst* features serenely quiet yet exotic-looking backgrounds that depict highly realistic environments just begging to be explored.

*Myst,* created by Robyn and Rand Miller and released in 1993 by Cyan, was a groundbreaking adventure game. What made the game such a phenomenon were the intricate and highly realistic worlds that gamers could move through as they solved puzzles to unlock more levels, or worlds, to explore. One of the unique aspects of the game was that it had several different endings, depending on what choices the player made during gameplay.

In Figure 2.4, notice the extremely realistic textures, the sky, and the curious structure in the center, entreating you to notice it and to come explore inside. The game is quiet, mostly a visual tour de force, with beautiful imagery like this at every turn.

Some of the adventure games available today are Telltale Games' *Jurassic Park* and *Back to the Future,* Pendulo Studio's *The Next Big Thing,* and Microids' *Dracula 3: The Path of the Dragon* and *Still Life.*

## Action-Adventure Games

Action-adventure games are a hybrid of action games and adventure games and may be the broadest type of game design in the industry. Adventure games tend to be more slowly paced and are focused primarily on storylines and problem-solving to get through the levels. When designers add some of the action elements described earlier to an adventure game, players can immerse themselves in the narrative of the game, experience more and varied personality types with their avatars, and enjoy faster-paced gameplay than in an adventure game while also solving puzzles and often experiencing a detailed and elaborate storyline. *Tomb Raider, God of War,* and *The Legend of Zelda* are prime examples of action-adventure games.

## Shooters

A shooter typically falls under the action game genre; however, it's a separate category here because of the massive number of games designed this way. These games tend to be violent and are usually played as first-person shooters.

Many people consider *Wolfenstein 3D* to be the first game produced as a shooter. It was created in 1992 by id Software and published by Apogee Software. Figure 2.5 shows a screenshot from the game with its simple graphics and easy-to-read statistics running along the bottom. Although basic-looking by today's standards, for its time, the highly textured graphics were innovative. During gameplay, the player saw a hand holding a weapon in front of him as he moved through the 3D world. That method of gameplay has been used extensively in subsequent shooters.

Fast-paced games can wear out a player, but slower ones can become boring. Action-adventure games combine fast moments with more in-depth storylines.

◄

Shooters are a subset of action games. They're combat games played in either a linear or a sandbox style.

◄

◄

The first-person shooter point of view is often called FPS POV.

**FIGURE 2.5** *Wolfenstein 3D* amazed players with the ability to turn in a complete circle in real time.

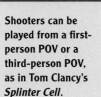

At the time, *DOOM* was unique because more than one gamer could play. Players entered the game from their own computers using phone-line hookups or local area network connections (LANs).

Shooters can be played from a first-person POV or a third-person POV, as in Tom Clancy's *Splinter Cell*.

In *Wolfenstein 3D*, you played a World War II POW named William "B. J." Blazkowicz, attempting to escape from a German castle—Castle Wolfenstein. Along the way, you picked up and used weapons including a knife, pistol, machine gun, and Gatling gun. Addictive and a massive hit for its time, the game holds a solid niche in game development history because of its success. In 1993, id followed on its success with *Wolfenstein* by releasing *DOOM*.

As these shooters developed into more elaborate, complex games, the abilities the characters could exhibit increased as well. Instead of moving over static backgrounds and observing gameplay from a bird's-eye view, gamers could run around inside a world—jump, duck, dodge, turn corners, and go through doors to encounter new locations as if they were immersed in the setting themselves.

Designers interested in creating shooters should keep in mind that the more immersive the game is, the more popular it tends to be. The more complete the immersion, the more the gamer can suspend disbelief. In *World of Warcraft*, for example, the environment changes to reflect time of day and exhibits weather that can include rain, snow, or fog. The game even has world events with quests and in-game prizes celebrating Halloween, Winter Festival, and so on. In the game *Thief*, conversations are overheard as the thief sneaks quietly about in the shadows, adding believability to that world. The more immersive a game is, the more players form an emotional attachment to their characters and feel like they're moving through a real world, regardless of how stylized it may be.

## Simulations

As previously noted in this book, simulations were developed primarily to help train people for difficult jobs. The military regularly uses them to prepare people for battle combat or operating large vehicles like tanks or jets and also to simulate using complex weapons systems without having to fire a single live round.

Simulators and simulation games are somewhat different. A simulator is a machine or device that mimics as closely as possible the real thing, like the cockpit of a plane. Figure 2.6 shows the game *Navy Field: Resurrection of the Steel Fleet.* This game has the player commanding a World War II ship to experience battle at sea. Although this game has RPG elements (the sailors you can interact with), the experience is essentially meant to replicate what a naval skirmish is like, right down to the historically accurately designed ships and weaponry, so this game would be considered a "simulation" as opposed to a "simulator."

Designers create immersive games by providing overlapping stimuli, such as realistic movement from characters or animals coupled with weather and sounds. Psychologists call this immersive feeling *presence*.

**FIGURE 2.6** In *Navy Field,* all the ships and weapons are as accurate as possible to enhance the experience of entering into a conflict.

Simulation games try to mimic real situations and tend to fall into one of these categories:

**Management/Construction**    *SimCity,* developed by designer Will Wright, is an example of a management/construction simulation game. In this game, you design whole cities. You also place inhabitants in the cities and look after their wants and needs.

**Life**    *Wolf,* developed by Manley & Associates, Inc., allows a player to live like a wolf. The player uses the wolf's senses to make decisions about how to evade hunters, or track down and kill prey in order to survive.

**Vehicle**    *Abrams Battle Tank,* developed by Dynamix, is a somewhat arcade-type game that allows a player to simulate driving a tank and deploying on missions to bombard the enemy or escort friendlies.

Simulation games, although designed to represent reality, can be used to teach or are played for fun.

Other types of simulation games focus on medicine, politics, science, police work, exploring space, diving in the ocean, and so on. The premise behind their design is that the player is the one making the decisions that affect not only his own outcome but also the outcomes for any virtual inhabitants of the world and often the environment itself.

## Strategy Games

Gamers can play against each other in a strategy game or go head-to-head with a computer. In 1996, chess champion Garry Kasparov lost to the computer *Deep Blue.*

*Chess* is a classic example of a strategy game; as discussed in Chapter 1, "Game Design Origins," so is the game *Go.* In this game style, the primary goals for the players are to determine methods for overcoming conflicts through planning and tactics. Strategy games tend to be designed for two players and are known as *turn-based games*—one player takes a turn and implements his strategy, and then the other player gets to play.

Sample strategy games include *Silent Storm, The Battle for Wesnoth, Civilization,* and *Age of Wonders.* The game *Civilization,* created by Sid Meier and released by MicroProse, is often referred to as *Civ.* The object of the game is to build an empire that will last; however, this empire is in competition with other civilizations. These civilizations compete for resources and technology and can go to war with each other for territory and other goods that can help them thrive.

# Clustering Game Types

So far in this chapter, we've looked at ways games can be categorized by their style. We can also categorize games according to their purpose and who the game is intended for.

## Designing for a Specific Audience

Instead of focusing solely on gameplay style, designers can choose to cater to a broader audience—casual, core, or hardcore gamers. Players may choose casual games to play, whether they're maze games or word puzzles or hidden-object games. By the same token, players can gravitate toward hardcore games that require substantial amounts of time to play through or have a darker or more violent game style, such as action or adventure games.

There are casual action games, and there are hardcore action games. They're differentiated by the level of intensity and immersion. You can use the same approach to categorize games in any of the gameplay styles we have looked at as either casual, core or hardcore. As a game designer, you may choose a certain type of gameplay to focus on, or you may determine what groups of different types of people tend to favor. By looking at a broader cluster of people, you may find ways to overlap or merge play styles to create unique and successful hybrids.

## Casual Games

A casual game appeals to gamers who like an easy-to-learn, light game that doesn't require a large amount of time to play. Casual games can fit any genre. The only distinction that sets them apart is that these games tend to be played for a short amount of time and are meant to be a fun diversion in the player's day. Although most games that are considered casual games tend to be light and fun, any game that players like to delve into for brief durations could be considered a casual game.

> ◄
> **According to the Casual Games Association, www. casualgamesassociation.org, the majority of casual gamers are female, are over 30, and play via the Internet.**

The majority of games that people tend to jump into for short periods of time are card games, maze games, puzzles, and so on. *Angry Birds* (shown in Figure 2.7), which was designed as a mobile game by Rovio but can also be played on a home computer using Google Chrome, is a popular casual game.

**FIGURE 2.7** In Rovio's casual game *Angry Birds*, the graphics are brightly colored and simple but highly engaging.

The goal is to slingshot different types of birds at pigs hiding in crude structures they have built to keep the birds out. The birds are angry because the pigs stole their eggs. This is a casual game because the gameplay is lighthearted and can be enjoyed in short chunks of time.

## Hardcore and Core Games

Hardcore games tend to be extremely large and complex and can take months, if not years, to play through. Hardcore games are often dark, violent, multifaceted, and made up of elaborate storylines and intricate characters with a wide array of talents/skills.

Examples of hardcore games are *Halo* (developed by Bungie Game and published by Microsoft Game Studios) and *Gears of War* (developed by Epic Games and published by Microsoft Game Studios).

Like hardcore games, core games immerse gamers for hours at a time. Core games are less dark and intense. The violence in core games tends to be more cartoon-based than in hardcore games.

Both hardcore and core games are favored by gamers who like to compete not only with the elements of the game but also with each other. These types of games can garner fans who create intricate websites devoted to their character or characters, guilds, in-game achievements, stats, and so on. These fan sites are filled with tips on how to master the game, screenshots showing in-game accomplishments, and blogs.

Figure 2.8 shows avid gamers queuing up to try *Cataclysm,* the 2011 release of the game *World of Warcraft,* from Blizzard Entertainment. *World of Warcraft (WoW)* is considered by many to be a core game; but because it has such a huge following, and gamers have admitted to playing for hours, sometimes days, at a time, some critics think it belongs in the hardcore category. However, even with its massive number of fans, as evidenced by this image, WoW lacks the dark, violent elements that are the benchmark for hardcore games.

WoW boasts fantasy characters such as dragons, orcs, and trolls, but it also has time travel and modern components like motorcycles and cars. *World of Warcraft* is the reigning champ of subscribed-to multiplayer online games.

## Multiplayer Games

Massively multiplayer online games (MMOG) and massively multiplayer online role-playing games (MMORPG) have grown substantially in popularity as more and more people have gained high-speed access to the Internet.

According to Satoru Iwata, CEO of Nintendo, the Wii U (successor to the Wii) was designed for the core (also known as midcore) gamer.

Because there are so many players, World of Warcraft is grouped into realms (individual servers) that can hold up to 20,000 gamers.

**FIGURE 2.8** Fans of Blizzard's *World of Warcraft* lined up in droves to get a first look at *Cataclysm* when it debuted.

Multiplayer online games tend to be real-time games that allow players to not only move through elaborate worlds, solve puzzles, experience intricate storylines, and master quests, but also interact socially. Players can talk to each other in the guises of their characters during play.

These types of games can encompass any and all of the gameplay styles discussed in this chapter. The first game to launch online with graphics was *Neverwinter Nights,* which debuted on America Online (AOL). Other, lighter versions of MMOG exist, such as *FarmVille,* shown in Figure 2.9, which most players discover through Facebook and which is actually considered a social game. In this game, developed by Zynga, players can grow crops, sell their harvest, and produce livestock.

Whereas *World of Warcraft* is a for-profit game (garnering profits in excess of $2.2 billion), and players pay for the initial installation then remain connected through a monthly subscription, *FarmVille* is free to play. Social games like *FarmVille* make money through the sale of virtual goods to players and by selling ads.

*Social games* run on a social network (like Facebook) and earned their name from that distribution platform as opposed to the games being "social."

**FIGURE 2.9** In the social game *FarmVille*, players grow crops and interact with each other online to keep moving forward in the game.

# Playing for Fun and to Learn

Learning theory suggests that we learn more and learn better when we have some fun doing it. Based on that theory, game designers are developing better-designed, more interesting educational games. Because these games aren't dull or boring, they have more staying power (people want to play them, and the more you play, the more information sticks).

The value of learning by playing is being embraced by more than the educational industries. These types of games are developed now to help train workers as well as students.

▶

**Most designers have adopted the term *digital game-based learning* instead of *educational computer games*.**

## Serious Games

Although this category sounds foreboding, serious games can be fun. Essentially, you can think of them as games that have problems designed into them that gamers need to solve. The term *serious* was derived from the book *Serious Games*, written by Clark Abt and released by Viking Press in 1970.

As you learned in Chapter 1, military leaders use games like *Kriegspeil* to help train troops. The business sector has also embraced gaming as an approach to training methods for all kinds of jobs, from accountants to surgeons to human resource managers and so on.

Because people do learn from playing games, developing games that help them solve problems and thereby better society or improve workers' job performance is becoming big business.

The Serious Games Initiative, a summit for game designers, first met at the Woodrow Wilson International Center for Scholars in Washington, D.C., in 2002. Its purpose is to provide a forum where designers can discuss serious game design.

## Educational Games

When designing educational games, you want to focus on making a fun game. If the design isn't fun, students won't play, and no learning can take place.

*Incidental learning* is a phenomenon associated with playing games. Marc Prensky, noted author of *Don't Bother Me, Mom—I'm Learning* (Paragon House, 2006) and *Teaching Digital Natives* (Corwin, 2010), says of gamers, "They learn to make good decisions under stress, they learn new skills, they learn to take prudent risks, they learn scientific deduction, they learn to persist to solve difficult problems, dealing with large amounts of data, they learn to make ethical and moral decisions and to even manage, in many games, businesses and other people." Prensky points out, quite well, that the conditions a game sets up offer learning opportunities even if the game doesn't appear to teach, reinforce, or test specific knowledge.

In the early 1990s, when home computers were becoming more common and educational games were being designed for that market, the creativity fell off substantially. Too often, games were designed as "drill and kill" games and earned the unfortunate moniker of "chocolate-covered broccoli."

Since then, the educational-games industry has been going through a significant learning curve. Many contend the industry is still learning how best to design games that can teach but are also fun to play.

Online sites that group several game choices together are contributing significantly to advancing good digital game-based learning. Students, parents, and instructors can peruse these sites and read reviews about the games, understand the teaching objective for each game, and then play for free or try before they buy.

The term *gamification* has been coined by serious game designers to describe how players use the mechanics of the game to help solve problems.

The goal for educational game design is not to teach, but to have fun. Learning is a byproduct of repeating the gameplay.

One such site can be found at www.funbrain.com, which is part of the Education Network and caters to K–8 students. The site hosts games to help improve math and reading skills. It also provides resources to parents and instructors and launched *Diary of a Wimpy Kid.*

**Educational games designed with a combination of learning material and entertaining gameplay are often referred to as** *edutainment.*

# Entertainment Software Rating Board

As noted, certain types of games tend to be violent. The Entertainment Software Rating Board (ESRB) rates games based on this and other criteria.

When designing games, you should understand what ESRB ratings mean and why they're important. Table 2.1 displays the seven ESRB ratings icons along with a definition of each rating.

**The ESRB was formed in 1994 as a nonprofit self-regulating organization by the Entertainment Software Association (ESA). To learn more about ESRB, visit** www.esrb.org.

**TABLE 2.1** ESRB Ratings

| Icon | Rating and Description |
|---|---|
|  | Titles rated *EC (Early Childhood)* have content that may be suitable for ages 3 and older. These titles contain no material that parents would find inappropriate. |
| | Titles rated *E (Everyone)* have content that may be suitable for ages 6 and older. Titles in this category may contain minimal cartoon, fantasy, or mild violence and/or infrequent use of mild language. |
| | Titles rated *E10+ (Everyone 10 and older)* have content that may be suitable for ages 10 and older. Titles in this category may contain more cartoon, fantasy, or mild violence, mild language, and/or minimal suggestive themes. |
|  | Titles rated *T (Teen)* have content that may be suitable for ages 13 and older. Titles in this category may contain violence, suggestive themes, crude humor, minimal blood, simulated gambling, and/or infrequent use of strong language. |

*(Continues)*

**TABLE 2.1** *(Continued)*

| Icon | Rating and Description |
|---|---|
|  | Titles rated *M (Mature)* have content that may be suitable for persons ages 17 and older. Titles in this category may contain intense violence, blood and gore, sexual content, and/or strong language. |
|  | Titles rated *AO (Adults Only)* have content that should only be played by persons 18 years and older. Titles in this category may include prolonged scenes of intense violence and/or graphic sexual content and nudity. |
|  | Titles listed as *RP (Rating Pending)* have been submitted to the ESRB and are awaiting a final rating. (This symbol appears only in advertising prior to a game's release.) |

Source: www.esrb.org

Although the rating system is voluntary, most commercial game producers choose to have their games rated because the majority of retailers in the United States and Canada only stock games that have the ESRB ratings on them. To get a rating, a producer fills out an ESRB questionnaire with information about aspects of the game that deal with drugs, sex, and violence. The producer submits the game, along with video showing scenes in the game that deal with any of those things, and scripts from the game. Three reviewers who are not associated with the games industry go over the material and then submit their findings to the ESRB along with their recommendations for what rating the game should receive.

Game designers should be aware of how the system works and how these ratings are derived, because in order sell your finished product through any retailer, you'll most likely be asked to produce your rating.

Designers often rework games that receive an unexpected or undesirable rating and submit their games multiple times until they hit the requirements for the rating they're after. Most games are targeting a specific audience to gain the most fans and/or sales; therefore, these designers want to make sure they have the ESRB rating on the box that lets a specific audience know the game they're buying is truly designed for them.

## THE ESSENTIALS AND BEYOND

You can decide what gameplay style may work best for an original game based on examples from existing games, and there is absolutely no reason you can't combine styles. Some games match the criteria for certain gameplay styles, but there are no hard and fast rules. These categories exist to help designers make choices on the best way to design their games. They also exist to help gamers search for new games based on their experiences with similar titles.

### ADDITIONAL EXERCISE

Go online and take a look at some of the sites where you can play games, such as www .kongregate.com, www.bigfishgames.com, www.candyland.com, www.gamenode .com, and www.addictinggames.com. Review the categories these sites use to classify their games. Pick at least three different games from different categories and play them, taking note of what type of gameplay style you believe the product to be. Does it match how the game was categorized? If not, why do you think the game was placed in the category where you found it?

Pick two games from one category—say, two adventure games or two action games. Play them both for at least an hour or two, and then compare how the games are similar and how they differ based on the way the gameplay styles were described in this chapter.

### REVIEW QUESTIONS

1.   Which is credited with being the first adventure game?

    **A.** *Wolfenstein 3D*          **C.** *Civilization*

    **B.** *Colossal Cave Adventure*    **D.** *World of Warcraft*

2.   True or false. If a game design becomes more immersive, it allows the player to suspend disbelief.

3.   Which type of game tends to be turn-based?

    **A.** Simulation          **C.** Action

    **B.** Adventure          **D.** Strategy

4.   True or false. The ESRB rating system is required for any game sold in the United States.

5.   What term do psychologists often use when referring to how immersive a player believes a game is?

    **A.** Spatial acceptance     **C.** Presence

    **B.** Delusion          **D.** Make-believe

# CHAPTER 3

# Core Game Design Concepts

*You have an idea* for a game, a vision in your head about how it can be played, so how do you begin to put it all together? Perhaps you've sketched out an amazing-looking character and want to spin an entire game around that. For the most part, that approach won't serve you as well as you may hope. There are sounder methods for developing a game.

Amazing characters and stunning environments are just part of the entire package. Developing the gameplay is the primary step, and that begins with the story, which helps define the actions of the game and reasons why things happen the way they do. Couple that with the type of game you're creating (refer to Chapter 2, "Gameplay Styles," for a review) and who your audience is, and you have a plan.

Start with an overview of the game, describing what the story is and the goal for play, and then flesh it out from there.

▶ **Writing the game**

▶ **Creating the characters**

▶ **Designing props**

▶ **Creating environments**

▶ **Understanding the basics of animation**

▶ **Understanding cinematics and cutscenes**

## Writing the Game

As you develop characters and environments for your game, the main thing you'll want to keep in mind is that gameplay should always come first. And although you're jotting down your initial ideas for the design (you have to start somewhere), when it comes to gameplay, the more you can design ways to let players discover through trial and error or by seeing how things are done, the more successful your game can be. In other words, if you have too many rules to read, most players get turned off.

To get started, write a short overview, or synopsis, of what your game is about. This will help establish characters, storylines, and events that need to be developed along with the lore. Don't get too detailed, just stick to the basics:

- ▶ Who is the game designed for? (Demographics are discussed later in this chapter.)

- ▶ What is the gameplay style? (Gameplay styles are covered in Chapter 2.)

- ▶ What is the goal or purpose of the game? Write this in one to two sentences, also known as the *logline*.

## Loglines

A logline is a device used by writers and designers to explain the entire project, boiled down into one sentence. For example, here is a one-sentence description for the game *Mario Bros.*: "Italian-American plumber, Mario, and his brother Luigi battle evil creatures that come from the sewers in New York City." That one sentence gives you the logline and provides enough information to write the overview of what the game is all about.

To help you write your own logline, try answering the following four questions.

- ▶ Who is the main character?

- ▶ What does this character want?

- ▶ What is going to try to stop the main character?

- ▶ What about the game is unique or compelling?

Loglines can be tough to write, and doing so takes some practice. An excellent way to do this is to look at loglines for other projects, especially ones you're familiar with. You can find loglines for thousands of movies at www.imdb.com and for selected movies with commentary at

www.norman-hollyn.com/535/handouts/loglines.pdf

These loglines are very similar to what you want to write for your game. The purpose is to give a good overview of what the project is about and to encourage others to read further. Keep it simple and to the point. If possible, include the game's genre to help clarify what the project is about.

To get more ideas on loglines for games, look at some of the catalogue listings of games for sale. Writers strive to create a one- or two-line description (the logline) of what a game is about to encourage buyers to look further at the game. The blog *My Day Will Come* has some pretty good loglines describing games: www.mydaywillcome.com.

The short descriptions used by *Academic Skill Builders* (www.arcademic-skillbuilders.com/games/) provide more examples of how you can boil down descriptions to get to the point quickly and efficiently without losing any flavor of what the game is about.

Once you've defined your genre and demographic and prepared the logline, write a few concise paragraphs with a bit more detail. Two to three paragraphs are all you need to broaden the information. For example, you can expand the logline for *Mario Bros.* to explain what the creatures are and *why* they're coming into New York in paragraph one. In paragraph two, you can explain *why* Mario and his brother feel compelled to try and battle them. You may choose to provide a third paragraph to explain how your gameplay will be unique and compelling.

In this example, your synopsis should explain why Mario does things, and why the creatures do things. This is the initial work that gets done on creating the lore.

## Creating Game Lore

*Lore*, in a nutshell, is the detailed backstory or narrative for any game. The lore outlines a series of events that have taken place beforehand (before the events that are happening in your game) and may explain the history of the worlds, the conflicts, the characters, and what is driving the current gameplay. Some games that have extensive lore are *Halo, Elder Scrolls, Metroid Prime, Fallout, Neverwinter Nights, Mass Effect,* and *World of Warcraft.*

The history of why lore has such a strong foothold in gaming can easily be traced back to story-driven tabletop games like *Dungeons & Dragons.* Lore is the mythology of the game. Most role-playing games (RPGs) are steeped in lore.

# Fans and Game Lore

Enthusiastic game designers spend a tremendous amount of time writing and cataloguing the lore for the worlds they create. The lore helps them generate the excitement that emerges in the gameplay. It provides the reason one faction wars against another and makes clear what instigates elaborate quest lines. It explains why cultures developed they way they did and allows fans to get caught up in the passion for why the game exists in the first place.

Some of this backstory can be revealed in the opening for a game; in addition, during gameplay the lore can surface in the form of quests, challenges, maps, diaries, logs, and charts related to the game. What makes this method of gameplay intriguing is that as players progress, they get glimpses into the mysteries behind why certain things happen. Information is revealed to them through their efforts, and most players respond favorably to this method of design. They're intrigued and usually want to learn more, especially if the lore is fun, unique, and captivating. Some gamers play to find out the end result of a quest line because it will add to their understanding of the lore.

Lore is one of the reasons many games develop fan bases. Understanding the basis for conflicts between heroes in the story, gaining a clearer idea of what you're fighting for, and knowing the history of people and places adds to players' attachments to their characters and makes the game world even more real for them. The lore you create should be apparent in the overview you write as the first short synopsis describing the game.

**Character specs are any special attributes a character may have.**

When avid fans get caught up in the lore for a game, they often create YouTube videos to show how to play segments of the game. These YouTube videos, along with tutorials on how to play character specs, can also narrate how the lore relates to the tasks being completed. Go to ThePinkkilla's channel on YouTube.com for examples of these types of fan videos: www.youtube.com/user/ ThePinkkilla?feature=mhee.

In addition to videos, players create blogs and entire websites devoted to explaining lore, showing screengrabs from gameplay, and creating their own new stories based on that lore. Just like some players *mod games*—that is, create their own levels to play in—they also take existing lore and write extended stories or create new characters for the existing world.

These fans, especially long-time ones, keep track of the lore and often present it more clearly than the official websites related to the games. Some games, like *World of Warcraft* and *Final Fantasy*, have such long storylines that it takes an act of love for the game by these fans to catalogue and present the material the way gamers like to see it. This isn't to say the official sites do a poor job. Rather, fans get so caught up in the lore that they rewrite it to make it clearer and then add screengrabs or videos to help illustrate more clearly what that lore is. Unless they have inside information (which occasionally happens), they don't know any more lore than what the game companies provide; they just tend to present it in a different way that appeals to a lot of gamers.

Designers can create lore for any game, regardless of how deep or light the project may be. They can then use the lore to create new storylines based on the backstory they have written. If your world is immersive with warring factions, then the reasons there are conflicts need to be written in detail. As you develop your game further, adding more quests and more areas to explore, draw on the existing lore, and then expand it where needed.

Adventure or action-adventure games tend to rely a great deal on lore. In *Lara Croft, Tomb Raider,* the main character's lineage and personal tragedies create much of the lore for her adventures. In other words, the events in her life helped to shape her character and the forces driving her to do what she does.

Lara (her title is Lady Lara Croft) is actually, according to her creators, an 11th-generation countess, daughter of Lady Amelia Croft and the dashing but scandalous archeologist Lord Richard Croft. Both her parents died before she came of age, and it was while she was a young student at the Abbingdon Girls School that her brilliance and athletic prowess were discovered.

The death of her mother was particularly stirring. Lara and her mother were on a plane that crashed while flying over the Himalayan Mountains. Lara survived the crash, but her mother was killed. Lara, just a young girl, survived 10 days in the mountains and made her way to Katmandu, where she walked into a bar, telephoned her father (of course, he was still alive at the time), and politely asked if he could come pick her up.

The lore for this game is learned during the opening cinematics, on the official site, and on a myriad of fansites. Players can learn more about Lara through a series of comic books; and as players tackle the game's quests, more parts of the lore are revealed at the conclusion of each quest.

Now that is fun lore! Who wouldn't want to jump into Lara's boots and race around with Olympic athletic abilities, leaping from broken edifice to massive statue in some remote undiscovered tomb, while evading evil henchmen so you can save a priceless relic?

Here's another example. Blizzard's *Diablo 3* uses a map (see Figure 3.1), which is an integral part of the lore for that game.

◄

**Often, games with extensive writing about the lore develop conflicts in the storyline. To resolve these conflicts, the lore is updated, producing what is known as *retroactive continuity* or *retcon*.**

**FIGURE 3.1** Maps, like this one from *Diablo 3*, can convey lore.

Maps, genealogy charts, and personal logs or diaries are designed to match the look and feel of the worlds that are written about in the lore.

This map shows Sanctuary, a haven for like-minded angels and demons and their offspring, the Nephalem, who wanted to live in peace. The area is infiltrated by other angels and demons who sought to disrupt the peace and started The Great Conflict, which essentially explains the basis for some of the lore that runs through *Diablo*. The lore covers centuries of time, and the map reflects that ancient look to help give weight to the stories.

The legend of the game—the lore—can be the basis not only for expanding an existing game but also for creating new games (either sequels to the first game or offshoots), books, manga, movies, and so on. The game *DOOM* is a perfect example of this. The game, which debuted in 1993, spawned several sequels, books, comics, and a movie starring Karl Urban and Dwayne Johnson, which was released in 2005.

The *Star Wars* franchise is a terrific example of how immersive and deep lore can be. The legends that George Lucas wrote about the Sith lords and the Jedi knights have carried through numerous films, games, comics, and TV shows (live action and animated). Fans have dedicated hundreds of websites to the lore and written their own stories based on what Lucas started with Luke Skywalker and his first adventure.

## MARIO BROS.: SPINOFFS AND SEQUELS

The *Mario Bros.* games have spawned numerous spinoffs and sequels. In the original story, Mario, an Italian-American plumber who lives in the Mushroom Kingdom, battles his nemesis, Bowser, who repeatedly tries to kidnap Princess Peach. Therein lies the lore for the Mario Bros. franchise. That simple synopsis has provided a framework on which to develop Mario's personality, the weapons he uses (think of all the tools a plumber carries!), and the locations where he can battle his arch-foe and save the princess.

Mario first appeared in the NES game *Donkey Kong* in 1981 and was the brainchild of Shigeru Miyamoto.

Game companies like Blizzard provide websites dedicated to the lore of their games and the worlds created for their games, and *World of Warcraft's* Azeroth is one example. You can visit www.blizzard.com to read about the lore and get a glimpse at upcoming projects.

◀

Many games develop communities to support fans' desire for immersion. Fans can access the mythology, write their own new stories, and compile existing lore to share with other fans.

## LORE SITES

*Final Fantasy,* an expansive and deeply immersive game that has spawned over a dozen sequels, maintains an enormous lore site at www.ffxivcore.com/wiki/Category:Lore. *Final Fantasy* and most other games are designed to be played without understanding the full lore, but once players get into the story and characters, many of them like to understand the backstory more fully. Lore sites are one way to provide that.

Not every game requires lore to accompany it; however, if you intend for your project to include any type of immersion or expansion, you need the framework of a backstory to work from.

### GAMES WITHOUT LORE

Not all games have extensive lore. Some have simple explanations to provide a quick overview of how the game is played. Good examples are the match-three games *Bejeweled* and *Jewel Quest*. In games like these, you're given basic instructions to swap gems in order to line up three or more to gain points and bring more gems into the playing field.

No lore is needed, just a simple description to get you started. Then the adrenaline starts to pump as the gems move faster and matches become more difficult to make. The driving force behind the gameplay lies in gaining points through increasingly difficult levels to make it interesting, rather than an involved story to provide the impetus for play.

## Developing the Script

**Telling the story through gameplay, rather than just through text, as Blizzard's *World of Warcraft* does, is effective for communicating lore and keeping players moving through the game.**

Scripts for games need to not only include dialogue the game may need, but also provide cues for when events happen. Events may include the arrival of a boss, challenges the player must overcome, and the arrival at a fork in the road where a decision must be made. Begin each scene of your script by describing the environment and time of day and weather (if that applies in your game), then add the secondary elements (music, background effects), and finally add in the events—what is happening in this scene, including dialogue.

### Storyboards

Use a storyboard to organize your ideas. This type of board should include written copy describing the following:

- ► Location
- ► Dialogue
- ► Actions
- ► Animations
- ► Additional effects (visual and audio)

Some examples of additional effects are ambient audio and secondary animations, such as background movements, weather, and text/map overlays with instructions.

Figure 3.2 is an example of one type of template you can use for storyboards.

| SHOT | IMAGE | DESCRIPTION / INTERACTION | TIME |
|---|---|---|---|

GAME Jake's Shadow  Jake's Shadow  
SEQUENCE Battle with Set  
BOARD ID Drr4.744.001  
SCENE 4.55.122  
ARTIST Sternberg  
PAGE 51/  
DATE June/09

**Location**  
Interior of Set's Sarcophagus

**Action**  
Jake confonts the god Set  2 sec

Boss emerges after Jake places stone  2.5 sec  
on the altar

**Effects**  
Animated star bursts from Set's hands

**Audio**  
Wind in caves, water dripping, footsteps

**Dialogue**  
Set: "Who dares to enter the  
realms of Osiris?!"

**FIGURE 3.2** Example of a boarded scene

This example of a boarded scene is from the game *Jake's Shadow,* which is about a little boy who ventures into the world of the ancient Egyptian gods to retrieve his stolen shadow. In the figure, art shows the god Set and basic information like dialogue, location, and so on. Boards are extremely useful to help organize story, actions, and more. They can also be scanned and cut into pieces, after which camera moves can be added in a program like Flash or After Effects as an animatic to provide a sense of timing for the action. That step is almost always done with cinematics (see "Understanding Cinematics and Cutscenes," later in this chapter).

> Creating storyboards and flowcharts helps others begin to see your vision.

## Flowcharts

You can create a flowchart to help map out where characters can go and how storylines may develop and be revealed. The flowchart shown in Figure 3.3, from the game *Pinkyblee and the Magic Chalice,* has been color-coded to show the start point (yellow), the departure point to a next level (blue), gameplay in this level (aqua), and a boss who can kill your character (red). Essentially, flowcharts can be created to enhance and explain gameplay to the artists, animators, coders, and others who are building the game, especially when you have large crews involved in a project. They don't have to be color-coded; they can be drawn in any manner and tailored to meet the vision of the designer and whatever seems to work best to communicate with the crew.

> Designers often create flowcharts like puzzles, keeping the events on pieces of paper or layers in Photoshop to move around and edit while honing the design of the game.

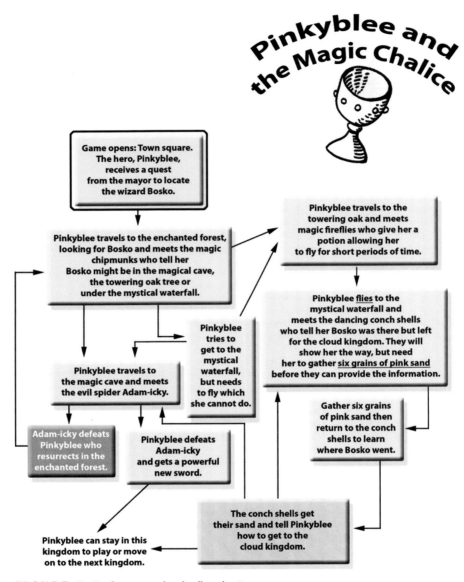

**FIGURE 3.3** One example of a flowchart

In this flowchart example of a nonlinear type of gameplay, a series of paths are plotted out for the character. The character can risk travelling directly to the boss to see if they can defeat it, or take a different route to complete more tasks and level up a bit more. If the character takes the longer route and completes tasks, they may choose to tackle the boss or bypass it and go to find Bosko.

Usually, tackling the boss and defeating it means many extra points and/or bonus items, so the player needs to decide the best way to exit this level.

The flowchart maps out the decision points of the game, and the written script fills in the prose and describes the visual and audio aspects of the scene. Figure 3.4 shows a sample piece of script from *Pinkyblee and the Magic Chalice*.

**The script is another method of getting ideas down, describing in writing the locations and most important, what the action is.**

```
EXT, day:  In the center of a quaint town, similar in
appearance to an medieval English village, several of
the townsfolk pushing rough looking carts filled with
produce and leading herds of sheep and goats meander
the cobblestone streets. An older man, dressed in finer
clothing than the townsfolk approaches a warrior.
PINKYBLEE, 28, female WARRIOR stands in the square
facing THE MAYOR of the town.

                    PINKYBLEE
                 My mission is to
                 defend this town.
           What deeds do you need completed?


                    THE MAYOR
         The defender of this realm has gone missing.
                We can only assume
                because of his power,
           an immense evil has taken him.


                    PINKYBLEE
           I can search for this defender.
                What is his name?


                    THE MAYOR
              Bosko, the Magnificent.
           He was last seen in the woods
              near the town. You would be
           well served to seek him there.

EXT, day:  Pinkyblee salutes the mayor then turns to exit
through the main gates for the town and enters the forest.
The woods are lush with a variety of flowering and
fruited trees. In the distance, a small river meanders
off into the distance while further to the east,
a small mountain range rises. The warrior walks along
the road until she reaches a fork, where two branches
of the road head off to the east and west. Across the road
is  a small meadow covered in flowers and a small, lesser
used path. The warrior can choose which direction to go in.
```

**FIGURE 3.4** This script excerpt includes descriptions, setting, and dialogue.

Flowcharts help the designer sort out where the characters go and what events happen. They also allow the designer to identify which events are major occurrences and which are minor ones that may allow the character or player the opportunity to gather more resources, build skills, or learn the interface better.

The script takes those sections in the flowchart and expands on them by adding good written descriptions of the locations and dialogue.

# Writing Dialogue

The dialogue, especially in RPG or action-adventure games, needs to be carefully written, because the words being spoken not only provide instructions, but may also offer up clues about how to solve quests.

In addition, the dialogue may tie in with information found in the lore for the game, shedding light on mysteries and helping to ignite that passion in the gamer to push on.

By understanding the type of character you're writing for, their personality, and also your audience, you'll have a better chance of creating successful dialogue. Good dialogue should be short and to the point. Long, flowery speeches wear on the nerves of gamers, especially those who may play multiple characters and have to hear the same dialogue repeated.

## BAD DIALOGUE

"You were almost a Jill sandwich!"

Many gamers and designers believe this statement to be one of the worst written lines in gaming dialogue history. The line is uttered in the first *Resident Evil* game by Barry, Jill's companion, when Jill is almost killed.

Video games are notorious for having bad dialogue, a fact you can easily research by looking online at the number of websites dedicated to collecting and showcasing some of the worst (or best, depending on your point of view) lines uttered in a game. This website offers a host of examples: `http://audioatrocities.com/`.

When writing for your game, be sure to use words that fit the comprehension level of your intended audience. Instructions provided in the game need to be clear and easy to follow. If your gamer begins to suffer frustration because the dialogue is muddled or too long, or the accent is too hard to understand, they will move on to another product.

In addition, keep the flavor of the game in mind. Accents, catchphrases, and in-game jokes are fun—sort of like adding Easter eggs—so you can spice a game with them here and there. But be careful not to make the game too difficult to follow. Special elements give gamers more to talk about outside of the game, and when fans form around a game and create mods or websites dedicated to the game, you've established an audience who will help promote your game for you.

*Mods* refer to modifications of the game made by fans. They can be entirely new levels or additions to existing parts of the original game.

## Testing Gameplay

While playing the first *Mario Bros.* game, players battled their way through castle after castle, defeating bad guys and hoping to save Princess Peach, only to see the annoying text "The princess is in the other castle" flashing across the top of the screen. Needless to say, that type of design was not repeated in subsequent games for the franchise. What can you learn from this design flaw?

As you write the gameplay for any game, keep in mind that players are working hard to get through all the challenges you have set before them. If a player is struggling to work through the game, and you deny them the reward again and again, you'll frustrate the player and they will walk away from your baby. Why would a player deal with constant frustration when there are many games out there that are well designed and provide challenges but temper the more difficult aspects with fun rewards?

The best way to determine if your gameplay is too difficult or too easy is to test. Test your game, then test it again, and then, test it some more. The importance of testing a game can't be overlooked or treated lightly. It takes a tremendous amount of time, effort, and often, money to make a game. Testing is a way to ensure that the game will be well received; and nothing is deadlier than releasing a game with bugs or errors that could easily have been caught and fixed in testing. If a game is released with problems, bad press will circulate very quickly, and all your effort to make the game will have been wasted.

As soon as your project goes into production and you have the first bit of playable game, begin testing—and keep testing right up until the game ships. The more people who test the game who aren't familiar with it, the more objective and honest the feedback will be.

Gaming companies have entire divisions dedicated to testing their games. Testing begins as soon as they have any playable game elements, even with temporary assets. Chapter 9, "Game Production Pipelines," includes a more thorough description of testing.

## Compiling the Game Doc

The *game doc* (document), also referred to as the *game design document (GDD)*, is the blueprint created from which to build the game. More information about GDDs is also covered in Chapter 7.

Small, independent games may have as few as one to three people building the game, whereas big AAA titles can have hundreds on the crew. The minute any game goes into production, money is being spent, so understanding exactly what everyone's job is and what needs to be created, along with deadlines for completing work, ensures as smooth an assembly as possible.

Not every game doc is the same, but they tend to contain the same basic information:

**Title Page**   This section includes the copyright information, logline, and production company. (See Figure 3.5.).

**Gameplay Style**   Provide the type genre here. This is generally written out as a one- to three-word description like this: *action-adventure*. The genre is usually italicized. (See Figure 3.5.).

**Demographic**   The information you need to provide here has to do with who the game is being designed for. Include the age, sex, and any other cultural markers that may help identify the audience. For example, you may be creating a sports game for teenage boys who like baseball: that is your demographic. (See Figure 3.5.).

**Game System**   Be specific about the platform for which the game is being designed. If your game is for a home computer, then explain that, along with telling whether it's for PC, Apple (Mac), or both (See Figure 3.5.). You can also include other information, such as the amount of RAM needed and video card requirements.

**Some of the systems that games play on include these:**

> ▶ Personal computers—PC and Mac
>
> ▶ Consoles—PlayStation, Wii, Xbox, Nintendo
>
> ▶ Handhelds—Mobile phones, Game Boy

> At this stage of development, don't make assumptions about what rating the ESRB may give the game. Once the game is done, you can decide whether to submit it for a rating.

## Weird Helmet

Genre: *action*

Audience: "E" for everyone

System: PC

Synopsis: Help Bob, the last member of this abandoned mining station in outerspace, get from level to level in his homemade helmet that can only hold a small amount of oxygen.

Copyright © 2009 Star Mountain Studios

**FIGURE 3.5** Provide basic information including title, logline, production company, gameplay style, demographic, art, and game system at the beginning of the GDD.

**Game Overview**   Start with the information you wrote for the synopsis. Get to the point immediately, and don't include any questions in the overview. You don't want readers guessing about anything regarding how the game is played. Write the overview clearly and directly. Explain how the game is played and what the goal is. Avoid the temptation to say something like, "Comedy ensues" or "and then the action starts!" No one in the industry will take a doc seriously if it's peppered with half-thought-out statements or innuendos.

The following is an example of an overview for the interactive hidden object game (IHOG) *Elder & Jung: The Frobish Riddles*:

## GAME OVERVIEW FROM THE GDD FOR *FROBISH RIDDLES*

Shortly after the disappearance of his brother "Old Bill" Putty, Sgt. Emil Putty was sent the bindings of a strange looking book. What was particularly odd was that it looked liked the book once held numerous pages but now only the first remained. Furthermore, that single page seemed to only contain nonsensical phrases. The book was a mystery. But Sgt. Putty was more concerned about the mystery of what happened to his brother. After conventional investigations turned up absolutely nothing on Old Bill's whereabouts, and everyone dismissed any connection the book had with his disappearance, Sgt. Putty was told about a most unconventional private investigator: Garrick Elder of the Elder & Jung Investigation Agency. Mr. Elder heads up the agency's Metaphysical Investigation department. This sort of case is his bread and butter.

The game follows the team's search through the abandoned Frobish hospital, where Sgt. Putty worked when it was still open, and where Old Bill was the caretaker after it closed. The hospital was Bill's last known location and the natural starting place for any investigation. And while Garrick doesn't always start at the most likely location, this time it seemed worthwhile.

Players can access three possible locations at a time, playing rHOGs, regular HOGs, mini games, and inventory puzzles to figure out where to find specific clues in each room. As more rooms are solved, a presence begins to assert itself, appearing from time to time. What is revealed at the end of the game is that the presence is the imprisoned spirit of Emil's twin brother, Old Bill. Old Bill was torn from the physical plane by a Djinn one night at the Frobish, and forced into service in an ethereal plane. Apparently Old Bill liked to dabble in the occult, and accidentally called forth this being.

*(Continues)*

## GAME OVERVIEW FROM THE GDD
### FOR *FROBISH RIDDLES* (Continued)

The Djinn wasn't very happy about it either. Fortunately Old Bill found an ally on the ethereal plane who helped him send encoded pages back to the physical plane.

The successful conclusion of the game results in Old Bill being returned to his earthly state and the evil creature that imprisoned him destroyed—or at the very least sealed within his ethereal realm.

## GAME CHARACTERS

**Garrick Elder**   48 years old, born in New Clacker, Pennsylvania. Historian, expert in ancient mysteries of paranormal, metaphysical, and bizarre lore. Garrick is a detective of sorts. He investigates cases that involve the metaphysical and chronicles them in novel form.

**Jacinthe Jung**   (JJ to friends, though Garrick calls her YuhYuh, keeping with the German Y sound of her names.) 28 years old, born in Flearshire, England. Her family was tragically killed in a house fire in Halifax. Being orphaned, Jacinthe was raised in a series of foster homes in England before she ran away and hid in the hold of a ship bound for the US. She applied for a job as a clerk with Garrick, who quickly discovered that Jacinthe was smart, quick-thinking, and a benefit to the agency. Jacinthe manages the day-to-day running of Elder and Jung and aids in the investigation of the cases through research and legwork for Garrick.

**Sgt. Emil Putty**   Emil worked on the police force for 20 years; then he retired and took a job as a security guard at the Wilhelm Frobish Hospital for the Criminally Insane. When the hospital closed, he retired for good.

**"Old Bill" Putty**   Twin brother of Emil, who recommended him for the job of caretaker of the Frobish building and grounds. Old Bill disappeared one night literally without a trace. He took the job because he thought it would be the perfect place to practice some of the occult stuff he had been reading about. He wasn't a Wiccan, Satanist, Voodoo priest, or anything of that nature. He was just fascinated with the rituals and thought they were kind of cool. Unfortunately for him, a little knowledge went the wrong way and he summoned forth the Mystical Djinn, Doooola. Doooola promptly ripped him from the physical plane and forced him into slavery.

**Art**   You may begin to add art to the project, usually concept pieces that show what the characters and worlds look like. For the *Frobish* game, some of the initial design work was for the character Mr. Putty and the world, which you can see in Figure 3.6.

**FIGURE 3.6** The distinctive look for the environments and world can be created in the early phases of production to help inspire other parts of the design.

The work on art at the beginning of development can also include what the interfaces might look like. The interface is what the player uses to interact with the game. The typefaces (fonts), colors, and overall look and feel of the art speak volumes about what the game will play like, as shown in Figure 3.7.

**Longer Description**   Expand on what you started in the game overview. In the longer description, you may want to explain more about the lore and provide histories for specific characters, cultures, regions, bosses, or specialty items in the game like a magic gem or powerful weapon that needs to be found or created.

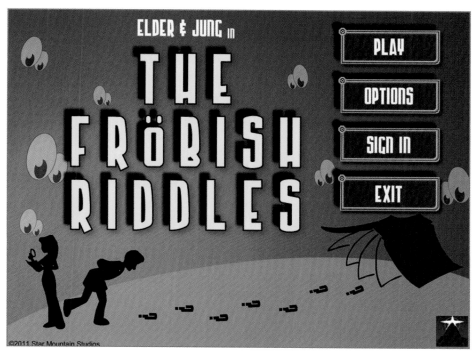

**FIGURE 3.7** Early art shows that *Fröbish* is a fun but slightly spooky hidden object game (HOG) in which the player sleuths around an abandoned hospital, looking for clues.

Work with maps to block out more areas where events can occur, and expand on your flowcharts. Development of the project at this point is a balance, going back and forth between writing out events and using visuals to help define the look and feel of the game along with plotting out where things will happen during gameplay.

**Narrative/Levels**   The narrative starts to get into more specifics for the actual game. In this section, you begin breaking the game into specific levels and describing what will happen in each level. Chapter 7, "Designing Levels and User Interfaces," goes into more detail about levels. You'll find an excerpt from an actual GDD from the game *Red Harvest* in Appendix C, "Game Design Document."

**Gameplay**   Explain how the player actually plays the game (for example, keyboard commands), the interface design (discussed in Chapter 6), options, and any features that will allow for customization of the game, including the ability to build mods. Mods can include new characters, weapons, quests, and abilities and are usually built on existing first-person shooters (FPS), real-time strategy games, and RPGs.

**Maps**    In this section, you can map out zones or areas for gameplay and begin to address how the player will navigate in the game. Navigation is covered in greater depth in Chapter 6, "Navigation and Interfaces."

Figure 3.8 shows an early version of a map created for the game *Fröbish*. It roughs out the basic layout of one floor of the hospital where the game takes place and shows the main path of navigation that players follow through the building to encounter other areas with quests, puzzles, and HOG items to collect.

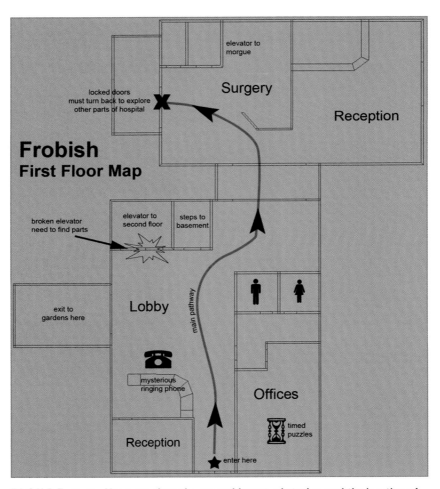

**FIGURE 3.8** Maps can show the general layout, obstacles, and the location of games or other activity.

In addition to showing the basic areas that are being developed for the game, the designer can select areas to develop in greater detail. In Figure 3.8, the main pathway has been mapped out; even in this early phase of development, the designer has already designated an area for a mysterious phone-calling game, indicated how to fix the broken elevator game, and shown that timed puzzles will take place in the offices. One of the reasons it's so important to map out these things is because frequently during this kind of gameplay, the player must go back to a previous location to obtain another clue or complete another task, and this lets the designer know how fluid those transitions can be.

**Audio Requirements**   Most games have musical scores, recorded dialogue, sound effects for weapons, monster sounds, clicking buttons on interfaces, ambient sounds, and so on. In your initial overview, you need to account for what audio the project needs. Chapter 8, "Sound," describes in greater detail how various kinds of audio are made.

**Schedules**   Begin to map out timelines for creating, completing, and delivering art, animation, audio, code, and so on. Each department will have its own time-line that needs to mesh with all the other timelines. For example, if the code writers need to work with specific completed animations, then write the delivery dates for animation to know when they must provide those assets. As the game goes further into production, some departments will need more time; others will be finished more quickly. You can adjust the delivery schedules as the project progresses and pieces are completed or excised from the game.

Writing the game doc can be the most arduous part of the process; however, unless a clear guide outlines what needs to be done, the game can quickly become overwhelming if the people working on the project don't have a solid understanding of what they're supposed to be doing.

## IMPORTANCE OF THE GAME DESIGN DOCUMENT

Game docs are large projects to undertake, but their importance can't be overstated. This doc spells out what each person on the project needs to be doing and helps to provide timeframes for work to be done. At the same time, it remains fluid; as the project gets deeper into production, the designer may still opt to change part of the game, and the game doc is where all those changes are catalogued.

## Preparing Pitches

Designers often write a game pitch to sell their concept to a company. They may also use the pitch to help potential game makers they wish to work with understand what they want to accomplish. Pitches are much less involved than game docs; however, they should contain much of the same core information:

▶ Title, including logline

▶ Overview

▶ Gameplay style and intended audience

▶ Concept art

▶ Playable first version (prototype or vertical slice)

The concept art and overview are necessary components of any pitch. A prototype of the game is optional but can be extremely helpful in selling the concept.

Pitches are intended to generate interest and excitement about the project and should not get too bogged down with details. At the same time, they must be inclusive enough that major questions are quickly answered. In addition to the key information listed, the pitch should address how long the game will take to make and potential marketing ideas.

> The prototype or vertical slice may be a partial or complete playable level, providing enough for someone to play and get a good grasp of the gameplay.

# Creating the Characters

Characters are, of course, important in most games. Well-made characters will become beloved, or deliciously hated, by players who immerse themselves in the game.

### GETTING INTO CHARACTER CONCEPT WORK

For many artists working in the games industry, character concept is a coveted role. Very few people find their way into that job, though, particularly those first entering the games business. Most artists who are doing concept work have been in the industry for years, working in other positions and learning the industry inside and out, before they get to create brand new characters.

Many people just entering the industry tend to do so in animation—inbetweens (part of the process in keyframe animation) for characters, secondary animations like background nonplayer characters (NPCs), or effects

*(Continues)*

**GETTING INTO CHARACTER CONCEPT WORK** *(Continued)*

animations for button pushes. Intro jobs may also include development of assets (creating art for interfaces or cleaning up art that is already in the pipeline). There are also entry-level positions for audio, level design, world building, game writing, coders, and content design. Most of these areas require some concept work; however, the majority of entry-level jobs have the person matching to existing styles. In other words, most people begin by working with existing styles and working as part of the team while they learn the ropes.

There tends to be a great deal of 3D modeling work as well. A good entry-level position can involve working on cleaning up existing models, adding rigging, or painting textures.

One of the first things you want to consider when developing characters is how immersive a game will be. Extremely immersive games have a tendency to allow players to form a deeper emotional attachment to their characters. Successful screenwriters and novelists challenge themselves to write characters that the reader will care about and possibly identify or at least empathize with. Successful game designers take that a step further, by having "living" creations that can become an extension of the player.

Therefore, developing characters involves not only their appearance, or look, but how they move and communicate and the types of skills they may need to use during gameplay. If the project is highly immersive, then developing a character that is rather complex tends to be the way to go. By the same token, less immersive, light-hearted games are the perfect arena for designing simpler characters. For either type of design, concept artists start with the game doc to get a clear understanding of what that character needs to be able to do in the game, what the gameplay is (what the character will be doing), and who the audience is.

Figure 3.9 shows concepts by Jack Keely for the character *Dagmar*. This concept compilation shows variations for her and enough visual information to provide a good understanding of how the character could appear in the game. For many design teams, it isn't unusual to have more than one artist working on concept for characters, because their final look and development can be critical to the success of any game.

◄

**Many concept pieces are posted on the website ConceptArt .org, an open forum where you can post work to get feedback and view the work of others.**

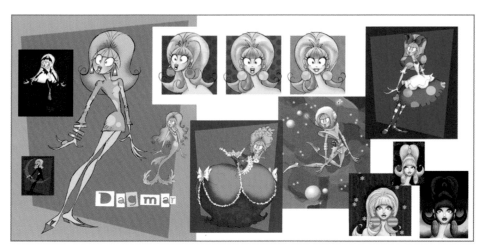

**FIGURE 3.9** These concept illustrations show possible variations for a character including character types, clothing, and hair and facial styles.

## Design

The look of characters can quite often be one of the most labor-intensive parts of creating a game. The characters are, after all, the stars, and they need to look amazing and perform with cool moves because in gaming, much of what a character does requires repetitive movements.

The concept artist needs to understand not only what types of things the character is required to do during gameplay (will it swim, fly, jump, run, fall down, or sweep its arms about during fighting or when casting spells?) but also what sort of personality it should exhibit. If designing characters attracts you, then studying anatomy as well as how people and animals move is critical to your education.

Many characters designed for games are idealized or stylized humans and animals that do extremely physical things. The artist who works on designs for such characters needs to know how muscle groups work, especially if the task involves making certain muscles look larger or specialized. In addition, if the task involves creating a character that is alien, having an understanding of anatomy allows the artist to build on that knowledge to distort or create something new that, although unreal or otherworldly, is logical. That logic allows the player to buy into the abilities of the creation.

In addition, learn to observe carefully. Watch the interaction between people and animals. Note how body language is displayed when there is anger, fear, or apprehension. Pay attention to what people do when they're lying or hiding something.

When designing characters for concept work or as they appear during different actions or emotional displays, it's deadly to simply draw what you think they should look like. You end up drawing the same things over and over again—that is, drawing from memory. To break out of that habit, study as many examples as possible of action and performance to add to your understanding of how people and animals react and move.

Practice gesture drawings to capture not a portrait of the people or animals you're studying, but the essence of their performance. When you do gesture work, find the inner line of action first (the red line in Figure 3.10) and sketch it in. Then loosely rough in the rest of the figure. Remember, you're trying to capture the action and performance, not draw a portrait.

**FIGURE 3.10** Gesture drawings capture action and performance.

If you don't study live models or videos of these types of movements and examples of emotion, then you're limited by your experiences and will fall back again and again on what you *think* the character should look like and how it should move instead of what it *actually* looks like. Learn throughout your entire career. Avoid making up characters based on what you have seen in other games. Get out in the world, look around you, see what is there, and draw it.

Another issue to keep in mind while designing characters is whether the final version will be 2D or 3D. 2D characters can actually show more of the physics of animation than 3D—like squash and stretch. *Squash and stretch* is one of the first principles of animation. If you watch a ball drop and hit the ground, just as it hits, it tends to squash a bit; then, when it bounces back up, it stretches a little before it resumes its normal shape. Being able to show that with animated characters helps breathe life into their movements and tends to be easier with 2D work. For that reason, using many 2D images can be highly successful for comedic, light games where very cartoony movements and reactions to in-game situations require over-the-top motion.

3D characters tend to be better suited for more realistic games and let players view the characters and their world from all types of camera angles. The 3D character lends itself well to highly immersive games where gamers often identify with the avatar they're playing.

**Animators who do 2D and 3D work start with the same skills: learning the physics of animation. Animators can be self-taught, but many schools teach animation.**

## Personality/Abilities

Understanding how human and animal bodies react to stress and emotional states will help you to design your characters. To reiterate, gameplay should be the first and best goal to designing any game. Focusing too much attention on the look of a character or its abilities won't create a successful game; however, character appearance and abilities add to the mix that makes for good gameplay.

As a designer, your job may be to create a character with abilities never seen in games before. In order to do this, you need to clearly understand what the character needs to do and a bit about the physics of its world. You may also be asked to work with existing characters that need to be updated or redesigned because gameplay has changed or the characters have new abilities.

**Sometimes, working backward from the endgame goals will help you sort out how your character can get there.**

To help sort out what abilities and personality traits your characters need, look at the goals for winning your game. If the game involves quests, then having the ability to walk, run, or move some other way, along with fighting skills, are some of the things you need to discover.

The game *Street Fighter*, from Capcom, provides several different styles of characters so the player can pick which type they want to use as their avatar. The lineup in Figure 3.11 shows the range of sizes and types of characters the game provides.

**FIGURE 3.11** In this character lineup, the designer includes visual clues for each character's abilities.

In this figure, you can see the characters' body language, poses, clothing, and, in some cases, weapons. Together these characteristics give a good indication of what abilities these fighters have. They may be small and fast so they can move in and out with quick jabs, or big and muscular and designed for punching, and so on.

Personality can also be conveyed through the way characters dress, what jewelry or tattoos they have, and the body language they exhibit during different situations. Some characters move in a comical fashion, denoting the type of gameplay, whereas others move with purpose or authority—again, all attributes that the designers can study from the way humans or animals move and behave in different situations.

# Bosses

Bosses are characters and should be treated as such when it comes to designing them. As with other characters, you need to understand the boss's appearance, personality, and physical capabilities. You also need to know how, if at all, it will react with other characters and the environment.

Bosses tend to be larger than the player or avatar, to add to the fear factor and make the adrenaline rise. Most gamers feel that it's more fun to defeat something much larger than they are. Figure 3.12 shows a boss known as The Beast from the game *Infamous*, about to face off with the lead character in the game.

**FIGURE 3.12** Bosses are often much larger than the player's character.

Bosses tend to have skills that players have not encountered before—or, if they have, in smaller doses. One of the aspects of good gameplay is a boss that is tough enough to defeat your character but can be defeated by figuring out the strategy to the fight. Bosses also tend to be unique in that no other character in the game looks or moves like them, although that isn't a hard and fast rule.

## Quest Givers

Quest givers can take on all forms in a game. They may be human or human-like, animals, animated objects like rocks or trees, road signs, or pages from a newspaper or journal with prompts or clues for the player to help decide what tasks to perform in order to move forward in the game. Whatever form the quest giver takes on, its role is to give scope and meaning to the task the player needs to undertake.

The design of the quest giver often reflects the look and feel of the game, and their appearance may be tied into the quest. For example, if your quest is to kill a boss that is harming the sheep that live nearby, your quest giver may be the shepherd or even one of the sheep.

The quest giver can also provide hints to the player. Often the player can return to the quest giver for further information if they get stuck. Most quest givers have an icon over their head or stand out from other NPCs so the player will approach them. In some games, the quest giver comes right up to your player if you're in the area.

Figure 3.13 shows a quest giver from the game *Vanguard: Saga of Heroes.* The player is receiving instructions about their quest along with crucial information on the dangers that lie ahead.

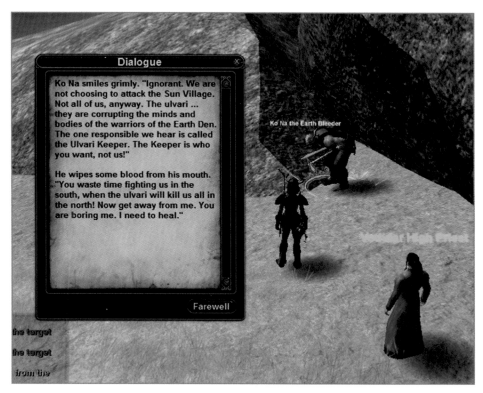

**FIGURE 3.13** This quest giver gives instructions and additional information to help the player find things to do in the game.

# Designing Props

When designing props for a game, you want to create pieces that will be useful as part of the gameplay (after all, it takes time to build them and animate them, and then they take up space in the game). Do some research to determine what props will work best with the gameplay. High-end sports games should exhibit the most current sports equipment, whereas shooters—especially military games—rely on accuracy in how the weapons look and work.

Many designers also work the *wow factor* into props. If a character needs to progress through various difficult levels, defeat bosses, fell dragons, and so on, part of the reward is a cool-looking prop.

# Creating Environments

You've written your script and designed amazing characters and props, and now you must build your stage. The stage for the game can define much of the game's look and feel. It sets up the mood, inspires, and amazes. With each subsequent game, designers are learning that audiences want bigger and better. In other words, if players experienced a stunning world in one game, they want to see more in the next one. Games that rely heavily on realism aim for even more realism in subsequent titles.

If you're attempting to design a game for a particular market, then you should look at the games that have been successful in that market and study the quality of their environments.

## 2D/3D

When you're designing environments for 2D gaming, it's useful to think of dividing the layouts into distinct foreground, middle-ground, and background elements. Being able to draw those areas helps to impart a sense of depth to the world being created.

Figure 3.14 shows a screenshot of gameplay from a 2D massively multiplayer online game (MMOG) called *Elgaill Town*. Notice how the foreground elements work well with the toolbar and statistics about the status of the avatars, while the middle-ground and far-background elements add to the look and feel of the world.

Whereas 2D worlds tend to be viewed from the same point of view (POV), 3D worlds are designed in a much more sophisticated manner. Whatever appears in the foreground may shift to the middle ground or background (or even be out of sight) if the player moves their avatar. If the avatar turns without moving off the spot where they're standing, you see the environment change as the avatar's POV shifts.

Figure 3.15 shows the development of a world from concept drawing to finished world. The center image is an environment built within the CryENGINE from Crytek. Some 3D backgrounds are built in 3D software modeling programs, such as Maya, 3ds Max, or Cinema 4D; other worlds are generated directly into engines that have been designed to create custom worlds and assemble the gameplay.

> **Parallax movement adds a sense of depth in 2D environments. As the camera pans, the objects in the foreground move more quickly than the objects in the distance.**

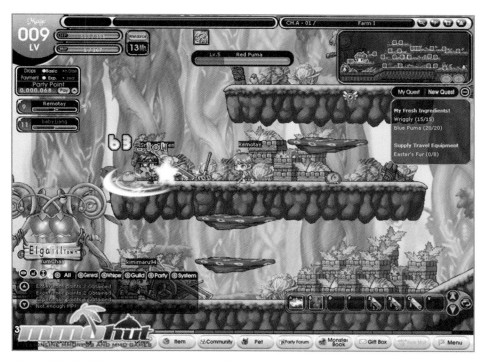

**FIGURE 3.14** 2D environments can still have a sense of depth.

Crysis 2. Image courtesy of Crytek GmbH.

**FIGURE 3.15** Three stages of environment development: concept drawing, 3D world being built using the Crytek engine, and the completed world

Not only do game engines drive the game, but they're also important for game development. Engines contain tools and components that handle the various basic elements of a game such as drawing the visuals, controlling the sound, and moving things around, and let the developer focus on generating data that gets plugged into the engine, like models/images, text, sound effects, and so on. A single engine can be used for a wide variety of games; it's the data put into it that makes the game unique.

This site has a tremendous list of free game-making resources: `http://gamemaking.indiangames.net/`

# The Physics of the World

Your environment might exist in the far reaches of outer space where gravity doesn't come into play, or deep under the sea where intense gravity impedes movement. There may be other factors to consider, such as weather, what surface the character is on (are they slipping across ice or slogging through mud?), or changing aspects like rock ridges or venomous plants bursting out of the ground.

Wherever your game takes place, one of the design elements you must consider is the physics of the world your characters need to maneuver. This process can allow for some fun gameplay design by adding twists and turns in the form of atmospheres that differ from what the player is used to (life on planet Earth).

*BioShock* is played deep under the sea in an abandoned city that is steeped in Steampunk design elements. As shown in Figure 3.16, a screenshot from *BioShock 2* (developed by 2K Marin), some of the gameplay occurs in air-filled rooms and hallways inside the city. At other times, the action takes place underwater.

*Steampunk* **is a style of art that combines science fiction and fantasy elements, which are highly influenced by the elaborately designed steam-powered machinery of the 19th century.**

**FIGURE 3.16** This image from *BioShock 2* shows the detail used to convey the physics of this world.

*BioShock* was built using the Unreal Engine, with Havok Physics added to allow for more realistic movements in the game. Specialists in programming water for games also worked on the project. As more games push the boundaries of realism or strive to build more elaborate fantasy realms, specialists in working with game engines need to be brought onto the project.

## Interactivity with the Environment

Is there a door to open? A window to close? A correct path to find? Difficult foliage to hack through? When designing elements in a world that the player will interact with, ask yourself these two questions:

▶ Will building in interactivity help with the goal of winning the game?

▶ Will adding the activity add to the fun?

Just because you're able to program interacting with the environment into a game doesn't mean you should. Unless that interactivity supports the gameplay, don't do it.

When you're adding an element that players need to interact with, make the piece a different tone or color to help the player find it.

Some games factor in an idle. If the player takes too long to find an interactive element, it may wiggle or do something to attract attention.

# Understanding the Basics of Animation

As mentioned in the discussion of characters, 2D characters can be flattened, stretched, and distorted much more than 3D characters. We have seen over decades of animated projects the incredibly wide array of movement and emotional states these types of 2D characters and their animation can demonstrate. Still, for many projects, designers choose 3D.

Designers begin with a 3D model. Once the model is completed, the figure is rigged with an internal skeleton that lets the animator controls manipulate it. Extremely complex characters take more work rigging and animating, so you need to test the models to make sure the rig will work as animation begins.

In order to animate 3D characters, you need to work with either keyframes or motion capture (mocap):

**Keyframe Animation**   A *frame* is the start point and the end point of any sequence that needs to be animated. The keyframes selected are usually large moves or weight shifts with the figure. Once these keyframes are created, then more frames (*inbetweens*) are created to make smooth animation from keyframe to keyframe. This type of animation is time consuming, but it allows the animator to use more of the physics of animation, such as squash and stretch and other cartoony movements.

**Mocap**    Short for motion capture, mocap is the technique of capturing the performance of an actor as an animated skeletal file. This skeletal data can then be applied to a character in a 3D application, mimicking that performance. The advantages of mocap compared to traditional keyframe techniques include the speed of animating lengthy sequences and the performance fidelity. Since its mainstream introduction in the early 1990s, mocap has become one of the major tools for 3D character animation.

The systems currently available typically utilize either optical markers or magnetic sensors, although contour detection (markerless) is slowly entering the field. The optical marker system requires multiple cameras ringing a capture volume. 3D points are derived from the intersection of the streaming 2D high-contrast images for the cameras. The markers are typically placed along the joints of the performers. A connect-the-dots approach is used to define the skeletal structure to extract rotational information. Cost of equipment and space and preparation time make optical tracking the most expensive approach, although it's also the most accurate.

Magnetic sensors are more easily set up and require no cameras. The person in Figure 3.17 is wearing a mocap suit; this particular rig is used by ElektraShock Studios in Venice, California (www.elektrashock.com). Using the Earth's magnetic fields, a sensor is able to give a discreet rotational value. Nesting the sensor data in a hierarchy, you can export an animated skeletal file. The only concession is that magnetic data has a much lower fidelity than optical data.

Most animation for games runs in cycles. In other words, you create short sequences that can be strung together as needed during gameplay. These cycles may be walking, running, flying, punching, or dying—this is just a short list of all the different types of cycles that can be created. Chapter 5, "Computer Graphic Basics for Game Design," provides a more in-depth discussion about animation.

The main constraints placed on game design these days are far less technical and more financial: how much detail can you afford to have people make, to complete the game in a reasonable amount of time? The most common technical problems tend to be related to the amount of memory available on a console for storing textures.

**FIGURE 3.17** An actor goes through his paces, producing movements that are captured using sensors.

## Navigating the World

Navigation is discussed in greater depth in Chapter 6; however, because much of the navigation in games depends on what the player sees in the environment, a short discussion is worthwhile here.

As you design the world, and as part of that ever-important gameplay factor, there may be things in the environment that assist or impede a player's progress. If the player must interact with elements in the background in order to move to another level or another room, then the designer needs to understand how obvious or how hidden that particular piece of the background should be. These interactive pieces of the background need to be incorporated into the script.

# Understanding Cinematics and Cutscenes

Cinematics and cutscenes are an important part of the process and should be considered along with core design concepts. Although neither one is inherently necessary for creating a game, their use has become so widespread that they have become their own visually stunning art form; they add flavor and help define the purpose and look of the game.

*Cinematics* are typically elaborate, animated short movies that help explain what the game is about. They're often used at the startup of a game to show the lore of the world the player is about to enter. They're also used extensively for marketing. Cinematics are easily accessible with any online video site, such as YouTube.com, and game companies regularly use them at large conventions like E3 and Comic-Con.

In the script for the game, note where cinematics are desired. However, each cinematic usually has a standalone script with dialogue, action, effects, and so on.

Like cinematics, *cutscenes* are short movies (the terms are often used interchangeably); however, cutscenes appear during gameplay. Cutscenes briefly take over the gameplay from the player and use animation and audio to explain the direction the game is going in, quickly and usually with intense, sweeping imagery. They can show in a short amount of time what would have taken pages and pages of text to explain in the past. Cutscenes should be included in the script for the game.

## THE ESSENTIALS AND BEYOND

By taking a look at some of the core elements involved in developing a game, you now understand that gameplay is the most important aspect to design first. If the game isn't fun or intriguing to play, then even the most elaborately and beautifully designed backgrounds and characters will fail to make the game a success. Some of the simplest art has been used to create games that have fun, intriguing gameplay that draw people to play them again and again. Designing a game that has longevity, or shelf life, is important because games take so long to make. You want your releases to continue to enthrall players while they wait for the newest game or sequel to be released.

### ADDITIONAL EXERCISES

Read the description of a character in a book or script, and then work on a concept for how that character would look in your game. Be very specific in writing what clothing,

*(Continues)*

## THE ESSENTIALS AND BEYOND *(Continued)*

armor, or weapons your figure would wear or carry, along with a description of their personality and a list of their abilities. After writing this attributes list, loosely sketch what your character would look like. Does your character look like it could be and do all the things you assigned to it in your list?

Write loglines for your own game or games you've played. Review the four questions from the "Writing the Story" section of this chapter to use as a guide:

▶ Who is the main character?

▶ What does this character want?

▶ What is going to try to stop the main character?

▶ What about the game is unique or compelling?

Part of this fun exercise can include reading existing loglines from movies, TV shows, or games and then trying to guess what the project is.

### REVIEW QUESTIONS

1. What is the most important thing to work out first when designing a game?

   A. Character concepts        C. Gameplay

   B. Environments              D. Quests

2. True or false. A good character designer should understand human as well as animal anatomy.

3. What is lore?

   A. A map                     C. The list of quests

   B. The backstory             D. Credits of who made the game

4. True or false. Flowcharts can be created as a visual guide to how the story is told in the game.

5. The physics of a world refers to which of the following?

   A. Foreground, middle ground, and   C. The kind of environment
      background

   B. The engine used to build the game  D. The number of interactive ele-
                                            ments built into the game

# CHAPTER 4

# Visual Design

*From concept to finished* art, designers must always ask themselves: do the visuals being developed work with the look and feel of the game? *Visuals* refer to the characters, props, environments, and interfaces built for the project.

Occasionally, an existing character is the starting point for a game, such as Marvel Comics' Thor or Luke Skywalker from the *Star Wars* sagas. An entire cavalcade of characters and exotic worlds had already been created for the *Lord of the Rings* trilogy. Those examples are well thought out, deeply developed entities that have their personalities and abilities clearly mapped. In such situations, the game and its gameplay usually develop around them.

In other types of design, the concept for the gameplay comes first, and then characters, environments, and so on are developed to match what the look and feel should be. Either way, the end result should be the same: a good balance between art and gameplay, to appeal to the demographic for which the project is being designed and to be appropriate for the gameplay style. All the elements have to work together to ensure that the final product is compelling and fun.

▶ **Developing concept art**

▶ **Previsualization**

## Developing Concept Art

Coming up with the concepts for innovative characters, props, environments, and interfaces is an important first step for beginning an original game design. These initial sketches help to carve out what the world will look like, where play will take place, and how the gamer will be able to interact with that world through the interfaces and avatars. Beyond the written word, where interpretation can be subject to the reader's own experience and imagination, actually seeing the first passes on art quickly gets the whole team on the same page.

According to game designer Daniel Cook in "Evolutionary Design" (in Game Design, www.gamedev.net), "The most common mistake of modern games is that they mistake setting for game design. A great plot does not make a great game. Nor does a great player model or animation engine. These merely provide contextual support for the game's reward system. If the rest of the game design is broken, a multi-million dollar investment in setting will still fail to produce an enjoyable game."

By now it's clear how important gameplay is, yet it's also highly subjective. Designers are faced with the task of building characters and other visual elements that will enhance the elusive quality of gameplay.

Many designers rely heavily on what has already been produced, claiming that visuals or gameplay that don't have a degree of familiarity won't appeal to gamers. Taking what has already been done but adding a twist to it, adding a little fresh design, tends to be the norm with many current games.

Being aware of this trend affects how concept work is approached in this industry. You'll be challenged to come up with designs that meet the needs of the project and are new and fresh, while also having a degree of familiarity.

## Where Do You Start?

To begin the process of coming up with the concept art, you need to know some basic information:

> ► Who is the game being designed for (demographic)?

> ► What is the gameplay style (discussed at length in Chapter 2, "Gameplay Styles")?

In addition to those two points, you should work with as much information as is available: backstory (or lore), script, goals of the game, and platform. (Platforms, or systems used to play games, are described in Chapter 10, "Designing Games for Varied Distribution").

Based on that information, you can make decisions regarding the look. Will it be cartoony, realistic, bright, somber, complicated, or intense?

It isn't uncommon for the concept artist to prepare three different preliminary versions of any visual that can work with the look and feel of the project. Three examples provide enough variety that the team can choose which one is going in the best direction for the needs of the project, or pick elements from two or all three that can be used to make another pass at the concept work. Starting with at least three variations also helps prevent the project from getting locked down too quickly with a specific look.

The concept work can be pencil sketches, sculptures, 3D models, or any other media that can convey the look and feel of the visual to people on the team. The concept artist usually includes color as well, because that can be such an important component of how the visual fits in with the game's look and feel. Color choices are often made based on how photoreal or stylized the game will look, so including them during the concept phase is a significant step.

Designer and animator Richard Sternberg started with this information for the game *Frozen,* created by Star Mountain Studios:

**Backstory (Lore)**   The story places a novice reporter, Samantha (Sam) Bloodworth, in Antarctica. Sam must reach safety after a volcano has exploded, stranding her on the remains of a shattered ice shelf.

**Demographic**   Everyone (no specific demographic).

**Gameplay Style**   Puzzle with a strong storyline.

Sternberg began with a modified Poser model to sketch in the initial design for Samantha. Figure 4.1 shows the original concept for Sam: a loose pencil sketch (left); the vector art adapted from that sketch, for cleaner line work (center); and the final color version, which was painted in Photoshop (right).

**FIGURE 4.1** Development of the character Sam from initial pencil sketch to line art (created as vector work in Flash) to the final version, painted in Photoshop

For the gameplay, Sam needed to be adventurous and athletic, on the young side, and dressed for the brutal weather that is prevalent in Antarctica, hence the dark glasses and parka (seen in the final version at right in Figure 4.1). There is enough realistic detail to help get across quickly that she is in a cold and dangerous environment; however, the bright colors and her energetic look work well with this being a lighthearted, fast-paced game.

Sam was designed as a 2D character and subsequently animated in Flash. The game *Frozen* is Flash based.

The software program Poser allows artists to pose a 3D model of a human or a wide variety of animals in various action positions as a drawing reference.

## Maintain a Balance

"We used to spend so much of our time on gameplay and today's games seem to put too much emphasis on graphics and sound. It's the game that makes a game fun, sometimes they forget that."

This comment by Larry Kaplan, one of the cofounders of Activision, reinforces the importance of balance between designing the visuals and the gameplay.

A good example of how this lack of balance can affect the success of a game can be found with PlayStation's *Rise to Honor,* which starred Jet Li (and no offense to Jet, because this author is a huge fan of his films!). The game captured the sweeping cinematic look and feel of an intense action film; however, the gameplay was repetitive and boring.

Looking at different platforms is a useful approach to get another perspective on design work for games. The *platform* is the system used to play the game. *Frozen* was designed for PCs (home computers), which tend to use good-sized monitors. The amount of real estate available allows for more graphics than something designed for a smaller, handheld device.

A boutique studio based in the UK, Mobile Pie (www.mobilepie.com/) creates original games (own-IP as well as licensed) for mobile platforms. The company designs and creates almost everything in-house, including characters, environments, and user interfaces.

According to Creative Director Will Luton, the artists at Mobile Pie take a very pragmatic approach to designing assets for games, going from the macro to the micro. To begin the design process, Mobile Pie answers the following questions:

▶ What is the goal of the game?

▶ What is the gameplay style?

▶ Who is it for (demographic)?

▶ What is the theme?

When the answers to these questions are clear, Mobile Pie generates an asset list and uses that to help prioritize how to segue the project into production. The asset list contains the number and types of characters, props, and other elements they may need to create. As color is worked into the art, reference images are used to help generate a palette.

*Assets* are characters, props, environments, and interfaces.

Your *demographic*, or audience, helps define the game's style. Understanding demographics means understanding the audience's age group, gender, and other key characteristics.

## KEEP THE DEMOGRAPHIC IN MIND AS YOU DESIGN

In *Game Over*, Nina Huntemann notes, "You know what's really exciting about video games is you don't just interact with the game physically—you're not just moving your hand on a joystick, but you're asked to interact with the game psychologically and emotionally as well. You're not just watching the characters on screen; you're *becoming* those characters."

When designing art for characters, keep in mind that the gamer is going to use your design to interact with the game itself, so that design needs to work for the demographic and gameplay style.

*Theme* refers to the setting or ambience.

*Reference images* can include a color palette or a look from a similar project.

The main thing to keep in mind in the early stages of developing the concept art is that this process is flexible. The goal is to keep things loose with room for change if it's needed, while giving enough detail to give a clear indication of what the final character can look like. Figure 4.2 shows an example of Mobile Pie's process. The character is roughed in with a pencil sketch.

**FIGURE 4.2** At this early stage of development, the concept art is roughed in as a pencil sketch, which helps keep things flexible.

While working on the concept stage of developing characters (or props, environments, or interfaces), keeping the work loose in the beginning is paramount. Don't try to settle too quickly on the finished look. The art director may still want substantial variations to take place. Nothing is more frustrating than investing an enormous amount of time in creating really finished-looking art during this early phase, only to have the client or art director review the project and decide that it isn't what they want. This type of error can lead to burnout.

Working smart—doing the upfront assessment of what the character should look like based on the macro-to-micro concept—is an excellent way to go. After creating a rough sketch, Mobile Pie takes it into a digital paint package or a 3D program, and a more finished product begins to take shape. This is a typical workflow for any game-design studio. Figure 4.3 shows an early render built in 3ds Max.

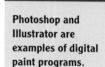

**Photoshop and Illustrator are examples of digital paint programs.**

**FIGURE 4.3** This image shows the final 3D version of the character.

One of the final stages of Mobile Pie's concept phase is mocking up screens to show all the elements in place. Because all the elements created for the project need to work together, you should generate mocked screens as soon as possible to see how well the art meshes with the gameplay. Figure 4.4 is an example of one of these mockups, created in Photoshop, showing characters and background pieces together.

**FIGURE 4.4** Mockups pull together concept work in all phases of design, from rough pencil sketches to more finished work, and help show the interplay of the art with the gameplay.

The *pipeline* for any project is the hierarchy of the workflow.

After going through the concept phases of designing assets for the game, a pipeline is created to help determine who will do what when it comes to developing the images further. The pipeline is examined in greater depth in Chapter 9, "Game Production Pipelines"; however, it's good to begin to get a rudimentary understanding of this workflow now.

The pipeline helps the creative director and artists focus their efforts where they're needed most. There is a lot of work to send back and forth between client and developer, so Mobile Pie, like many organizations, finds ways to effectively communicate not only the images but also the comments related to them. During the critical phase of creating final art, Mobile Pie uses a private blog that hosts comments along with the images to facilitate communication.

Methods for communication between team members or the client and developer vary from studio to studio. Some companies maintain a private website with a login feature, where work is posted and team members or the client can log in to view work in progress. Others use the blogging system, FTP sites, or simply email work back and forth. There are also services that allow users to send large files, such as MailBigFile and Dropbox. Dropbox has a drag-and-drop feature: users can drag files into their dropbox and share access with others who can pull those files onto their own computer systems as needed.

# Inspiration and Originality

Many times, I have counseled students to avoid drawing from memory. Artists or students occasionally draw what they think something should look like (how they remember it) instead of what it actually looks like. It's also too common for artists new to concept work to simply create a variation of a character they're familiar with from another game or similar medium, such as animation or a comic book.

The point is that in order to create a new type of character, it's important to reach outside of your current frame of reference and strive for something new and original. How many times have you sat down to draw, say, a house or a dog, and had it always be the same type of house or dog?

# Designing Original Characters

It's understandable to have a fear of coming up with something new. It's comfortable to keep drawing the same things over and over, kind of like doing a loving portrait of an old friend. But put yourself in the shoes of gamers who will immerse themselves in the world of the game you're creating and interact with the characters you're designing. You sit down to play, install a new game, marvel at the splash art, and are swept away by the intro music and stunning opening cinematics. Then you become entranced and amazed at some remarkable *new* character you've never seen before. And the best part is, you get to interact with this character.

Having well-designed characters—their appearance and also how they move, sound, and interact with other elements of the game—lends itself to making the game not only playable, but re-playable, and that is one of the components of successful gameplay.

# Where to Find Inspiration for Original Designs

Sometimes, though, your task may be to create an orc or elf or dragon or knight— a type of character that has been used frequently in games. Even in these cases, don't limit yourself by falling back on doing variations of what others have done. Where do you go for inspiration if your only source for ideas might be the last game you played?

The world. No: the universe all around you!

There is so much from which to derive inspiration that you'll do yourself a disservice if you don't explore other sources of motivation. You can

▶ Observe microscopic life that you can only see under a microscope. Some great beasties live in a petri dish.

▶ Look in the sky, marvel at the beautiful cloud formations, and imagine what those might look like animated.

▶ Leaf through a book about strange and unusual plant or animal life (make sure you select a book with lots of photos).

▶ Listen to a piece of music that inspires you.

▶ Watch the sublime movements of a dancer.

Inspiration is all around you.

You may also derive stimulation from how other creative people have worked at creating original work. Franklin Sterling III, an artist and designer living in Los Angeles, creates 2D/3D work for books and the simulation industry (we discussed simulation in gameplay styles in Chapter 2). Sterling is an avid fan of Matt Groening, the creator of *Life in Hell* and *The Simpsons*, and derives inspiration from the simple yet acerbic quality of Groening's work. Figure 4.5 shows a character named Weldon Price, whom Sterling created for an animated series of shorts titled *Out There* that is being adapted to a side-scrolling Flash adventure game by the same name.

**FIGURE 4.5** Weldon Price is a character whose inspiration came from the unique storyline for *Out There*.

*Out There* is a funny, lighthearted adventure about mild-mannered Price, who travels the world with his uncle. He literally falls into one escapade after another from the dilapidated balloon they travel in. As quaint, sweet, and nonthreatening as Weldon appears, his origins were strongly influenced by the conceptual methods H. R. Giger used while creating his award-winning monster for the film *Alien*.

Giger's frightening creation was built on a design from an earlier painting he had done called *Necronom IV* and was further designed based on studies he made of old Rolls Royce parts, rib bones, and snake vertebrae.

What inspired Sterling about that process was how Giger was able to study shapes and create such a fantastic creature. So what shape did Sterling settle on?

A peanut.

Sterling felt it was an odd shape and might work, so he used that shape to design Weldon Price.

Not all of Sterling's work is based on such simple concepts. In a project called *The Red Bedspread* that he is working on with fellow writer Karen Soliday, the lead character, named Henry Theodore Finch, is a little boy about 5 or 6 years old who overhears his dad talking about how he lost his job.

Believing this "job" is some sort of tangible object that his dad misplaced, he puts on a cape (the red bedspread) and searches all over town for the object. The character design and environments are more complex, which suits this character, who must go through the emotional ups and downs of helping his unhappy father. Sterling wanted to have the character interact with a more complex background as well, so he designed the initial layouts, shown in Figure 4.6, in 3ds Max. The image appears gray because it has not been painted with color or texture yet.

The character of H. T. Finch is certainly more complex than Sterling's Weldon Price character. He sports Chuck Taylor shoes along with tape holding his thick glasses together, to help show his vulnerability. The character was generated as a pencil sketch and composited over the background on a layer in Photoshop. The character and background were then painted out completely in Photoshop, and Sterling was able to use the shading of the shapes he had created in 3ds Max to help paint a believable world with correct perspective. Figure 4.7 shows the final render.

FIGURE 4.6  The design for the environments in *The Red Bedspread* were created with 3ds Max, so that the artist could create believable volume and perspective.

FIGURE 4.7  The finished art for *The Red Bedspread* was accomplished by rendering the 3ds file as a 2D image and then painting over the gray mesh in Photoshop to create the final world where Finch exists.

## RENDERING 2D IMAGES FROM 3D SOURCES

Quite a few 2D backgrounds or characters can be designed in 3D. One of the advantages of this approach is that the camera in the 3D program can be moved around the image to get just the right angle the artist wants to use to then paint the finished 2D piece. The focal length of the camera lens can also be adjusted. 35 mm is the standard length for the lens and is meant to mimic the way humans normally see things. Changing the focal length of the camera allows the viewer to create the impression of being closer to or farther away from objects, without physically moving closer or farther away. Changing the focal length tends to be something to adjust when rendering out backgrounds, however, it can be used to alter the appearance of a character or prop.

Once the render has been created from the 3D program and opened in Photoshop, then the following steps are one approach to creating beautiful images that show believable volume (shadow and highlight) and perspective.

- ▶ Open the image in Photoshop.
- ▶ Duplicate the layer.
- ▶ Multiply the top layer. (This will leave the shadows. Multiply can be found in the blending modes at the top of the layer menu.)
- ▶ Create layers underneath and paint in color or add real textures.
- ▶ The multiplied layer on top will automatically provide believable shadows over the paint and texture layers underneath.

Reading can be another source of inspiration. Nick Kozis, animator and character designer, says, "Choose anything from novels, short stories, and poetry. Do whatever it takes to get your imagination working. At this point I just read and try to limit my visual exposure to the subject matter. I enjoy focusing on what I am reading and let my imagination run wild. In doing this I try and get a fresh look. With the amount of visual references available to artists these days, it's easy for anyone's work to become derivative."

## CREATING A CHARACTER

Nick Kozis offers his process for creating a character, along with some resources and advice for designers.

**Start with the basics: "Visually, when I begin to develop a character, I like to start with the basics."** "In this case the character is posed in a standing position. The best are 3/4 front stances."

*(Continues)*

CREATING A CHARACTER *(Continued)*

**Use a variety of references:** "There are a lot of photo references that are available for artists. Try and show the character in an action." "After I establish a pose I can use, I begin to gather references of subjects that I would find interesting to draw. I combined some photos of dinosaurs and images of tribal humans. It's important to have as much detail in your reference materials as possible. The more you are looking at, the more you may use in your final painting."

**Think about your character from the inside out:** "A good practice is to start looking at skeletal structures. Then look at muscular systems, followed by textiles and costumes. Work a design from the inside out. This will give your imagined characters a degree of believability."

**Love what you're doing:** "You should always draw what interests you. If you want to get good, challenge yourself. Embrace the process and don't worry about the end product. The process is everything; if you love doing it, you will get good at it."

Nick also recommends looking at what others in the field are doing. This is part of staying current. It's good practice to be aware of how other artists work, study their methods, and pick up tips on how they derive inspiration from blogs and sites like www.conceptart.org, where numerous projects are posted with comments on how they were created.

Staying current also means understanding what trends exist in the industry. Trends give you information on what kinds of games are popular; what kinds of characters, props, and environments are popular; and what the next big interest is likely to be. Popular culture is another good indicator. The Harry Potter books swept the world with their tales of magic and spawned a series of über-successful movies and games. Graphic novels, classic stories, popular movies, fashion trends, comic books, toys—whatever people are talking about (and you can easily uncover this by reading blogs or news sites or walking through the mall) can be a source of inspiration.

# Functionality of Characters

What types of things does this character need to do?

When you work as a professional in the game industry, you're essentially a professional problem solver. Your problem is how to design the character's functionality to best meet the needs of the project. One of the first ways to determine this is to understand some of the physical things the character must do in the game. Does your character need to do any of the following?

- ▶ Jump
- ▶ Run
- ▶ Fly
- ▶ Swim
- ▶ Turn invisible
- ▶ Talk
- ▶ Sing
- ▶ Dance
- ▶ Carry one weapon, or two, or three

> **A *platform* is the playback system used to play a game.**

What your character needs to be able to do is story- or gameplay-driven, but how you portray these actions depends on your platform. Examples of platforms are

- ▶ Your PC
- ▶ Cell phones or other mobile devices
- ▶ A console—like a PlayStation or Wii
- ▶ A video arcade machine

Be sure you know what the technology you'll be working with can support. Small games designed for mobile applications like cell phones or iPads need to have simple, larger graphics with clear, easy-to-see movements. Some game engines can support complex movements, whereas others are limited to simple ones.

The concept drawings for your characters should be expanded to include action poses. And if the gameplay will be complex enough to show close-ups of the characters, the concept drawings should provide variations in the faces to include an emotional range and lip sync.

Again, I can't stress enough that in order to do this well, you need to avoid copying too much what is already out there. Go back to the basics. Use a mirror to study your own face while you form vowels and consonants or show emotion. Watch other people or animals while you're out and about, and notice their body language. These things will give you ideas for how to pose your characters and design faces for intrinsic movements.

As the concept is refined, additional sketches can include a lineup of characters, to indicate how large they are next to each other, along with different outfits, props, and any items that may be worn, held, or interacted with.

Designing props goes through the same type of process. The gameplay style and storyline describe what kinds of props are needed (for a shooter, you need shooting props; what kind will depend on the setting and other story details). As with character detail, platform limitations affect prop design.

## Functionality of the Interface

Even in the early phases of doing concept work, you need to focus your attention on the design of the interfaces. These visual elements also need to fit in with the game's look and feel and are a major component of how gamers will interact with the game.

An interface can be any of the following:

▶ Sign-in screen

▶ Options page (where the player can change video and audio settings, among other functions)

▶ Toolbar

▶ Maps

▶ Navigation panes

▶ Inventory panes

During the initial phases of designing visuals for the game, the type of gameplay and the goals of the game indicate which types of interfaces the game will need. For example, if the player must collect a certain number of elements before the game can be won, then an interface needs to be designed to hold those elements (such as an inventory bag or bank). Interface design will be covered in greater depth in Chapter 6, "Gameplay Navigation."

## Backgrounds

Creating concepts for games—especially ones that involve moving characters in real time through 3D space—can often mean elaborate and sweeping backgrounds to help convey the grandeur or complexity of the story.

Naughty Dog games, located in Santa Monica, California (a subsidiary of Sony Computer Entertainment America LLC), created the video game series *Uncharted. Uncharted 3*, released in 2011 and designed for the PlayStation, is a big, bold action-adventure game about fortune hunter Nathan Drake, who travels from one climatic extreme to another in search of treasure.

Figure 4.8 is a concept painting for the game that shows not only the multifarious environment, but also the character Nathan Drake and elements of gameplay (the gaping hole to be explored).

**FIGURE 4.8** The incredible distance, level of detail, and atmosphere help add to the immersive quality of *Uncharted 3*.

## OH WOW! ROOMS

Often, the complex, elaborate paintings created as part of the concept are grouped together and hung in one room called the *Oh WOW! room* while production is underway on a project. People coming on board a project who want to get a sense of what the game is all about can immerse themselves quickly in the look and feel of the game by hanging out in the Oh WOW! room for a while. Oh WOW! rooms can also be digital. These concept pieces (background, characters, and props) can certainly be viewed digitally as well.

Fans can enjoy collections of the paintings that are gathered and printed in books that are sold with collector's editions of games. These pieces can also be used in game trailers, posted online for fans to enjoy, and given away in contests. What fan wouldn't want an original concept piece used to inspire a game?

Methods for creating concepts for backgrounds depend on a few things:

- ► 2D or 3D
- ► Gameplay style
- ► Demographics
- ► Genre
- ► Playback systems

Again, as with the characters, some of your parameters for the concepts are based on the game's technology and whether it's 2D or 3D.

If you're working on developing backgrounds for 2D games, you'll need to know if the game background will remain static or will move, as in a side-scroller like the *Mario Bros.* games. Backgrounds in games are not only stages for the action taking place; they can also become an integral part of the gameplay. Characters or other elements from the game may need to interact with the background, as in adventure games where doors open or parts of the background move or fall away to reveal clues. Hidden object games' (HOGs') backgrounds tend to have dozens of items that need to be found, laced throughout the environment.

When designing backgrounds, come up with the look for the environments: those concept pieces that often find their way into Oh WOW! rooms. From there, you can begin to come up with more detailed layouts that the designers can use as temp art pieces to begin actually building the game.

If the game is 3D, then background designers work with either a 3D package or the game engine itself. For many backgrounds, especially 2D, creating a pencil sketch and then painting that in a software package like Photoshop is an ideal way to go. You can see the result of that approach in Figure 4.9, a background created by Franklin Sterling III for his *Out There* project.

◄ Until finished art is ready to put into the game, temp art can be roughed out and used during game builds.

◄ Maya, 3ds Max, and CINEMA 4D are examples of 3D packages. Crytek is an example of a game engine.

**FIGURE 4.9** *Out There* needed to have a large-world look (the main characters literally travel the globe) while remaining simple enough to work with the character design.

While creating backgrounds, it's important to understand which paint package will be used for the final render. Photoshop, using raster images, can be used to create massive amounts of detailed textures and lighting. Vector images tend to be flatter, although you can create some truly astounding lighting and impressions of depth and distance with a bit of clever manipulation of the software, particularly using gradients. Figure 4.10 shows a background from the game *Weird Helmet,* created by Star Mountain Studios. The background was created first as a pencil layout and then painted in Flash. All of the texture shown on the toolbar at the bottom was created as separate, small vector pieces. The finished effect is one of an aged, highly textured background, but because it is vector, it is highly scalable and a much smaller file size than a raster image.

**FIGURE 4.10** The background for *Weird Helmet* needed to convey an impression of being in outer space using just flat color and vector art.

Even though a game may be designed strictly for 2D gameplay, occasionally a more realistic world needs to be created. Although pencil layouts work well for this, using a 3D package to build a rough layout of the environment works exceptionally well. One of the benefits is that the designer can rotate the camera inside the environment and decide which view is best for the scene being worked on for the game.

In addition, if a 3D package is used, the camera's focal length can be shortened to make the background look warped, curvy, and somewhat comical; or lengthened to appear more photorealistic. The camera can look down into the environment, showing establishing shots or areas of the room where clues in the game may be hidden; or dropped low to look up, giving a spookier appearance. Figure 4.11 shows the rough 3D render for a background from a haunted-hospital game created by Star Mountain Studios along with the finished version. Once the camera angle was decided on and the image was captured, the final paint was done using matte painting techniques in Photoshop.

**FIGURE 4.11** For the background in this haunted-hospital game, the rooms were roughed out using Maya, the camera was rotated to provide the desired angle, and then one frame was rendered out. That frame was used as the layout for the 2D paint.

Backgrounds designed for full 3D movement are trickier. Designers are aware that they have to deal with the x- and y-axes (up and down/right to left), as well as the z-plane (depth). Games that allow for 3D movement render each frame as the game is played, so the game engines are usually used to lay them out and paint them; but many of the more detailed assets, such as houses and foliage, are built in a 3D package and then imported into the engine.

Another approach for creating backgrounds uses an engine with elements that can be used to build the background. The company Crytek has an engine that will create all types of backgrounds, from dense jungle to a wide range of architectural building styles. Figure 4.12 shows a background created using the Crytek engine. During gameplay, the scene you're seeing is redrawn in real time, frame by frame, as you, the controller, move through the environment.

**FIGURE 4.12** This background was created using the Crytek engine.

## Understand the Physics of the World

While working on concepts for a game, keep in mind the physics of the world you're creating. Is it underwater, in outer space, or in high winds? Is there weather, and if so, what kind? These things are essential to understanding what needs to be in the worlds you're creating—including props and backgrounds.

In addition, by reading the lore or script, you'll note that perhaps a character or characters always fly through the world; if so, you'll need to consider designing bird's-eye views (what the world looks like when the character is flying through treetops or between mountain peaks). By the same token, your character may travel the world by boring through the Earth's crust, in which case you'll need to design worm's-eye views for some of your scenes.

Understanding basic perspective is also critical when doing drawings. Because part of your job, when creating backgrounds for a game, is to give the sense of depth and distance, reviewing one-point, two-point, and three-point perspective is helpful. One-point perspective shows a dead-on view of the world, as if you're standing on railroad tracks and seeing how they disappear on the horizon line. Two-point perspective gives a more interesting three-quarter view, and three-point helps you draw bird's-eye and worm's-eye views.

# Previsualization

*Previsualization* (*previs*) is an overarching term that refers to any aspect of designing the concept work for the game's visual elements and making decisions about how the final work needs to be produced. If, during the concept phase, art is created to show examples of a character as a 2D element and also as a 3D element, then a decision must be made about how the final design will be implemented: 2D or 3D. Once that decision is made—let's say the decision is 3D—then the final design and production of the character go to the artist or department that specializes in creating 3D work.

## TYPES OF PREVIS

Previs can be broken down into five categories:

**Pitchvis**    Shows potential for an unproduced project; a pitch

**D-Vis**   Design visualization

**Technical Previs**   Dimensional work

**On-Set Previs**   Real-time work, usually done on the fly during production

**Postvis**   Refinement after production is underway

Because there are so many specialties when it comes to creating a game animation, 3D model building and rigging, 2D and 3D environments, programming, animation, sound, and so on, previs helps sort out who is going to make what.

When you're planning a scene for a trailer or deciding how sequences in the game need to be executed, the mechanics of actually building it is one of the things previs can help sort out. During the previs phase of development, decisions are made such as who will build the 2D elements, 3D, animation, music, dialogue, sound effects, special effects, and so on. There are a great many details to track while building a game, and using previs to refine what needs to be done, by whom, and when is critically important.

Previs can indicate what needs to be done, and it can also point out gaps for design elements that had not been considered yet, or show problems with production that may be too expensive or pointless to pursue.

## Storyboards

When it comes to designing characters and planning how they will work together with other characters, bosses, quest givers, and anything else they might interact with in the game, entire sequences may need to be *boarded out* (depicted in a storyboard) to gain a clearer understanding of how the story is being told, how actions need to be planned for, and what other elements need to be designed, redesigned, or eliminated.

Storyboards are essentially blueprints, or roadmaps, if you will, that can communicate to members of a design and production team what needs to be created and how events will unfold. They help save time and money once a project goes into production, because they indicate what things need to be created and where people need to focus their time: they can also provide insight to help you eliminate unnecessary elements.

Games, like most projects, have one or more creative directors associated with the endeavor. After making creative decisions, their most important goals are as follows:

▶ Communicate the vision to other members of the team.

▶ Allow team members to offer feedback, based on the vision, on ways to implement, change, or enhance the design.

Storyboards are an important tool to accomplish both of those goals.

You may wonder how a game can be boarded out if characters can go in different directions. Don't think of them like storyboards created for a movie or TV show, where the story and action unfold in a linear manner from opening scene to final credits. Storyboards for games help plan actions and events that need to be created by the character/prop designers, background artists and animators, engine designers, and game coders.

Storyboards are also used extensively for *cutscenes* (also called *cinematics* or *in-game movies*) and trailers for games.

Your flowchart (see Chapter 3, "Core Game Design Concepts") helps point out decision points in the game. Storyboards are created to help design more detailed interactions for major plot points.

## ORIGINS OF CUTSCENES

The first cutscenes in games were created as a type of intermission, or interlude, during gameplay.

In 1980, the game *Pac-Man* had little animated movies that showed Pac-Man being chased around by the ghosts he battled during gameplay. These original cutscenes were silent; it wasn't until *Donkey Kong*, in 1981, that audio was added to them.

*World of Warcraft: Cataclysm* has cutscenes throughout the game; however, when your unique character reaches a plot point where the cutscene starts, the game engine drops your character directly into the movie. You don't interact with the other characters or elements of the scene, but it makes it more fun to see your character moving around in the movie.

Usually, cutscenes are linear movies that play from start to finish without interaction. Technology is coming that will allow players to interact with them.

Just as for film or TV production, game storyboards tend to be a combination of graphics and text. The graphics are loose drawings that provide a visual blueprint of what is going on in the scene; they can be drawn over several panels to show progressions of the actions. The text is generally any dialogue that is spoken, voice-over narrations, instructions for things that need to be created for the scene (effects, animations, assets, and so on), and identifiers, such as the scene number or date.

Again, at this stage of production, the storyboards are meant to be a flexible design tool. They communicate the vision of the project to other members of the team, and they also identify gaps in the gameplay, or what I like to call *boat anchors*—graphics, animation, or any gameplay element that doesn't work and will drag down the whole project.

Figure 4.13 shows a basic storyboard panel template. You can create your own storyboard, stringing together several panels on a vertical or horizontal page, depending on which works best for you.

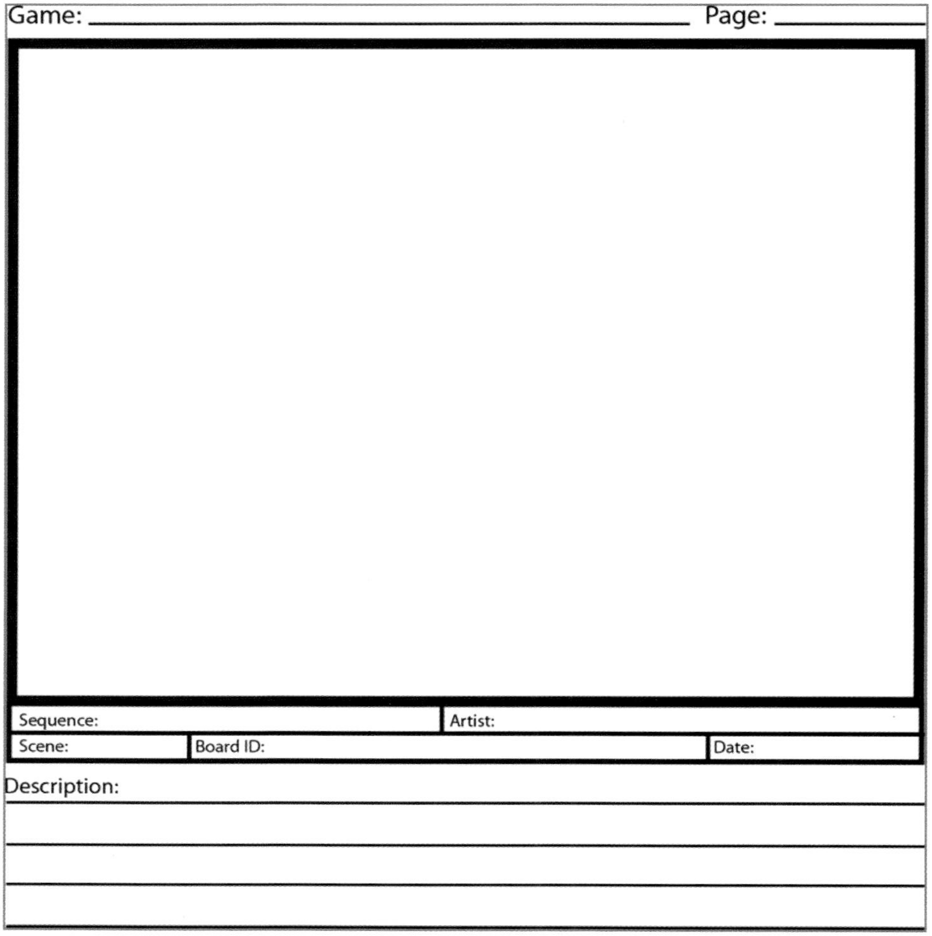

| Game: | Page: |
| --- | --- |

| Sequence: | | Artist: | |
| --- | --- | --- | --- |
| Scene: | Board ID: | | Date: |

Description:

**FIGURE 4.13** This image shows a form of storyboard template.

In professional game production, once boarding has begun, dollars are being spent; therefore, the most focused, efficient method for producing storyboards is the way to go.

Boards may be more or less elaborate, depending on the needs of the project. Some storyboards are just walls covered in sticky notes or 3×5 cards tacked to a corkboard. Some people write directly on the wall, while others scribble on tablecloths during lunch. I have seen all kinds of storyboards in numerous formats. Again, it all comes down to someone communicating a vision and information to someone else. In other words, although I'm showing you a template here, that doesn't mean you have to use it. You may choose to design your own and fill it with the data your project deems important.

# Animatics

*Animatics* are a previs tool used to help show timing. Storyboards can communicate massive amounts of information—what characters, props, and backgrounds are needed for specific parts of the game; camera angles; and how cutscenes will work. One of the things storyboards can't do effectively is show the timing involved.

You may write on your storyboard how long an event will take; however, that information tends to be difficult to perceive. Experiencing events over time is tough to communicate unless you can show someone how long an event will need to take place. That's where animatics come in.

Taking storyboards and animating the images using a time-based editing program allows the designer the luxury of showing how long an action or event really takes. In addition, the camera can move (zoom in or out, pan, and so on), and transitions between scenes can be added (cut, dissolve, or other transition effects).

While timing is worked out in this process, along with camera moves and transitions, audio is also added, such as dialogue, voice-over, music, and sound effects, to further enhance the movie.

**There are several editing programs to choose from when creating an animatic, including After Effects, Final Cut Pro, Premiere, and Movie Maker.**

# Pitches and Vertical Slices

If you're in the process of pitching a game idea to try to sell the concept, a previs reel can help by creating a movie with movement and audio that draws your audience into the world you want to create. Should you get the opportunity to take the next step in a pitch—that is, to let someone get a sense of your game's gameplay—you'll want to create what is known as a *vertical slice*. Essentially, it's a short section of your game that has been produced as a playable piece. It might be a level, or a boss fight, or just moving through a section of the world to clearly show someone how the gameplay works.

The vertical slice is still part of the previs stage, because after it's completed, changes continue to be implemented. The vertical slice is just enough of the game to give a sense of the gameplay; it isn't meant to represent what the final game would look like. Often, vertical slices are full of temp art, animation, and audio.

In this business, talking about a game doesn't do much to further getting it made if you're seeking assistance from other artists, designers, coders, financial backers, and so on. You can wave your arms around all you want; but once you show someone how things will work with your previs reel, or let them run around in the game and play a piece of it with the vertical slice, your brainchild will speak for itself.

## THE ESSENTIALS AND BEYOND

We revisited the concept of gameplay and how everything you do related to designing a game should support that. Characters can indeed be stars of the game; however, all that you do when it comes to designing and creating them needs to support gameplay. The same approach should be kept in mind when you're creating backgrounds or other elements that support the game, such as cutscenes and trailers.

Studying articles about design and development is an excellent thing to do as you continue to learn about designing and producing games, whether you're interested in character creation, world building, or the game itself.

Sites like www.gamasutra.com provide excellent articles and blogs related to all phases of game design and development, from the pitch to production to post-mortems. They show in depth how existing games were created—including the pros and cons. You should study games that are well received and have good design. You should also study games that have poor design, to learn what to avoid. This is very important!

When you do research about how games are made, pitched, marketed, and so on, you can get ideas about how to apply the same principles to your own projects, or where you might like to work in the industry based on some of the jobs and challenges you discover.

### ADDITIONAL EXERCISES

Coming up with a unique look for a character can be a wonderful challenge, and fun as well. Pick one of the following scenarios:

▶ You're a timid little animal living underground on a distant planet. The colony, which contains thousands of other timid animals, is running out of water. Your grandfather told you tales of a secret well, deep in a dangerous mountain range, far from the safety of your colony. You decide to travel on your own to find the precious liquid that can save everyone. What do you look like?

▶ You exist in the dreams of a little girl living in a poor part of a big city. While she sleeps, you whisper to her, telling her how special and wonderful she is, and that she will grow up to be an important person. She does: she becomes president of the United States. Now she faces an unusual crisis: the first alien visitors have reached our planet, and they're hostile. You resurface in her dreams to help give her strength and support during these hard times. What do you look like?

While you work on your design, list the special attributes your character should have, and use those to help you sketch what your character will look like.

*(Continues)*

## THE ESSENTIALS AND BEYOND (Continued)

Another fun exercise is to select a favorite character from classical literature, such as Hercules, Icarus, or the Minotaur. Read stories related to these characters, and uncover the following:

▶ Where did the character live? (Determine the setting: what the world this character moved through and interacted with looked like.)

▶ What special abilities did the character have?

▶ Did the character have flaws?

▶ What things did this character need to do?

Based on what you uncover, come up with two or three different sketches, and see how one drawing alone can't work. Coming up with different looks shows you how diverse design can be and that you don't need to be limited based on pre-existing drawings of similar characters.

### REVIEW QUESTIONS

1. Why is it a good idea to come up with more than one initial concept design for any game asset?

   A. To avoid getting locked too early into a design that may later prove impractical

   B. To have a variety to choose from

   C. To keep as flexible as possible while the design process evolves

   D. All of the above

2. True or false. A vertical slice is just a small section of a finished game.

3. Demographic means _____.

   A. The geography created for the environments

   B. Genre

   C. Who the audience is

   D. A demo of the game

4. True or false. When designing a character, supporting gameplay should always take precedence.

5. Which of the following is not a type of previs?

   A. Pitchvis

   B. D-Vis

   C. Concept-vis

   D. Postvis

# CHAPTER 5

# Detailed Development of Visuals

*Now that you've looked* at methods for previsualization and concept work, let's examine a bit more closely how you can further develop the look of the characters, props, environments, and interfaces for your game. A great many games today use 3D graphics; however, 2D is also still used in developing and producing games.

We'll examine different methods for creating graphics and look at how animation is created for cinematics and in-game play.

Topics in this chapter include:

▶ **Overview of designing graphics**

▶ **3D models**

▶ **Color, texture, and lighting**

▶ **Animation**

## Overview of Designing Graphics

Designing graphics for any game is a juggling match. The designer must make decisions taking all these concerns into account: making the gameplay work, using the graphics to add to the appeal (eye candy), and helping players to—especially in immersive games—identify with their onscreen persona. Designing a game that achieves all these things is a challenge for the designer, albeit a fun one.

The first digital games were text based, like the *Colossal Cave Adventure,* which used written descriptions to create the characters, props, and environments. These games used just 16 colors and 255 symbols (IBM-extended

ASCII character set) and were extremely simple in appearance by today's standards for visual complexity, but they provided gripping gameplay.

While playing text-based games, players used their imaginations to invent what the characters and environments looked like. In creating games for today's market, game makers assume that task.

One of the first things a designer needs to consider is who the intended audience for the game is. This is known as the *demographic*, and research regarding what exactly a demographic may want in a game tends to be an ongoing compilation of data from game sales, interviews, Q&A testing, and observing focus groups.

## Who Is Your Audience?

You have a great idea for a game and are ready to jump right in and begin designing. Before you even write out the short synopsis, you need to identify the genre, or gameplay style, and the demographic. In other words, who is your audience?

## Demographic Traits

Designers identify demographics for games by studying some of the following traits:

- ▶ Age of the player

- ▶ Gender

- ▶ Amount of time spent playing games

- ▶ Gameplay styles preferred

This information is gathered through phone interviews, analysis of market surveys, and trade journals. According to the 2011 *Sales, Demographic and Usage Data* compiled by Entertainment Software Association (ESA), 72% of American Households play digital games. ESA also found that the average age of the game player is 37, but the average age of the most frequent game purchaser is 41.

The ESA provides good information about the distribution of the age of players, as seen in Figure 5.1.

ESA also identified the distribution of players by gender, as seen in Figure 5.2.

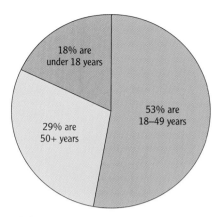

**FIGURE 5.1** According to the ESA, most players are 18–49 years old.

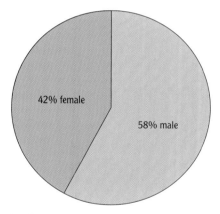

**FIGURE 5.2** According to the ESA, slightly more than half of all players are male.

> **Women age 18 or older represent a significantly greater portion of the game-playing population (33%) than boys age 17 or younger (20%).**
> **—ESA 2010 demo-graphic survey**

# Researching Game Sales

Figure 5.3 shows sales grouped according to their ESRB ratings. Although there are plenty of slasher, killer games with lots of killing and gore, sales figures indicate that the market for those types of games is smaller than the market for products designed for the whole family. The data was collected and analyzed by the NPD Group (an independent global corporation that gathers consumer and retail information).

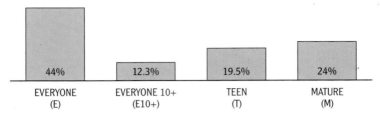

**2010 Computer and Video Game Sales by Rating**
by UNITS SOLD

| EVERYONE (E) | EVERYONE 10+ (E10+) | TEEN (T) | MATURE (M) |
|---|---|---|---|
| 44% | 12.3% | 19.5% | 24% |

**FIGURE 5.3** According to the NPD Group, a large percentage of all games sold are designed for the entire family.

The number of gamers has increased substantially over the past few decades, and the demographics indicate that more adults, including women, are enjoying them. Whole families play together, and according to the ESA compilation, these are the top four reasons they play:

1. It's fun for the entire family (87%).
2. Because they're asked to (83%).
3. It's a good opportunity to socialize with the child (75%).
4. It's a good opportunity to monitor game content (60%).

Mary Ulicsak, Martha Wright, and Sue Cranmer, in a Futurelab report, came to similar conclusions: "Video gaming as a family has the potential to bring generations together, provide experience of digital technologies to all ages, and develop social skills such as turn-taking—all in activity described as 'fun.'"

> Be sure you research as much as you can about your demographic to understand their likes, dislikes and the types of games they like to play.

The statistics presented here should give you a clear indication that games aren't just for kids, nor does your demographic have to be extremely narrow.

That said, the demographic is an extremely important aspect to understand when designing the graphics for a game. If you're designing a game for little girls, say, 5–8 years old, then working with somber earth tones and using just stone and rusty metal textures would not be the best way to go. But how do you know what *will* work for a particular demographic?

Unfortunately, too many game makers rely on their own personal experiences and likes and dislikes when designing games. One way to work past this dilemma is to incorporate a thorough research/design phase for any game being constructed. Do the legwork to learn about your demographic, even if you're working on a game in a niche you enjoy and you believe you know everything there is to know about that niche.

Learn everything you can about your demographic, such as the following:

- ▶ What are the most popular games for your demographic?

- ▶ What are the least popular games for your demographic?

- ▶ What do players have to say about games geared toward your demographic?

- ▶ What colors, styles, and interface designs are popular in existing games for your demographic?

To get this information, you can consult several sources:

- ▶ Market surveys

- ▶ Reviews of existing games

- ▶ The games themselves

- ▶ People in your demographic

- ▶ Review services from games portals

Conduct, purchase, or locate online market surveys for the demographic you're focusing on. According to Nielsen, gaming has grown 10% over the past year (2011) and now accounts for 10% of all U.S. time spent online; and consumers, in 2010, spent $25.1 billion on game content, hardware, and accessories (ESA).

Because of the massive sales that gaming now enjoys, many third-party researchers, like ESA, conduct demographic surveys and offer their information to help designers further target the groups for which they're creating their games. The International Game Developers Association (IGDA) also conducts surveys to gather demographic information. Some third-party groups, like NPD, do market research and offer highly detailed sales and demographic information for a fee. If you're about to seek millions of dollars to launch a new game or gaming company, having detailed information about sales is an important facet of your business plan.

In addition to survey data, look for and read reviews posted about games geared toward your demographic. For example, Big Fish Games allows players to freely post their thoughts about games for sale on the company's site. Comments

**Websites like Gamasutra.com offer post-mortems on how games were made. Review best sellers to see what works. Study the flops to identify mistakes to avoid.**

about games are fairly numerous. Take note of both positives and negatives. You can learn a great deal from mistakes and avoid making similar ones yourself.

As you compile your information, save images from the games and reviews you're studying to understand more clearly how not only the gameplay, but also the graphics are talked about.

Look at—and play—similar projects that have been produced for your demographic. The Internet makes it easy to view games for the audience you're designing for. You may want to look at sites like these:

▶ Big Fish Games: www.bigfishgames.com

▶ Kongregate: www.kongregate.com

▶ Gamespot: www.gamespot.com

▶ Gamasutra: www.gamasutra.com

▶ Game Rankings: www.gamerankings.com

▶ The Game Reviews: www.thegamereviews.com

You can also check findings released by the Entertainment Software Association (ESA): www.theesa.com.

## What Do They Have in Common?

As you view projects that were designed for a demographic similar to the one your game is targeting, notice things they have in common, such as the genre, the color palette, the style of artwork, and how the interface looks.

**Big Fish Games allows players to download and play for free for an hour—plenty of time to form an opinion about the success or failure of graphics and gameplay.**

For example, a review of games designed for young girls at sites like PopCap Games and Big Fish Games found many games that had girls raise baby animals, play dress-up, sing and dance, or do veterinarian role playing. Other games were highly colorful shooters like *Peggle* or social games like *Farmville* and *Animal Crossing*. All of these were designed as casual games, with big, easy-to-read text and brightly colored graphics. Figure 5.4 shows images from *Animal Crossing* and *Peggle*.

In addition to compiling research, make a point of playing the games yourself. Look for free demos to download and play (try to review at least 20–30 similar games). You don't need to play too long to get a good sense of whether the graphics that were designed work with the gameplay and seem suitable for the demographic.

**FIGURE 5.4** These games were designed for a demographic of young girls: the graphics are brightly colored, and the objects the player interacts with the most are painted to look more 3D and invite the young player to touch them.

After you've conducted your research and work begins on creating the graphics, you may want to show the work to people in your demographic. If you're able to, at an early phase in design and production, expose the work to your audience. Locate family and friends who fit your demographic, or reach out to your potential players through a website where you post art or small, playable sections of the game, and ask for feedback. This will allow the project to become more player-centered.

Quite a few of the larger gaming companies like Electronic Arts (EA) and Blizzard allow their players access to beta versions of upcoming releases to get feedback before the game goes to market. This is known as *user-centered design* and gathers useful information through beta testing and focus groups.

Some portals, like Big Fish Games, offer a service that lets you submit your game to them, in progress, and they will provide a review. This is a good service to take advantage of, particularly if your goal is to market your game through a portal (see Chapter 10, "Distribution and Marketing"). Portals that offer reviews base their comments on knowledge they acquire about how your demographic has responded to similar games. The portals tend to be honest about their assessment because they make their money by marketing these games and establishing good relations with the indy game companies.

In short, when you consider the design for your game and look to the demographic to be targeted, doing research on your own is essential. Look at games that were designed for the same gamers you want to design for. Third-party researchers like ESA and the IDGA will provide you with critical information on how to find games to study and how large the demographic is.

*Player-centered* means you involve players in the design and production process whenever feasible.

How games look these days has become an important aspect of game design. Playback systems are much faster, allowing for more complex imagery, highly elaborate animation, and using the camera to help make the experience more immersive.

# Camera Angles

A locked-down camera keeps one camera angle throughout the game.

Earlier forms of games were all 2D. The camera tended to be locked down, allowing the player to maneuver through a playing field that usually had obstacles to get past. Some of these games that kept the locked-down camera were *Donkey Kong, Mario Bros., Duck Hunt, Sonic, Resident Evil*, and *Devil May Cry*.

Although the camera is locked down, plenty of games still use 2D, such as solitaire, mahjong, and chess. This format is also a huge favorite for designers of casual games, as evidenced by such favorites as *Tetris, Angry Birds, Classic Doom, Sinistar* and *Zombies Ate My Neighbors*.

With the introduction of 3D graphics, greater complexity was incorporated into games, and allowed the designer to place the camera in different locations to create a significantly different gameplay experience. Shooters are an example of how this ability to move the camera around during play significantly changed the experience. The flexible camera angle allows the player to turn and see who is shooting at them.

One of the drawbacks with 3D is tiny spaces in the game environment. The camera may need to raise up rather high in order to see the character and the environment, so using this type of camera can be tricky in confined spaces.

Point of view (POV) affects the camera angle. You can design games to be played from a first- or third-person point of view (TPS POV). As with so many elements, the designer must choose which POV to use so that gameplay isn't sacrificed.

Many game makers enjoy designing for the first-person POV (FPS POV) camera because it can let the player really get into what their character is feeling and doing. It also adds more realism because players watch the game unfold through the character's eyes. For example, if you hear something coming up behind you or see a shadow cross your path, but you can't see yet what is casting it, this adds realism; the level of suspense soars because essentially you're seeing and experiencing what the character is.

A good example of the type of immersion experienced using FPS POV is in the game *Half Life* from Valve. The gamer assumes the role of the lead character Gordon Freeman, and through the game interacts with other characters who come right up to him (the player) to have conversations. The player sees Gordon's hands appear in front of them as if they were extensions of their own hands when he tries to open doors, use weapons (such as his trademark crowbar), or touch other items in the game.

With shooters, though, the weapon your character carries can sometimes obscure much of the image. The FPS POV also creates a limited field of vision because you're only seeing the scene through the eyes of the character you're playing.

Quite a few gamers seem to enjoy the TPS POV more than the FPS POV because they feel in greater control of their character. The TPS POV provides a broader view of what is going on during play, which can be helpful in fast-paced combat games. This method of design also allows the gamer to see their onscreen persona all the time, and that is helpful in role-playing games.

One of the most popular games utilizing the TPS POV is *Max Payne*, developed by the Finnish company Remedy Entertainment, produced by 3D Realms, and published by Gathering of Developers for Windows. Later versions of the game were ported to the Xbox, PlayStation 2, and Game Boy Advance by Rockstar Games. The game is a noir tour-de-force and pits the hero, Max Payne, against enemies terrorizing New York City. One of the fun features of this game is that, instead of cutscenes placed between levels, the story progresses through a series of comic-book-style graphics.

During gameplay, if Max gets into a firefight, the speed of play changes from a normal pace to one showing bullet time, or slow motion, so the player can savor all the action.

Figure 5.5 lets you compare first- and TPS POV. On the left is an image from the game *Max Payne*, where the gamer can see Max and the extensive environment and other characters to interact with. Contrast that with the image on the right, showing the POV of the player who has assumed the role of Gordon Freeman in *Half Life*, where you see that he (the gamer) is fighting with a crossbow.

**FIGURE 5.5** Compare the TPS POV on the left with the FPS POV on the right.

Whether to use first person or third person is a choice the designer needs to think through carefully. If you want to give the gamer more control during gameplay, then third person is likely the way to go. If you as the designer want to control the experience more as the gamer plays through your game, then first person is probably what you want.

Also, as you design a game, take into consideration how much realism you wish to provide the player. For a more realistic experience (what you as the character hears and sees), a FPS POV may be more desirable. However, if you have incredible environments to see and explore and hazards to negotiate, the TPS POV might be the way to go so the gamer can move the camera to watch their character and see more of the world they inhabit.

An interesting combination of the two POVs can be found in the game *Ratchet & Clank,* developed by Insomniac Games and published by SCEA for the PlayStation. The gamer can choose to switch between FPS and TPS POVs. This is an unusual approach to design and allows the gamer to choose how they wish to see the game. Blizzard's *World of Warcraft*, through the use of the mousewheel, allows players to zoom in so close that they see the game as a first-person POV as well. This option gives the gamer some variation in how they play the game, but doesn't really affect gameplay. Most players tend to jump into the FPS POV for short spurts, just to up the adrenaline a bit; however, most prefer to drop back to the TPS POV.

In addition to choosing a point of view, you must decide where to place the camera. Options for the camera position include bird's-eye view (overhead or helicopter), *projection*, side-scrolling, and faux 3D. We'll look at these four options next.

## Bird's-Eye View

**Bird's-eye view is also known as top down, overhead, or helicopter view.**

The bird's-eye view has the gamer looking down onto the playing field. A classic example of a game that uses bird's-eye view is *Frogger*. This view lends itself to games that involve exploration. In addition, games that require strategy often use this approach because you can coordinate a map. Games that use the bird's-eye view are often known as *board* games.

Figure 5.6 shows a screenshot from the game *Weird Helmet,* made by Star Mountain Studios. The goal of the game is to turn tiles on the game field so that the avatar can race across from one portal to the next in outer space before he runs out of the air he carries in his "weird helmet." An overhead view is ideal for gameplay of this type because of how quickly the player must be able to anticipate which tiles to turn in order to make a pathway from start to finish for the racing hero.

**FIGURE 5.6** This overhead (or bird's-eye) view of the game board for *Weird Helmet* lets the gamer see all the tiles they can chose from to make a path for the avatar (seen at upper left in this image), who moves very quickly across the field.

These top-down and side-view games often use what is known as an *orthographic projection*. This type of projection lacks perspective: objects don't recede, or get smaller, as they get closer to the horizon. Oblique projections are occasionally used, although they aren't as popular because images can appear severely distorted. However, for some games like *Pac-Mania, Ultima VII,* and *EarthBound,* the distorted look matches the gameplay quite well.

A variation of side-view games is the side-scroller, where instead of the avatar moving across a static field, the environment actually scrolls side to side or up and down to create the illusion of the character moving.

In parallax scrolling, foreground elements move faster than those in the background to add to the illusion of depth.

# Side-Scrolling

Side-scrolling games are viewed from the side, and players can pan back and forth. A good example is *Angry Birds*. This type of game occasionally adds parallax scrolling to give a greater sense of depth. A few games, such as *Fly Hard* and *Shmusicup,* use this same design approach but scroll vertically instead of horizontally.

Scrollers can support games that call for exploration but also allow for rapid action. These types of games are often referred to as *platform* games.

Scroller games are popular, as you can see in racing games like *Mario Kart*, beat 'em up games like *The Simpsons*, and platformers like *Super Mario Bros.*

# Faux 3D Backgrounds

Designers are able to combine the top-down and side views into a faux 3D type of environment using a projection. These aren't true 3D worlds. Instead, they use 2D graphics (sprites and tileable pieces) to give the impression of a more dimensional world, but the computer doesn't have to scale the 2D sprites or tiled elements used to create the backgrounds.

This approach was excellent in earlier games (*DOOM, Duke Nukem 3D)* because the machines that ran the games didn't have the computing power of most systems available today. In those early games, the engine used to run the game created the world on a two-dimensional grid using closed 2D shapes called *sectors* and then added structures as flat, simple objects that were the *sprites.*

A *sprite* is a graphic object with its own z plane, which allows it to appear in front of or behind other objects. It can move, but it doesn't have to.

Today's systems can run true 3D and allow the gamer to move throughout a more realistic world; however, faux 3D (or 2.5D) backgrounds are still used in some games. For the purpose of discussing faux 3D backgrounds in this chapter, the topic is being limited to creating the graphics for the environments.

2.5 D refers to either

> ▶ Pseudo (fake) 3D used for games like *Baldur's Gate*
>
> ▶ 3D games that are played entirely in 2D, such as *Pandemonium* and *Clockwork Knight*

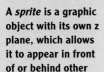

In an axonometric projection, there are no discernible vanishing points, and the scale for all objects remains the same whether they're in the foreground or the distance.

Let's take a step back and review what we know about creating the illusion of depth. Perspective is used in a drawing or painting to create a believable environment (depth). This sense of depth is accomplished by having a horizon line and vanishing points. Figure 5.7 shows how two points fixed on a horizon line can be used to draw shapes with correct perspective.

Projections are a bit different. A sense of depth is created, but there are no discernible vanishing points. With parallel projection (also known as *axonometric projection*), unlike top-down or side views, the graphics are rotated slightly to reveal other facets, thereby creating a faux 3D image.

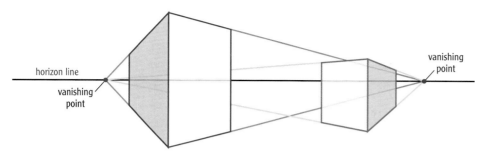

**FIGURE 5.7** Two-point perspective shows a facing corner of an object, such as the rectangles in this image.

Axonometric views can be isometric, diametric, or trimetric. The most common type of axonometric projection, know as *isometric views*, projects three-dimensional space onto a two-dimensional picture plane, as do diametric and trimetric; however, the face sizes are equal. This projection again allows for infinite scrolling over the background. Isometric is also known as *3/4 perspective*. All three faces are drawn on the same scale, as shown in Figure 5.8, and the axes are oriented at the same angle to the projection.

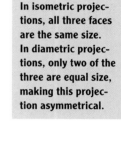

In isometric projections, all three faces are the same size. In diametric projections, only two of the three are equal size, making this projection asymmetrical.

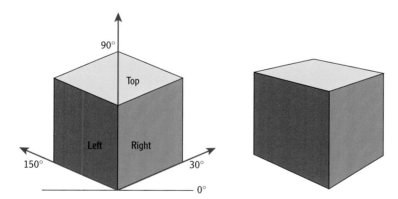

**FIGURE 5.8** In this example, the box on the left has been drawn using an isometric method, while the box on the right was drawn in perspective.

## SKYDOMES

*Skydomes* or *skyboxes* are a method for creating backgrounds where objects far in the distance in-game are painted on the cube enclosing the entire level.

The unique aspect of using isometric projection is that regardless of the position of the axes, the angle between the projections is always 120 degrees. Figure 5.9 is a perfect example of this from the game *Baldur's Gate,* from Black Isle Studios, Interplay Entertainment: the buildings don't appear to scale, but they do appear to be facing in different directions.

**FIGURE 5.9** The game *Baldur's Gate* uses axonometric projection for the backgrounds. Notice how the buildings in the distance are the same size as those in the foreground.

2.5D backgrounds can be created in 3D, but the camera is locked down so the projection is isometric. 2.5D can also be created using a 2D digital program like Photoshop. Again, the images are rendered with an isometric view showing at least two faces of any building and some of the top.

## SCROLLING AND AXONOMETRIC VIEW

Using faux 3D environments allows for infinite scrolling over backgrounds, and generally the viewer can see two sides and the top plane of any object in the background. A great example of this, from its historical origins, can be found in Chinese scroll paintings like the one shown here.

*(Continues)*

**SCROLLING AND AXONOMETRIC VIEW** *(Continued)*

These types of paintings were designed as a form of narrative. The viewer can fix on any area of the painting and understand the story being told there, regardless of how wide the scroll is and without any optical distortions created by vanishing points or strong light sources. The projection the Chinese invented to create this unusual perspective is known as axonometric, or *dengjiao toushi* in Chinese, meaning "equal-angle see-through." The term *axonometry* means "measurable from the axes."

Regardless of the approach to creating the faux background, the result is the creation of a bigger world in which players can move up and down and side to side without straining the capabilities of the computers running them. This approach is still used, especially with games that are playable online.

# 3D Models

Whether your game is designed to play in a world where you can move 360 degrees or is a flat 2D game, characters, props, vehicles, and environments can be designed and built using a variety of 3D programs. These are some of the commonly used software packages:

► Maya: http://usa.autodesk.com/maya/

► 3ds Max: www.autodesk.com/3dsmax/

► CINEMA 4D: www.maxon.net

Open source also has a 3D package called Blender that you may want to take a look at. Blender is a free program that can be downloaded here: www.blender.org.

**WHICH 3D PROGRAM?**

Maya is an excellent program that, like CINEMA 4D, 3ds Max, and Blender, can be used to create 3D models, animate, and do compositing, match moving, and other visual effects. Maya tends to be the preferred program to use because of its versatility for creating organic models and the robust nature of the entire package—it has everything you need for modeling and

*(Continues)*

Polygons are used to create the 3D models. A low-poly model, or *mesh*, has fewer polygons, appears a bit blocky, and is used for slower engines and playback systems.

Some designers prefer to sketch characters out using pencil and paper or roughly blocking in the image using a graphics tablet and their computer. Others prefer to start with a simple shape in a sculpting program like ZBrush or Mudbox, and carve away, using the 3D capabilities to sculpt the forms they're looking for to create a character or prop. In some cases, you may be adapting an existing 2D character into a 3D package for a project that is being upgraded to a more immersive environment and complex gameplay. Regardless of where your project starts, there are a few important things to keep in mind when working with 3D models.

*3D models*, even the most organic-looking ones, are created from a series of flat *polygons* linked together. The more polygons, the smoother and more organic a model may appear; however, getting a complex, high-polygon figure to animate is a different story. Simply stated, the more polygons used to create your model, the "heavier" the model is, and the more computer resources are required to get the model to animate.

If a model needs to animate for an intro or trailer, then a higher-poly figure usually will work fine, because the frames are rendered out and played back as an existing, complete, pre-rendered movie.

The *frame rate* for 3D games is generally 30–60 frames per second (fps), which is the same as video (30 fps).

If the figure needs to move in-game, then the computer must animate that figure *live*, in real-time, which can take up an enormous amount of a computer's resources. To keep the figure from slowing down the *frame rate*, you'll generally use a lower polygon mesh with more detailed textures. Ideally, you'll use normal maps to increase the topological detail of the object without add-ing extra polygons, but you should use at least high-quality diffuse maps with a greater amount of detail painted in. More information about these maps is out-lined in the "Painting 3D Images" section of this chapter.

As examples, a game like *Gears of War* might create a very high-resolution model in a program like ZBrush and then export normal maps to be used on a lower-resolution version of the model. *World of Warcraft* uses a much lower polygon mesh and paints the details into the diffuse map. *Gears of War* also uses diffuse maps in conjunction with the normal maps to allow the greatest amount of detail while keeping the poly count manageable. Most modern games use the normal/diffuse map combination.

**Diffuse maps are sometimes referred to as *skins*.**

Texture-map size is often determined more by the power of the graphics hard-ware; it isn't as much a consideration for a low frame rate (although it does have an impact). The number of polygons moving around, and any special effects going off, are the first targets of poor frame rate.

Main characters in games tend to have about 3000–4000 polys; however, depending on the platform the game is designed to run on, that number can vary a great deal. Figure 5.10 shows a completed character model from Artery Studios (www.artery-studios.com) with a low-poly mesh.

**FIGURE 5.10** Artery Studios specializes in creating models for all types of projects. This model, an example of a character for a game, was created using a low poly count. The polygons are visible in the figure at far left. The skin was painted with greater detail to make the figure appear more realistic.

When your sketch is completed and you're ready to begin modeling, you may want to start with a basic, or primitive shape, like a cube, which has six faces. By using the tools in the program—*extrude* (pulls new faces from existing faces); *tessellate* (also known as *tiling*: repeats a shape covering a plane without gaps or overlapping); and *bevel* (cuts off the corner where two shapes meet, creating a new face and giving a slightly rounded appearance along the corners of a model)—the modeler expands the faces of the cube, pushing and pulling to add more polygons and flesh out the form. This process is referred to as *box-modeling*, but there are also other methods you can use.

Some artists prefer to work with existing basic human forms or import their drawing into the program on image planes to see front and side views and then model from that.

## Rigging

Finished characters, props, and vehicles that need to move in-game or be animated for introductions and trailers require a rig for the animators to use to make the form move. The concept is similar to moving a puppet, except the mechanics are buried inside the model. You can shop at a variety of websites for completed models that are rigged and ready to animate, including www.turbosquid.com; or you can find free ones at www.blendswap.com. Rigs can be added to models after they have been sculpted in a 3D program if you're creating your own, unique figure.

## Cel Shading

Also known as *toon shading* (short for *cartoon shading*), *cel shading* allows the designer to create a character or prop in a 3D program but render it like a 2D graphic. Toon shading is a stylistic choice that takes advantage of being able to animate directly out of the software or place the camera to meet the needs of how a figure needs to be posed or moving.

An excellent example of this technique can be found in the game *Gravity,* from Vita, as shown in Figure 5.11. The look is reminiscent of comic books or graphic novels. For games that originate from or emulate those sources, this approach is ideal.

In order to create a toon-shaded object, you essentially turn off the lighting for the model, thereby creating a flat look for the art. Figure 5.12 shows primitives rendered out of 3ds Max.

▶

*Primitive* **is a commonly accepted term for a simple geometric shape generated in a 3D program.**

**FIGURE 5.11** Toon shading, or cel shading, is a method for rendering 3D models to look like comics while allowing for animation.

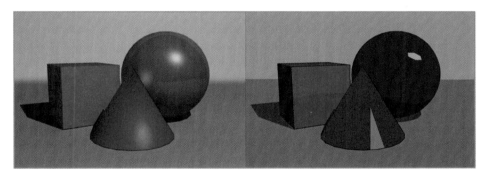

**FIGURE 5.12** The images on the left are rendered with the lighting turned on, creating the highlights and shadows necessary to make them look dimensional. The image on the right has been toon-shaded.

Different programs have different steps to making the model appear toon-shaded. The manuals specifically written for the programs have sections devoted to lighting models and how to toon-shade them. Numerous sites like MangaHelpers (www.mangahelpers.com) and Second Picture (www.secondpicture.com) have online tutorials as well.

Both of these sites also have extensive tutorials for numerous aspects of working with the creation and animation of 3D models along with loads of useful tips for working with Photoshop. Photoshop is the preferred program for painting the skins for models.

In addition, you may want to review the tutorials offered by Digital-Tutors (www.digitaltutors.com).

The black lines often seen on toon-shaded objects are created in a secondary step, also in the 3D program.

# Color, Texture, and Lighting

2D images can be painted a variety of ways, using Photoshop, Illustrator, Flash, or any of the many methods for traditional paint—like acrylic, watercolor, and so on. 3D pieces are handled a bit differently, especially if the object being modeled needs to be animated as a 3D element.

## Painting 2D Images

For decades, game designers have used 2D graphics—and they continue to do so. Flash-based games use them, and there are a variety of programs you can use to render images including backgrounds, characters, props, and vehicles.

Photoshop is still the workhorse of the industry. It's used for everything from creating storyboards to animatics and previs, painting in-game assets, and even drawing the art for the box. This versatile program can create vectors along with raster images, so it can be used to cel-shade individual frames of animation and do photorealistic work for environments. Whatever the visual task, this program can handle it.

Raster images are made of pixels. The more pixels used, the more detailed the image; however, file sizes start to get large as more pixels are used.

Most studios work with Photoshop, so you should learn the interface for this program. Information about Photoshop, created by Adobe Software, can be found on Adobe's website: www.adobe.com/products/photoshop.html.

Numerous other sites offer online tutorials for learning how to manipulate this program. Here are a few of them:

Vector images are created using a mathematical equation in 2D or 3D space. They scale well and have smaller file sizes than raster images, but they can't display as much detail.

▶ Photoshop Tutorials: www.photoshoptutorials.ws

▶ Good-tutorials: www.good-tutorials.com

▶ Photoshop Roadmap: www.photoshoproadmap.com

▶ Adobe Design Center: www.adobe.com/designcenter/

Many of the websites you may stumble across with Photoshop tutorials offer step-by-step lessons on how to create a specific special effect with text, or how to make and use your own brushes. Those are fun to play around with and help get you used to finding and using the tools on the program's interface.

As an example of what Photoshop can do, look at Figure 5.13 from a game called *Frobish,* created by Star Mountain Studios. The image on the left was created in Photoshop using multiple photographs, textures, and digital paint. The image on the right was also created using Photoshop, in this case using all digital paint. The point of doing the two versions was to come up with two different looks for the game so the designers could choose which approach to use when making the game.

Keep in mind that you can create 2D graphics digitally using programs like Photoshop, Flash, Illustrator, and GIMP, to name a few. Indy designers with fewer resources at hand may want to consider GIMP for creating graphics. Like Blender, which we looked at in the "3D Models" section of this chapter, GIMP is a free online graphics program. Information about GIMP and the features it offers can be found at www.gimp.org. You can also use traditional methods like pencil or paint on paper or illustration board and then scan the images into your computer to work from.

**FIGURE 5.13** Photoshop was used to paint both images, providing a remarkably different look for the same layout.

## Painting 3D Images

At this point in the process of creating your art, you've designed your character (or prop), scanned it into your computer, imported this into the 3D program of your choice, and built your model. The goal now is to add color, texture, and details onto the surface of the model.

Some programs, like CINEMA 4D, allow the artist to paint textures directly onto the model. Other types of 3D programs, like Maya and 3ds Max, require the artist to map a skin onto the finished model. The skin is called a *UV map* (UV refers to the x and y coordinates of the model), also called a *diffuse map*. Other maps can be layered on the UV or diffuse map to add additional dimensional texture (*bump maps* and *normal maps*) and *specular values*, thus creating skins that are lifelike and realistic.

A program called BodyPaint 3D can be used to create skins for characters, props, and backgrounds with CINEMA 4D, Maya, and 3ds Max.

Figure 5.14 shows a model of a goblin character named Goblinko, created by artist Richard Sternberg. After sketching the figure, including front and side views, he imported those drawings as image plane into 3ds Max. The image on the left, an exploded view of the goblin, shows what that map looks like before it's attached to the mesh. Sternberg then used the program to generate the finished model on the right.

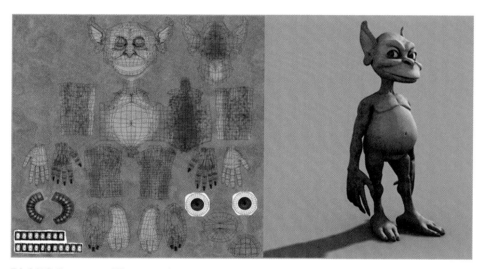

**FIGURE 5.14** When creating a texture map for a 3D model, a program like Photoshop allows you to paint all kinds of details that are then applied as the skin.

As a quick review, the *mesh* is another word for your 3D model; the terms are used interchangeably. There are different methods to apply a skin of texture and color to that mesh (model):

**Normal map**   This method for painting the map for the model uses a fake lighting technique of bumps and dents that add more detail to the figure without increasing the number of polygons.

**Bump map**   This is a form of normal mapping, where wrinkles or bumps are made to appear on the skin you're painting for the 3D model by adjusting the lighting without having to change the polygons of the model. This a grayscale version of the color map.

**Specular map**    Specularity refers to how bright or shiny the surface of the model appears.

# Animation

Animation for games falls under two major headings:

▶ Animating for non-interactive elements

▶ Animating for in-game or interactive elements

Non-interactive elements, such as trailers or the introduction to the game, are fairly straightforward. The *animation* is done using 2D or 3D techniques and approached in the same way you would create animation for a TV show or movie. The animator usually works from a script and/or storyboards and animates in a linear fashion, from the beginning to the end of a scene or scenes.

In-game animation is a bit different because it isn't a pre-rendered movie, like a trailer. It's animation that happens in real time.

Cutscenes used to be rendered out as movies; however, most games now run them in real time directly from the engine, thus avoiding huge rendered movie files.

Animation for gameplay doesn't address certain things an animator might normally work on, such as creating facial deformations to match lip synch. Most playback systems just don't have the speed and capability to render the frames in real time with that much complexity, so most animations for games are limited to cycles that can repeat. The majority of characters or props that will be animated in game are simplified to limit the strain on the system.

You'll want to plan for a variety of elements to be animated. The most obvious animated elements are the characters—you want to see them move and have some sense of realism to add to the fun of the gameplay. Props and vehicles (including horses or other mounts that might be used) are treated much the same as characters and animated in repeatable loops so their animation can be rendered in real time as the game is played. Other elements that are animated in games can include weather, which is usually particle-based animation. Although the designer of a game generally doesn't create the actual animation (that falls to the production crew), it's useful to understand how the process works so the designer will be able to plan for the different cycles required to create the game.

*Particle animation*, or *system animation*, is a technique for animating soft or diffused things like smoke, clouds, fog and dust in a 3D program using an emitter.

# Characters, Props, and Vehicles

We discussed camera angles earlier and revisit them now in relation to animation. The animator needs to understand clearly how and where the camera will be used in game. If the game uses a FPS POV, then the camera will be locked just behind the player and look through their eyes. In other words, the player sees what the character sees.

The approach is quite simple to create and program; however, it limits the amount of animation for the character because you primarily see just their hand or hands. Using the TPS POV, multiple elements in the scene may need to be animated, including the lead character/s, secondary characters, non-player characters (NPCs), vehicles, animals, foliage moving, and so on. Again, how immersive the designer wants the game to be will dictate how much animation needs to be created.

Most animations for games tend to be generated in short cycles that can, if necessary, be strung together to show complex movement. For example, a character can be animated to kick, and then there may be other movements like jumping or punching; if you play them back to back, the final result is a seamless transition from one cycle to the next.

When you begin to plan animation for your game, create a list of things you want that character (or prop) to do. The more animations you plan for, the more work is required, and the bigger the strain on the playback system, so make sure these are the movements needed for the game. These movements tend to be used over and over again, so it's good to plan for a variety or variations of the same types of movements.

These are the basic moves used for in-game animations:

▶ Idle

▶ Running

▶ Walking

▶ Reactions, such as cringing in horror or shaking from fear

▶ Falling down

▶ Getting up

▶ Specialties (the figure may need to fly or make other specific movements, such as casting a spell.)

Characters that aren't moved by the gamer tend to move slightly, such as shifting their weight or looking around, to give the impression that they're alive.

Depending on the type of game you're making, you'll want more or less of any of those types of animations. A fighting game may need more animations that can be strung together for kicking, punching, jumping, and so on. Sports games will need a variety of movements for throwing a ball, catching a ball, hitting a ball, and so on.

As you develop a game, an asset list is generated based on the script and flow-chart and gameplay desired, so the animators will have a good idea of how many cycles of animation they're building. Keep in mind, the more cycles you have, the larger your game gets, and the more work the engine has to do. If you're building a casual, downloadable, "try before you buy" kind of game, anything greater than 100–200 MB will put off any potential buyer; so, make sure you need the animation before including it in the game.

Asset lists include all elements that need to be created for a game—graphics, animations, effects, and sounds—to help keep track of the numerous tasks involved.

The actual mechanics behind the creation of animation can come from a variety of sources. Objects (characters, props, and vehicles) can be animated using keyframes or motion capture.

*Keyframes* are starting and ending points for any transition and generally show dramatic changes such as weight shifts or movement of the character. This work is done by hand, by the animator, who positions the character (whether it's a 3D model moved by its rig or a 2D image that is drawn) to show these major movements. An animating program then draws the inbetween, to smooth out the transitions.

*Motion capture*, which is becoming more prevalent, is used for 3D animated movies, special effects in film and TV where 3D graphics are created, and games. Detailed information about this form of animation can be found in Chapter 2, "Gameplay Styles."

## Clickable Items

Some items in games, such as navigation buttons and items to be found or interacted with in the environment, require some animation. These tend to be simple, repeatable animations like showing a wiggle, a color, or a value change if the player mouses over something that needs to be clicked.

In *Apparitions: The Haunting of the Red Reef Inn,* created by Star Mountain Studios, players can record and review evidence of a possible haunting in the hotel. The player can mouse over the entire surface, and clickable items shift color. In this case, the images become lighter by 50%, as shown in Figure 5.15 where the cursor is positioned over the Peter Wren Agency icon.

Mousing over an object means literally moving your mouse (or other controller) until the cursor is positioned over the clickable object.

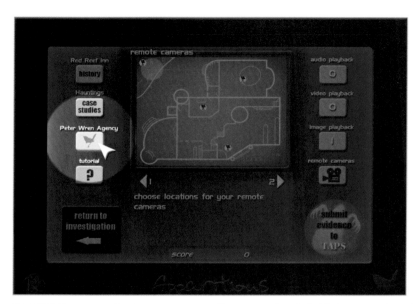

**FIGURE 5.15** Designers create a rollover state for clickable items so that when your cursor moves over the object, it will wiggle or change color to let you know it can be clicked.

Any item that shows a value change can be clicked; and when clicked, a simple animation shows the button appear to depress and then rise again. This type of animation has a resting state (as shown for all the buttons in Figure 5.15), a rollover state (the value change shown by the Peter Wren Agency button), and a click state. The click state is created by duplicating the button in Photoshop, offsetting it to the right and then down a few pixels, and reversing the lighting in layer-style effects (bevel and emboss).

Reward animations also tend to be repeating types. On the plus side, using repeating animations allows the game to use assets over and over, thus reducing the strain on the system and giving the designer the possibility of investing more animation in the main characters. The downside is that some rewards, which are meant to be fun and a big "wow" factor in games, can get boring when seen repeatedly. Designers often try to solve this dilemma by creating a few variations of reward animations (fireworks, explosions, star bursts, fairy dust, and so on).

The designer needs to figure out where they will get the most bang for their buck when it comes to investing the assets of the game with animations. A game that doesn't have any animation these days tends to be ignored by players.

So how much animation should you use? Start by understanding how much animation the player is used to seeing.

Play games that are similar to the one you're designing. Note how much animation is used, and what is being animated. Are you seeing only a character or prop animate, or do other things like buttons wiggling or background animation such as birds flying in the sky or fish swimming in water give the game a more realistic, immersive feeling?

Once you have a sense of how much animation is expected, develop an asset list to plan for what types of animation you'll need.

## THE ESSENTIALS AND BEYOND

In this chapter, we took a look at how some of the graphics are designed and created for games. Many traditional methods are still widely used, such as 2D graphics; however, 3D introduced a new wrinkle in the design process, including new ways to create 2D imagery.

The look and feel of games can be dramatically affected by the placement of the camera, and that decision alone can make or break a game's success.

Now that you have had a chance to review some of these important design essentials, look for them in games you play, and try some of them with your own projects to see what results you get. Do your choices in your own projects, or choices you see in existing games, enhance or hurt the gameplay?

Improved animation, more immersive play, and sequel upon sequel designed and built for successful games keep products moving. In addition, new improvements in technology for faster animation and improved graphics, more fascinating storylines, and updated versions from classic games ensure a steady stream available to avid game players.

### ADDITIONAL EXERCISES

▶ Play one of your favorite games, and write down how many repeatable animation cycles you see, including the idle.

▶ Play one or more games, and take note of the kinds of animation you see. In other words, look at the characters, backgrounds, and other elements, and see what is animated and what kinds of movements you see. Then, review any trailers you find for the game, and note the difference in quality between the animation and art. Is there a difference? If so, how would you describe it? Some trailers draw their material directly from screen captures during gameplay, while others invest a great deal of time and effort into making original mini-movies. See if you can spot the differences.

*(Continues)*

## THE ESSENTIALS AND BEYOND *(Continued)*

► Play a few games, and determine what the intended demographic was. Then compare your notes with what the manufacturer says the demographic is. If they differ, why do you think that is?

► Examine and play 3–5 games. See if you can figure out which type of camera angle the designer chose.

### REVIEW QUESTIONS

1. Which type of axonometric projection is most commonly used in games?

   A. Diametric                     C. Isometric

   B. Trimetric                     D. Skybox

2. True or false. The demographic for a game is based on who the designers are.

3. True or false. The majority of games that are played are violent.

4. Which two types of POV are used in games that have characters in them?

   A. Second person and third person     C. First person and second person

   B. First person and third person      D. Second person and fourth person

5. True or false. An advantage of faux 3D backgrounds is that objects do not change size as the player scrolls the playing field.

# Navigation and Interfaces

*Designing navigation refers to* guiding players through the game, including how to adjust sound, graphics and animation, special attributes for the avatar (including the name), saving games, tutorials, and so on.

Whether the game is designed for play on home computers or a playback system like the Wii or handheld devices, players need to have the ability to adjust gameplay and personalize aspects of the game, such as adding their name, choosing avatars, and selecting customizable color palettes or even textures for the backgrounds.

For players who have slower computers, navigation screens can also provide ways to adjust how fast or slow the game can run so they may optimize performance.

The player interacts with the game through a series of interfaces: clickable menus or other elements such as inventory, points, maps, and so on.

In addition, in this chapter, we'll review methods for testing games and see exactly when testing should start and its incredible importance to the overall success of the project.

▶ **Guides for the player**

▶ **Interface design**

▶ **Testing!**

## Guides for the Player

For the most part, guiding players through games is fairly standard, and for good reason. If navigation screens are too unique or unusual, most players won't stick around to figure them out. These screens, such as the splash screen and main menu, are an integral part of any game design. Players purposely look for these screens to help them get started.

You need to take care to figure out how much information and how many interactive elements to add to each screen. Some screens carry a great deal of information (how much usually depends on the complexity of the game) or are broken into sequences of screens. Some are extremely simple and filled with eye candy. One thing is true for almost all games: these screens are the first thing any player interacts with when starting a new game. When coming up with the look for the splash (or title) screen, you should not only provide a good visual that communicates the look and feel of the project, but also entice the player and make it easy for them to get right into the game (finding what buttons to push, and so on).

Use words, colors, and graphics that appeal to your audience. If the game is designed for little children, then select bright colors, use text that's easy to see and read, and consider having animations that actually jump up and down and point at things the child needs to interact with in order to play the game. Be careful of cluttering screens for children's games. It's tempting to fill them with all kinds of cute things, but if your goal is to entice the child and let them run the game, then they need to see clearly what they have to interact with.

## Languages

All the screens for the game need to be checked for typos, and the complexity of the words and grammar should align with your audience. If your game needs to be translated into other languages, use a professional service. Copying and pasting text from a free online translation site will yield iffy results.

### MOST COMMONLY USED LANGUAGES

According to the Summer Institute of Linguistics (SIL)'s 2009 census, the most common languages in the world are

1. Chinese (Mandarin)—1,213 million speakers

2. Spanish—329 million speakers

3. English—328 million speakers

4. Arabic—221 million speakers

These numbers are based on the numbers of people in the world who speak the languages. Significantly more people speak Chinese than speak any other language. The languages listed for numbers 2, 3, and 4 change from time to time, as the populations adjust and census methods vary, to include Hindi, Bengali, Portuguese, Russian, and Japanese. Although there are more Chinese speakers, the English language is the most widespread.

*(Continues)*

**MOST COMMONLY USED LANGUAGES** *(Continued)*

Although deciding the languages into which a game will be translated generally falls to the publisher, the game maker needs to know if the game will be translated for the following reasons:

► Space for areas that hold text may need to be enlarged.

► Colors may need to be adjusted due to cultural influence.

► Characters or environments may need to be designed and then swapped out to make the game more appealing to other audiences.

Usually, games are translated into other languages after their completion; however, the game makers are often brought into the loop during this phase because areas on the screens sometimes need to be made larger to accommodate more text, or colors need to be adjusted. Although certain colors were selected during the initial design phase, swapping those out for colors that are more appropriate for players from other cultures is often part of the process.

# Everything Needs to Be Tested!

As you work on the navigation screens, you should also be preparing for testing. None of the planning will let you know if your game is going to be successful or not, until the game gets to the testing phase. (See "Testing!" later in this chapter for more information about this important phase of game design.)

Consider the design for a car. On paper, it looks fantastic—the concept art shows it be the coolest vehicle ever to roll over the face of the Earth. But if a driver gets behind the wheel and discovers that the car drives terribly or not at all, then it's a failure. Keep this analogy in mind as you design anything for a game. Designing a cool car that also drives like a dream (that's the gameplay!) is your goal.

# Launch Icons

Whether you're launching the game on your home computer, handheld device, or playback system such as PlayStation or Wii, the game needs to have some type of icon or shortcut to click to start it. For home computers, those graphics tend to be $256 \times 256$ pixels; so whatever the graphic is, it needs to be clear and easy to read at such a small size. Various playback systems and gaming portals specify sizes they require, and they can be as tiny as $32 \times 32$ pixels.

**Games come with desktop icons that can be used to launch the game. The player can easily see these unique icons on the desktop or user interface for console games.**

Programs such as iConvert, IcoFx and LiquidIcon allow you to make your own customized icons on your home computer. You can also use Windows 7, which has features to let you make customizable icons.

To create a launch icon:

1. Create the graphic at $32 \times 32$ pixels.

2. Save to your desktop as a `.png`.

3. Change the file extension to `.ico`.

## Launch!

When you launch a game, most designers feature an intro screen, which can be the splash art, title screen, startup screen, loading screen, or any combination of those. This screen usually includes a button that players can click to proceed to the main menu (alternately, they can click anywhere, and the game will proceed). Some designers also add some of the elements that are associated with the main menu (see the section "Main Menu").

To get to this first screen, players need to click a launch button. For players with home computers, the launch button appears as an icon, generally on the desktop. Figure 6.1 shows a close-up of what a launch icon typically looks like on a computer desktop. This icon launches the game *Apparitions: The Haunting of the Red Reef Inn*. The logo is used through the game and its marketing, making it easy to spot on the desktop.

**FIGURE 6.1** Launch icons are unique to any game or software program.

## Interface Design

Game makers continue to improve graphics, animation, sound, and gameplay in an effort to engage the player more and more. Getting players involved in a game is almost like drawing them into a movie or TV show, but games are set apart in a few distinct ways. Whereas a film or TV show is a linear experience, pulling the viewer along from scene to scene, games can be nonlinear, and they also allow the gamer to interact with events in the game.

There are a few different forms of interactivity:

**User-to-technology interactivity**   This type of interactivity can occur when someone accesses a website like an online dictionary. You can type in a word, and the website returns information to you.

**Player-to-technology interactivity**   This is the type of interaction generally found in a game, where the player can pick up an object or turn something on that affects the gameplay.

**Player-to-player interactivity**   Social games and massively multiplayer online games (MMOGs) offer this type of interactivity, where players can interact with each other in game.

The ability of the player to interact with a game occurs through interactive screens. These screens, known as interfaces or the user interface (UI), tend to fall under two main categories:

**Dispensing information**   These tend to tell the player things such as how much money they have, how much life they have left, and so on.

**Allowing for action**   These aspects of a screen allow the player to do something in the game such as pick up an object, fire a weapon, jump, and so on.

## EARLY IDEAS ON INTERFACES

In 1945, Vannevar Bush, a scientist at MIT, wrote an article titled "As We May Think." In it, he proposed a method for making data more accessible on microfilm using hyperlinks. This was the first thinking that helped develop UIs.

# GUI and HUD

One common type of interface is a *graphical user interface (GUI)*. In other words, you can see and then click something. In contrast, with a command-line interface (CLI) like the one you encountered in *Colossal Cave Adventure* in Chapter 2, "Gameplay Styles," you type in commands. The GUI and CLI are both examples of UIs.

The GUI is often referred to conversationally as the "gooey."

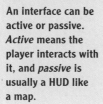

Many HUDs in games are designed to appear as part of the game world. For example, in a racing game, the player sees dials that could be part of a car's dashboard.

An interface can be active or passive. *Active* means the player interacts with it, and *passive* is usually a HUD like a map.

The *HUD* is the *heads-up display*. The term comes from a type of display that was created for fighter pilots: they were able to see critical information displayed as transparent images on the visors of their helmets or windshields so they could access that information and also maintain visual contact with what was in the area. This let pilots keep their heads up instead of having to look down at controls in the cockpit.

For gamers, HUDs can appear as pop-ups in the center of the screen or off to one side. This allows them to quickly see the information without losing sight of what they're doing in the game. The HUD in a game can also be part of the toolbar or any other display that is kept up during play. HUDs typically show the health of the character, points accumulated, time elapsed or a clock, weapons and ammunition, and so on.

## Important Aspects of the UI

The look and feel of the UI need to match the look and feel of the game.

The most relevant information needs to be provided to the player with as few button presses as possible. If this interface is too complicated, it can clutter up the playing field and cause the player frustration. Nothing is more annoying than being involved in a big battle, or coming to the conclusion of a fast-paced race, and not being able to find the right button to push to complete the actions.

Games can combine elements that are part of the game world (diegetic) or not (non-diegetic), as they suit the needs of the game. The goal is to keep the UI simple, yet match the look and feel of the world while also being functional. Don't have buttons on the interface just because they look cool. If they don't have a function, don't clutter real estate with them.

In the game *Apparitions: The Haunting of the Red Reef Inn,* interfaces are on all screens during gameplay. This is typical so that players can interact with the game, access other features such as the Options menu, or exit.

Figure 6.2 shows an interior in the game where the player—in this case, a ghost hunter—is studying an abandoned spiral staircase. Along the bottom, the toolbar has several buttons that can be clicked.

Figure 6.3 is also from the game *Apparitions.* A critical component of gameplay is being able to review data that the player (the ghost hunter) has captured while investigating the hotel. This interface is a bit more complex and has many buttons that can be pushed to capture photos, audio clips, and video; view the past history of the hotel; and submit findings to the *Ghost Hunters* (SyFy Channel), Jason Hawes and Grant Wilson.

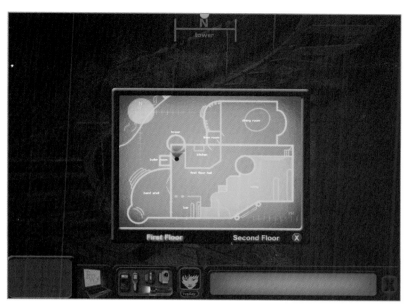

**FIGURE 6.2** This toolbar from *Apparitions* is a non-diegetic example of a UI. One of the buttons on the toolbar brings a map forward full screen: the player can click this type of HUD to navigate to other areas of the hotel where the game takes place.

**FIGURE 6.3** Clicking the open laptop on the toolbar displays a new screen that is all interface. This is where players can play back and review data they have collected. Looks like they captured something!

# Spatial Relationships

There are a number of ways to classify interface types. For example, interfaces can be diegetic or not non-diegetic:

**Diegetic interface**   This unique interface is incorporated in the world in which the gamer is playing. As the player moves around the world, they may encounter things to interact with, in the environment or on the character, and these are diegetic. This type of interface lets players immerse themselves more fully in the world of the game they're playing.

**Non-diegetic interface**   This is the most common type of interface players encounter in games. The interface is seen and heard by the player, but it isn't part of the game world. For example, in a racing game, the player may see a steering wheel or speedometer on the screen that shows what is happening to them and their vehicle in the race, but the display isn't part of the actual race going on in the game world. A HUD is an example of a non-diegetic interface.

Figure 6.4 shows a terrific example of a diegetic interface from the survival game *Dead Space 2*, which is a third-person shooter. The game, developed by Visceral Games and published by Electronic Arts (EA), doesn't use any HUDs at all.

**FIGURE 6.4** In *Dead Space 2*, you can see the player in the foreground wearing his unique suit. The dashed blue bar down the back indicates health, and the circular one on the right shoulder indicates the stasis meter.

Working with spatial elements can alter the gameplayer's experience:

**Spatial elements**   Objects may appear in the game world that aren't part of the action designed to help the gamer understand what is happening. For example, an object the player needs to interact with might glow or jump, drawing the player's attention to it. These elements appear in perspective, matching that of the environment.

**Meta elements**   These objects may appear during gameplay, but they don't match the perspective or the world. For example, in some games, when a character is shot, blood splatters appear on the screen as if someone flicked them onto the monitor from inside the computer to indicate that damage has been inflicted.

Interfaces can also be classified as manual or visual:

- ▶ *Manual interfaces* usually involve the hardware used to connect with the technology, such as a keyboard, game controller, or footpad.

- ▶ *Visual interfaces* that the designer works on involve the creation of graphics, animation, audio, and special effects that appear on screen.

## Different Types of Screens

Once launched, games usually provide the following screens, and generally in this order:

- ▶ Licenses (EULA)
- ▶ Splash (or title) screens
- ▶ Loading
- ▶ Main menu
- ▶ Instructions (also called the tutorial)
- ▶ Options
- ▶ Toolbar
- ▶ High scores
- ▶ Credits
- ▶ Exit

**Any type of interface created for the gamer to use needs to be functional and easy to use and should, whenever possible, match the look and feel of the game.**

## Licenses

The *end-user license agreement (EULA)* is a document provided with any game that tells you who owns the copyright and what rights or permissions the buyer has. The EULA may be the first thing presented to the player or can come after the startup screens.

The game designer is usually tasked with creating an interface in which the player can read the information provided in the EULA and then click to accept it or decline (in which case the game usually shuts off). Even though this can be fairly dry reading, it's still a legal document, so all of the information needs to be easy to read; however, most designers create an interface that matches the look and feel of the game.

## Splash Art

One of the most fun types of screens to design for a game is the splash art. This screen can often become the signature look for the product. It may be used on the homepage of a website designed to support the game and is often used on the box art (or a variation of it, depending on the shape of the box).

Figure 6.5 shows a fun, simple launch screen that is also the splash art for the game *Findola*. This is an amusing, fast-paced game in which the goal is to match tiles on a game board and rack up points as quickly as possible before hazards begin to get in the way, such as ice that forms on some tiles and blocks the possibility of making a match.

> Splash or title screens can be static or include clickable items or movies. Instructions may be static or movies, too.

**FIGURE 6.5** The art on this splash screen, with its dynamic imagery and bright colors, communicates to the player that the game is lighthearted and fast-paced.

Figure 6.6 shows an example of another launch screen, designed for the game *Frozen*, which clearly shows that the gameplay takes place in a snowy environment—in this case, Antarctica. The page also includes instructions for purchasing and registering the game, an Exit button, and the splash art for the game (at lower left).

The designer for *Frozen* chose to include more information on the launch screen because the game is more complex than *Findola*. *Frozen* also has more options for gameplay variations than *Findola*, as well as a backstory that can be accessed during play.

As you play more games and consider their design, you'll discover that these screens (interfaces) can have many different combinations of sign-in features, options, features, art, animation, and so on. The designer's job is to provide screens that help guide the player through the process of learning how to use the game, or customize the game and still keep its look intact through the selection of art and animation.

**FIGURE 6.6** The launch screen for *Frozen* provides more detail, including the splash art and a link to the company website.

Keep in mind that no matter what information you as the designer feel a screen should have, the player must be able to use it.

## Loading Screens

Loading screens are fairly typical for most games and usually feature some type of animated graphic indicating that the player needs to wait for a few moments while the game loads.

Even if a game is already installed on your computer, your machine needs a few moments to access any stored information that is required. The animation lets the player know how much longer they need to wait for their game to load; in the case of long loads, the animation also lets them know that their computer hasn't crashed.

In *Frozen,* once the player chooses which option they want from the launch screen, the full-screen splash art comes up next with an animated graphic of ice cubes along the bottom, indicating the game is loading. For this design, the splash art is also the loading screen. You can view this loading screen for free, by accessing the game at www.starmountainstudios.com.

For standalone loading screens, the designer can create a simple animation that lets the player know the game is loading. You may want to consider adding an animation here because it acts as a type of timer, indicating how quickly things are loading, and also lets the player know (if they have to wait a few minutes) that their machine hasn't frozen. In Star Mountain's game *Kotsmine Hills,* shown in Figure 6.7, a standalone screen with animation reflects the look and feel of the game: it's a spooky but fun hidden object game (HOG) in which players hunt for objects and clues to unmask a mysterious killer lurking in the town.

**FIGURE 6.7** In this loading screen for the game *Kotsmine Hills*, a spotlight plays from left to right across a series of tombstones that spells *loading*.

Loading screens are fun to make, but be careful not to use too much animation. The more animation you place in the game, the larger the file gets. For games that must be downloaded, files that are too large are prohibitive.

## Main Menu

The majority of games, after they launch, take the player to a main menu. This screen usually has art associated with the look of the game and lets the player change modes and adjust settings that affect the look or performance. This menu typically contains all or some of the following:

**Choose or create player name**   Players enter their name or an alias they will play under.

**Continue or change player**   If more than one player is saved to the game, the player selects the appropriate player.

**Log in**   You may need to provide your login name along with a password. Passwords are generally required for online gameplay in the larger MMOGs like *World of Warcraft*. Designers may choose to provide them with any game, so that players who share a computer with others can protect any aspects of their customized game from being deleted.

**Exit**   Sometimes you launch a game and then decide not play, so the designer may provide an Exit button with the launch screen.

**Splash art**   In *splash art*, designers use art, assets, and the color palette, textures, and logos to brand the game. This art is often also used in marketing or for the box or website related to the game.

**ESRB R**   If a game has gone through the ESRB ratings process, you'll generally see the rating here. (For more information on ESRB ratings, see Chapter 2.)

**Other**   The launch screen may also display other features such as the official website address (often clickable), fansites, and links to reviews or other clickable locations.

Figure 6.8 is an example of a main menu from the game *Frozen*.

This menu offers the player the option of which type of gameplay they wish to experience. After that selection is made, they have access to more menus they can use to adjust the game's performance, look, and other elements. Because each unique game option has specific attributes, one main menu for all would be too complicated and cluttered. The menu shown in Figure 6.8 also lets the player see the avatar for the game, Samantha Bloodworth, and her trusty sidekick, a little robot named PEDRO.

**FIGURE 6.8** In this example of a main menu, the player is provided with information about how to play the game before they choose a gameplay mode.

Figure 6.9 shows another main menu example. This is a casual HOG. The main menu gives access to certain features such as selecting the player, a clickable link to the designers (Star Mountain Studios), the Options button, and of course Play! The name of the game, *Kotsmine Hills,* is etched into the tombstone, giving the player a pretty good indication that this game will be a bit spooky—albeit spooky fun.

The main menu is an important center point for the designer to work with. Like good web pages, main menus should make features easy to see and understand and contain graphics and/or animation that help brand the game. The moment any navigation screen—especially the main menu—becomes so complicated that the player can't understand how to use it, your game is likely to be discarded.

If reviewers include a graphic from a game, they often choose the main menu because it provides the look of the game and additional information.

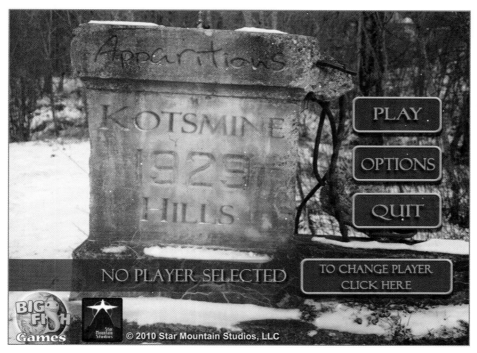

**FIGURE 6.9** In this example of a main menu, the spooky look and feel of the game are clearly evident from the snowy tombstone behind the buttons that access different aspects of the game.

## Instructions

Providing instructions for gameplay can be a slightly tricky undertaking. As discussed previously, part of the fun of a game is figuring it out. Designers need to make gameplay clear without boring the player with too much detail.

At this stage of game development, the genre and demographic should be fairly well established, so begin by putting yourself in the shoes of your target player. Try to anticipate players' needs and questions.

Instructions can come in the form of tutorials at the beginning of the game. They can be either static images with words describing what the player needs to do or movies explaining how to play. These tutorials can also be interactive. For example, at the beginning of a game, players may be allowed to play through part of a level, with help; their performance won't affect the final score they achieve for the game as long as they're in the tutorial mode.

*Weird Helmet* has a specific look, showing lots of weathered metal but bright colors. That look was carried through all the tutorial screens to not only provide the player with important information, but also keep them immersed in the look and feel of the game. The goal of the game is to get an avatar from the door on the left to the door on the right by turning tiles to make a path for the fast-running character. Players have the option to run a tutorial explaining how to play the game. The first screen of that tutorial is shown in Figure 6.10.

**FIGURE 6.10** The first screen of the *Weird Helmet* tutorial shows the gameboard filled with all the possible powerups and hazards that can appear during play.

The tutorial continues with directions, as shown in Figure 6.11. These are text based and include images to help the player understand the toolbar and powerups.

**FIGURE 6.11** After seeing what the gameboard looks like, the tutorial continues with specific information about how the powerups and certain parts of the toolbar work.

At any time during gameplay, the player can click the Options button on the toolbar and access a Help screen to review the instructions (as shown in Figure 6.12). These tutorial screens also appear at the beginning of the game for first-time players, right after the EULA is agreed to, although the player can opt not to run them.

**FIGURE 6.12** The Help screen from *Weird Helmet*

Players can change the volume, turn off music and leave dialogue, or reduce ambient sounds and decrease but not turn off the music or dialogue.

Typically, performance is adjusted by modifying levels of graphics detail such as overall screen dimensions, texture detail, particle effects (often used for weather), and anti-aliasing.

## Options

Options screens for games can include the following:

▶ Adjust sound

▶ Adjust playing speeds to help performance for slower machines

▶ Adjust performance

▶ Restart or reset the game

▶ Change playing modes

▶ Change players

▶ Access other levels that may be saved and are in progress, or start a new level

▶ Access websites associated with the game

▶ Access the tutorial

▶ Exit

Figure 6.13 shows us the options screen from the game *Frozen*. Notice how it ties in with the look of the splash art and main menu. (The logo for Star Mountain, is actually just the star and the mountain; however, the designer added snow to the logo to stay with the look and feel of the game.)

**FIGURE 6.13** Options screens usually allow the player to adjust sound and graphics and reset game modes.

This options screen also has a few other fun features such as the ability to check the weather in Antarctica and view screens that contain information about wildlife. None of these features affect gameplay. The designers included them to allow players of this casual game to immerse themselves a bit more in the game's world.

Many buttons and tools that are built into games but aren't used on a regular basis, such as adjusting sound or gameplay or resetting things, tend to be relegated to the options screen. This way, they don't clutter the playing area and use up precious game real estate.

## Toolbar

The toolbar is a navigation aid that can appear as soon as gameplay starts and remains in place as long as the game is open. Designers may provide an option for players, usually a keyboard shortcut such as Alt+Z, to hide the toolbar until the same shortcut is pressed again.

Toolbars usually contain general inventory items that are needed quickly and often during gameplay, such as weapons, equipment (for example, different golf clubs for a golfing game or a variety of weapons for a shooter), powerups, maps, and saved items (such as objects collected in a hidden object game or adventure game).

Most toolbars contain the following features:

**Inventory**   This can include items picked up and carried during gameplay or elements to help the player get started. For example, if you're playing a game where you need to enter a mine and gather specific ores, the inventory might contain a pick for you to use.

**Options**   Clicking this takes the player to the options screen.

**Help**   If a player gets stuck, clicking this button on the toolbar should take them to a screen with suggestions. The help screen is often set up in a Frequently Asked Questions format.

**Exit**   If the player wants to leave the game, they click this. In some games, when you click Exit, another pane or a pop-up window asks if you really want to leave, and gives you the options Yes and No; or you may be asked if you want to save the game.

Figure 6.14 shows a toolbar from the game *Apparitions: The Haunting of the Red Reef Inn.* The features are labeled for you. At far left, the player can access

The term *real estate* describes the physical visual area designers have to work with.

Allowing players to hide the toolbar helps reduce clutter for those who like to take screenshots during gameplay.

The Help button is often in the toolbar, but it may be anywhere on the gameboard.

a map that lets them click any other site on the gameboard and be transported there.

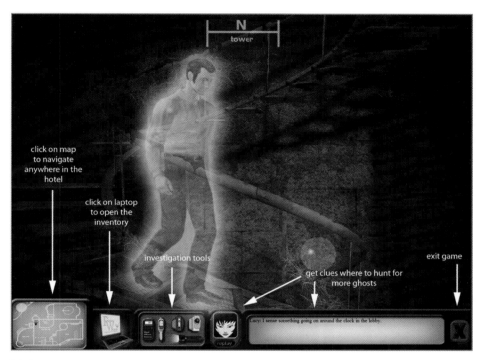

**FIGURE 6.14** Most toolbars are oriented across the bottom. It's natural for the player to focus on the game and then glance down to access different tools.

Because the inventory of things collected in this game is extensive (it's a ghost-hunting game in which the goal is to gather as much evidence as possible and determine whether the observed phenomenon is paranormal), there is a separate set of menus for those items. As stated earlier, toolbars often contain inventory items that are needed frequently and quickly, so investigative tools such as cameras and flashlight are included here. In addition, there is an in-game help feature in the form of a character named Lucy. Click her icon, and she will type out a message suggesting good places to hunt. At far right is an Exit button.

Toolbars, like all the screens discussed so far, are unique elements that designers create to help the player move around the game. They provide methods for adjusting gameplay.

Most toolbars are oriented along the bottom of the visual screen. However, they can be placed anywhere as long they remain functional and don't impede play.

Study toolbars for various games that have different gameplay styles, to see the most prominent elements. Odds are, the more action-packed the game, the more prominent tools or weapons. In slower adventure or hidden object games (HOGs), the collected inventory can become more important and prominent.

## Scores

Many games allow players to post their scores online. This lets players not only to try to beat the game, but also try to outdo other players.

Some gamers just like to open a game and wander about, poking at this or that and having fun with the graphics, animation, and so on. It's safe to say, though, that the majority of gamers are more competitive, and that means providing a system to show scores. Most scores appear on the toolbar or in their own area on or next to the gameboard.

Scores can use any type of denomination that fits your game. They don't have to be sequential numbers. For example, sports games such as tennis and football use sports scoring, which may award more points for a more challenging play. In football, a touchdown is worth more points than a field goal, and so on.

Other scoring methods can be how much gold or how many gems or other objects the player gathers during play. Scores can also include the number of extra lives acquired, quests completed, levels bested, and so on. Basically, any type of measurement can be used to tally a score. Don't be afraid to be creative or unique when it comes to how your gamer can tally scores (maybe they collect golden apples, beating hearts, or live squirrels), but do be clear and understandable.

## Exit

Pop-ups usually contain information that is important only at certain times. Using real estate on the toolbar or playing field for this information is a waste of space.

Exit features, as part of navigation, might seem to be a no-brainer; however, you need to make good decisions about their design. If you place the exit feature in an awkward area or use a poor design, you may cause some players to click the button accidentally and exit before they want to. This leads to player frustration and, quite likely, the player tossing your game.

## Pop-ups

You may want to include pop-ups from time to time. These can be little messages that pop onto the screen with help, advice, timers, clues, rewards—all types of additional messages that haven't been directly covered in the categories so far.

They can pop up over the playing field, temporarily pausing the gameplay without the player risking any losses. Again, these are assets that can add to the game's final file size. Although they don't increase the size a great deal, you should still use them sparingly.

Many players find too many pop-ups annoying.

*Sharkbites* is a fast-paced version of hangman. If the player fails to select the correct letters used in the game (they have 10 tries, as indicated by the number of steps on the gangplank), then they plop into the water and get eaten by the trio of hungry sharks. If that happens, a pop-up appears on screen, encouraging the player to try again and avoid those pesky sharks. Figure 6.15 shows a pop-up that appears when the player wins. This pop-up covers real estate that would normally be used in gameplay, but only while the game is paused as part of the reward for the player. After it disappears, the next round begins.

**FIGURE 6.15** In this pop-up from the game *Sharkbites*, the player has won the round. The pop-up stays on screen for just a few seconds while the game is paused.

As you've seen so far, you can design several types of interfaces to aid the player during the game. For the most part, they epitomize the look of the game and offer clickable areas to access other menus or locations to travel to.

# Testing!

Now that you've had a chance to look at how navigation and the user interface are created, and all the text, graphics, animation, and interactive elements used in the process, testing becomes paramount. Any game should go through a substantial amount of testing. Many pieces go into a game, and any designer or group of designers can only anticipate so much. Testing will indicate if something is broken, doesn't work the way it should, or is too complicated or confusing. For example, navigation systems in games are tested extensively.

Games generally require a great deal of time and, often, money, to create. It would be foolish for any designer to invest so much in the creation of a game and then release it with mistakes or bad gameplay, when those things can be caught during testing.

Departments in gaming companies that test games are generally referred to as Quality Assurance and Software Testing (QA). Testing tends to fall under two major approaches to gathering data:

**Qualitative**   Testing gauges emotional responses and reactions to the game. This information is generally gathered by observing players or asking them questions related to likes and dislikes related to gameplay.

**Quantitative**   Testing records hard data such as number of wins, number of deaths, amount of money won, and so on.

The more testing you can do, the more useful the information is to the designer. Many companies contract testing to third-party companies that can be more objective about gathering and analyzing data.

When selecting participants, try to find subjects who fit into the demographic the game was designed for. Lots of feedback is an essential part of game design. This process tends to discourage new designers, but seasoned creators know that this invaluable information can help refine their hard work. Embrace the information that testing provides, and then test some more.

## THE ESSENTIALS AND BEYOND

In this chapter, we examined how navigation refers to physically finding your way around environments as well as finding your way around how the game is played. Good navigation design requires an appreciation for logic and creating art and animation that fit the game's look and feel.

Navigation screens designed to help guide the player are often the first things the player interacts with when playing a new game, so they need to be useful, be attractive, make sense, and be fun.

*(Continues)*

## THE ESSENTIALS AND BEYOND *(Continued)*

Methods for navigating through the space created in a game will continue to develop as technology changes. We have seen this spatial aspect change dramatically from low-end 2D games to the more modern, high-end 3D games. As spatial design becomes more complex, with overlapping elements in highly immersive environments, providing guidance systems and maps for the player is opening up areas for designers of those types of interfaces.

Along with controllers, a keyboard, and a mouse to help move around in these worlds, companies are exploring the possibility of upping the experience by having the player interact with the world as much as possible. Some companies are experimenting with head-tracking systems, where the game can track what you're looking at and move the avatar in that direction.

Game systems like the Wii provide such direction interaction that movement in the worlds designed for that system let the player physically move and create actions and reactions within games such as bowling, baseball, and fishing.

Technological changes will continue to affect the design and creation of games. Over the past few decades, technology has dramatically changed the look and feel of games. The logic behind interacting with them remains fairly consistent, so the challenge is to keep refining these interfaces to match the ever-improving technology.

### ADDITIONAL EXERCISES

1.  Review at least five different games, and compare the splash art for each one. What similarities do you find? What are the differences? Does the look and feel imparted by these splash screens tell you what the game is going to be like? Do any of them appear to be badly designed and confusing? If yes, what poor design elements do you see?

2.  Have you ever found a bug in a game? This happens quite a lot. If you do find a bug, write up a report answering the following questions:

    ▶ What were you doing when you found the bug?

    ▶ Where in the game were you (physical location)?

    ▶ Did you try to do the same thing to see if the bug would repeat (if yes, note that)?

After you write up your report, contact the company that made the game and send it to see what sort of response you get (reputable companies are usually grateful to have such bugs reported and are often quick to fix the problem).

*(Continues)*

## THE ESSENTIALS AND BEYOND  (Continued)

### REVIEW QUESTIONS

1.    True or false. QA stands for quick and accurate.

2.    HUD stands for _____ .

    **A.**  Honor under duress         **C.**  Homing utility device

    **B.**  Heads-up display            **D.**  Help user detail

3.    True or false. A diegetic UI displays clickable buttons outside the gameplay area.

4.    True or false. Linear games focus on encouraging players to follow narrow story lines.

5.    What is the EULA?

    **A.**  End Users License Agreement     **C.**  Easy Use Learning Application

    **B.**  Equal Use Loading Aid           **D.**  Extension Upper Layer Addendum

# CHAPTER 7

# Designing Levels and the Game Design Document

*Coming up with the* idea for your game and deciding on the gameplay style, the narrative, and the look of your characters are major parts of game design. An important aspect of making the game is how you create and present the content and how players interact with it.

This chapter discusses level design, which starts by planning the world, what happens, and where it happens. Then you populate the world by determining where the action, key events, and cinematic locations for the game will be. Imagine you're leaving your home for a trip around the world. You'll want to look at a map to plan where you'll go and what you'll do along the way, including the points of interest you want to see, events you may want to attend, and people you want to meet.

While "level design," or content creation, is vastly different depending on the type of game being created, for ease of use this chapter will focus on level design as it is identified in the genre of action-adventure.

In addition, in this chapter we'll look at the Game Design Document (GDD), which is the predominant tool game developers and publishers use to catalogue a game as it's developed. All the things addressed in this book eventually make their way into the GDD.

▶ **Level design**

▶ **Spatial design**

▶ **Hub-and-spoke design**

▶ **The Game Design Document**

# Level Design

Level design can be as simple as designing one room in your game or as complex as designing an entire continent or galaxy. Essentially, the level designer is creating playable content for the core features to be used inside the world.

Start by imagining yourself in the world (which is another word for *level*). As the designer, determine where you want to go, where you'll start, where you'll end up, and what you'll do along the way. Couple all those experiences with what you'll see and hear as you travel, and those are the basics of level design.

## WHICH LEVELS ARE WE TALKING ABOUT?

Let's clear up the difference between levels and leveling up. In this chapter, *level* refers to the map or areas designed for the game. *Level* can also refer to the degree of difficulty related to any part of a game. *Leveling up* has to do with gaining points or skills to reach a new level with a character during gameplay.

Our focus in this chapter is level design: how to map out the worlds where your game will take place and what happens in them.

## Determining Waypoints

Don't feel that you have to begin the level design with the start point. Some designers do; others begin with the key event in the level. For example, if you have a critical battle to fight, a quest to complete, a puzzle to solve, or treasure to find, that is the highlight of the level. A good approach is to decide where that event will occur and work backward, or out, from that point. Determining waypoints tends to relate more to RPG types of games, but any game you design will have start points, endpoints, hookups to other levels, and areas where more intense or less intense play occurs. Plotting out these areas of varying intensity is part of designing the pacing for the game.

In order for gamers to find these waypoints, they needed to be guided in the correct direction. Planting guideposts to help the player, such as giving them a quest, is also part of the level designer's task. As the player heads out into the level, the designer also needs to provide clues so they don't get too far off track. This is a delicate balance during the design phase, because clues that are too weak, obtuse, or far apart may leave the player lost and frustrated. Too many clues amounts to hand-holding, and that can remove some of the challenge. You want the level to be challenging but not frustrating.

More than one major event may occur in a level. Decide where those events will occur. If a treasure will be unearthed, will it be in a cave deep below a mountain, somewhere under the sea, or in a castle floating in the clouds? As you plot where those events will happen, you may want to provide enough physical space between them that players will have time to enjoy the world you're creating; they should also have enough area to complete potential minor tasks before they turn the corner and face a boss or have to decrypt a significant puzzle.

The first passes on designing a level can be simple sketches that plot where some of the major events occur and the basic layout of the land. Experienced designers knowledgeable in gameplay can estimate how much time it will take a player to navigate any given area and its obstacles. The level will go into a build as soon as enough art, animation, and programming exist to begin testing. Figure 7.1 shows a very rough initial sketch of a level. In this sketch, the designer has created a lake filled with flying sharks, brambles to cut through, a river to cross, a bandit-filled forest to traverse, and a town in which the player can barter for enough gold to buy a boat. Upon entering the level, the player must first find a quest giver to point them in the right direction. Along the way, the player will encounter other obstacles and other helpers (the talking sheep) before reaching the cave where the chalice is hidden.

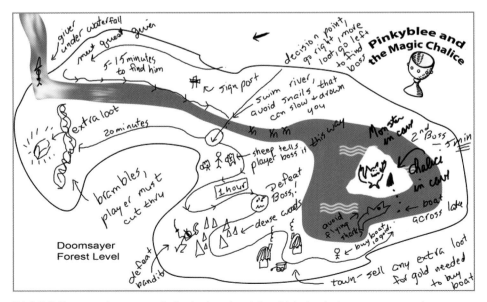

**FIGURE 7.1** A very rough, beginning sketch in which the designer maps out where events can occur.

Close your eyes and imagine yourself wandering through the world in your game. For example, if it's a golf game, think about where the first tee would be. Is a clubhouse or pro shop in view? Probably, because the player is likely to need to go there to get better gear or other elements to enhance the gameplay.

In addition to imagining what is around you, think about the space above and below you. In the level you're designing, can the character or characters go upstairs in tall buildings, or onto a mountaintop? Will they need to go downstairs in buildings, into sewers, or underground into caves?

## SECRET LEVELS

Some games have *secret levels*. Players who find them may encounter new weapons, lore, power-ups, or just the joy of having a new level to explore and win.

The secret "cow level" in Diablo II was one of the highlights of the game. In order to find it, the player had to complete a series of quests to open the rare red portal, allowing them to battle the Cow King.

For large adventure or action games, a safe haven is a good entry point for the level. These safe havens can provide areas where players can repair weapons or armor, barter or buy new goods to aid them during gameplay, or just avoid battles for a few moments while they decide on a strategy or figure out the interface (how to operate the controls). If a player learns a new skill, they will want to practice it in an area containing relatively easy hazards before confronting a final boss.

Here are a few questions you'll want to answer:

▶ What kind of environment is it?

▶ How long should it take the player to navigate the terrain?

▶ How much time should they spend there?

When thinking about the kind of environment, consider whether it's hostile or friendly. The player may be underwater in a cavern, far out in space, in a shrouded forest, or deep in some dark and dangerous urban jungle. Is the environment traversable? Does anything change if it's played multiple times? What are the technical limitations?

Flat terrain is likely to be traversed quickly. If the designer wants to slow the player so they can earn more experience and extend gameplay a bit, obstacles can be added, such as a ravine that needs to be crossed, quicksand, thorny trees, or creatures that must be avoided or killed. This is also a good time to keep in mind the physics of the world.

For example, if you add water, and the character needs to swim, then their movements should be slower (unless they have some special ability to run over or swim rapidly through it). Using physics to add to the gameplay is part of the level designer's job. If high winds can occur in the world, then the designer plans where the winds will begin to affect the player or redirect them. Again, there is a delicate balance between adding so many obstacles that the gameplay becomes frustrating and the player quits, and making it so easy that the player gets bored and quits.

As games are roughed out in the initial design phase, the designer can determine approximately how much time it should take the average player to complete the game. Knowing about how long it should take (AAA games usually take 10–20 hours to play) is important because gamers have grown accustomed to the average length of time they expect their money to buy.

The amount of time a game is expected to be playable is established during the planning phase (concept), when the game's goals and level parameters are decided upon (in other words, the game's scale).

Start to write down your ideas. Let them gush, and record all the possibilities that you can use as fodder to begin designing levels for the worlds in your game. Add everything that comes to mind; then, as you start to rough out the levels, keep and develop what seems to not only work for the look and feel of the game but also contribute to the gameplay.

# Research!

Research and development (R&D) is crucial to the concepting phase. Making games is big business and very expensive. Spend time in research before you begin sketching out the game or characters. Double-check your rough plans before you flesh them out. Even then, many other bits can go wrong and balloon the development cycle.

R&D is all about the possibilities. Dreaming up cool stuff is arguably one of the most fun parts of development. Then you need to implement your ideas. Not everything can be done. What *can* be done depends largely on budget, time, and expertise, but you can achieve many goals by doing things cleverly. If the title is meant to be real-life accurate, then R&D is swayed in that direction. If the game is an RPG, then whole civilizations will need to be fleshed out and made believable so players can fully immerse themselves in the illusion you're trying to create.

If your goal is to make an immersive game, then you need to throw yourself into as much research as you can so you understand the nuances of the world you're creating. Thorough research helps you achieve the level of detail required to create a believable world.

One way to make your world believable is to avoid "drawing from memory," or drawing or designing the same things over and over again based on what you *think* they look like (as discussed at greater length in Chapter 4, "Visual Design"). Instead, do some research when you start your design so you understand better what things and places *actually* look like.

Imagine for a moment that part of your game takes place in a cave. Do you have an image in your mind of what a cave should look like? Do all caves actually look alike?

Figure 7.2 shows three different images of caves and demonstrates how remarkably different they can be in our own home world. At far left is a shot showing narrow confines in the Shasta Caverns of California. In the middle is an image of a glacier cave in Alaska, with slit-like passages. On the far right, the massive Deer Cave in the Mulu National Park of Borneo, Malaysia, could house a small city.

> **Immersive worlds include not only visuals, but audio components as well. We'll examine the use of sound in Chapter 8.**

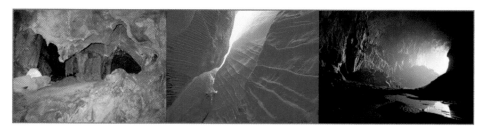

**F I G U R E  7 . 2**  The differences in these caves illustrate the importance of research in creating environments.

What do you know about caves? How are caves formed? How was the cave formed in the world you're creating? Is it manmade (like an abandoned mine), was it created by water or a lava tube, or did an earthquake cause the earth to open? Is it made of rock, or is it an ice cave? Does it contain water, or can wind whistle through? Do animals live in this cave, or is there evidence of a prehistoric civilization? Does the cave have a large mouth, a hidden opening, or perhaps openings to even more caves?

Doing research is half the fun of designing the levels for games. Putting yourself in the shoes of the characters or creatures that will roam your world is paramount. Start with the research, and then let your imagination take flight.

Too often, new designers copy what they have seen or played, so too many games look derivative. Even if your game isn't meant to appear realistic, and your goal is to produce a stylized or cartoony world, research will help you get out of your head and away from beloved memories of games you've played. Research can help you experience something new and get your creative juices working.

As you gather research materials, especially images, movie files, and sound, save them in a resource/inspiration folder so all designers and artists on the project can refer to them. Creating resources such as reference materials is invaluable to the level-design development cycle. Both level designers and artists will benefit greatly. These resources should be created jointly by the level designers and the artists because they're doing separate work, but on the same piece of content.

Creating a *comparables list*—relevant titles, songs, books, and so on—is part of the R&D process as well. Understanding your demographic, genre, and competitors (or peers) allows you to make the right choices when creating the game. You need to be able to imagine it on store shelves, reviewed by critics and enjoyed by fans, to really understand what you want to make and be able to achieve it.

## OK, Now What?

You've written down ideas; sketched out concepts for the world on a napkin while at lunch; walked for miles on city streets and through museums, the local park, the forest, and a mountain meadow; and perused every book, magazine, and web page you could find related to your ideas.

How do you begin to put all that together?

The ancients had a pretty good handle on how level design can work. Look at Figure 7.3, which shows an antique map of the city of Jerusalem produced in 1584. You see the layout for the streets, locations of buildings and parks, and features such as Calvary Hill (at lower left) with the story of the crucifixion of Jesus taking place.

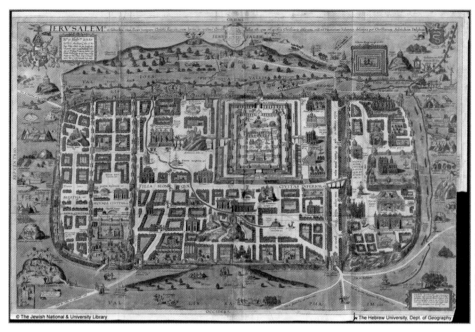

**FIGURE 7.3** This ancient map of the city of Jerusalem combines a bird's-eye view of the street layout with side or three-quarter views to show architectural details. This portrayal of the city, which includes events and special locations, looks very much like a modern level design.

This map provided not only a means for navigating the city, but also images related to areas where special events occurred, to (or away from) which a visitor might want to navigate. That is the basis for the way some levels are approached, drawing inspiration from real life.

Figure 7.4 shows a rough level design for the game *The Seven Sigils*. This portion (level) of the game takes place inside a massive cave system with an underground city and two lakes. In the layout, the red grid indicates square footage, and specific areas are plotted out where events related to the gameplay will occur. The general layout is shown at center right. Above it, you can see where this level fits into the complete world. The concept art at the bottom helps you visualize what the world could look like.

This action/adventure game requires that the player enter the cave (notice the tiny black figure at upper left, shown inside the circle for scale) and solve certain puzzles in order to obtain an essential clue in the old ruins (far left, shaded brown).

> Notice the enormous lip ring on the stone head in the concept art. It was added to help appeal to the teen market for this game.

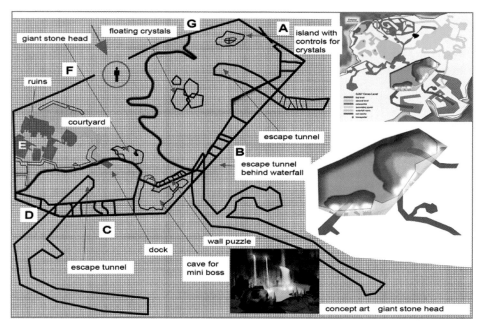

**FIGURE 7.4** This detailed level is part of the enormous world for the game *The Seven Sigils* (completely mapped out at upper right) and includes a concept painting to help you visualize what the world could look like.

The puzzles are in the form of huge, wall-size tiles that need to be moved around; they then point to floating crystals that must be aligned just so in order to shine a light on a hidden cavern at the bottom of the lake, where a key to a room in the ruins is hidden, and so on. Of course, while moving from puzzle to puzzle, the player needs to battle monsters and figure out how to get up and down the massive cliffs and waterfalls in the cave using bits and pieces of rope and equipment found lying around.

In this level, the most difficult and critical areas of the gameplay center around the floating crystals and events that occur within the ruins. Because those are intense areas, they're kept fairly far apart. The level was built based on their locations to provide lots of eye candy and elements for the player to explore.

Figure 7.5 is another level design, this one a bit more polished, that shows the vertical layout of a game called *Vostok*.

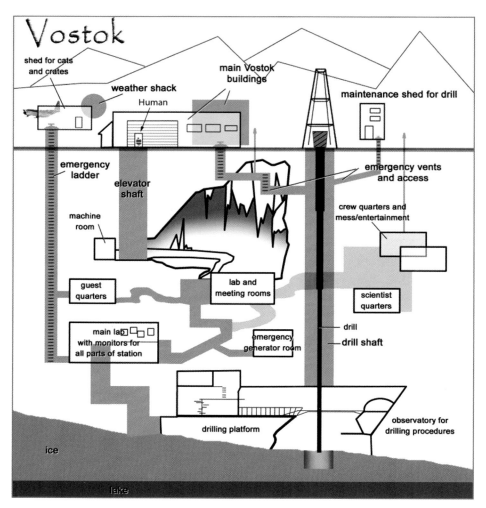

**FIGURE 7.5** This level design for *Vostok* shows where all the levels are and the rough look of one of the main areas, the large cave in the center.

*Vostok* is also an action-adventure game. A reporter travels to the remote base of Vostok in the Antarctic to write about scientists exploring an unusual underwater lake. The reporter gets trapped when a nearby volcano erupts, flooding the upper areas of the subterranean base with steam, boiling water, and lava.

An unusual challenge of this overarching level design (it's *overarching* because it maps out where all the game levels will be as opposed to looking in detail at specific areas where localized gameplay can occur) is that Vostok is a real place, the lake under it actually exists, and scientists have been studying it. Through research, the designer learned about the local geography (Vostok is surrounded by miles of snow, ice, glaciers, and high-peaked mountains) and that the base consists of a small building on the surface, which is sketched out in this design. It was up to the designer's imagination to decide what any underground features might look like. No information was unearthed about whether a physical study of the subterranean lake is being, has been, or might be conducted.

## THE STORY BEHIND *VOSTOK*

Vostok, Antarctica, holds the record for having the coldest temperatures on earth. Lake Vostok, which is 160 × 30 miles in length and width, was discovered by the British in the early 1970s during airborne ice-penetrating radar surveys; it's located two miles under the ice. Scientists would like to drill into the lake to study its prehistoric contents. This true story provided an exciting inspiration for the game.

The designer studied maps of mines along with geographic features that could be underground near volcanoes. Notice the twisty tunnel leading from the guest quarters to the lab and meeting rooms—those are based on what a lava tube looks like.

The drilling area at the lake is the site of some of the most intense action for the game. For that reason, this area was provided with more physical space.

Another important area is a large, naturally formed cavern just below the surface. The long, dagger-like ice stalactites hint at some of the visuals to be built for this area. After the player descends in the elevator from the main Vostok buildings, this will be an enormous, beautiful, terrifying maw of ice, along with dark, spooky depths that provide a tone for the game—awe-inspiring beauty married with the deadly terrain of Antarctica.

## Adding Gameplay

An important thing to keep in mind about level design is that if you allow a player to move from point A to point B, they're usually able to get back to point A unless the designer prevents them from doing so.

In *Vostok*, although the main elevator shaft is damaged when the volcano blows, the player needs to find a way back to the surface. At first, the emergency ladder seems like the way out, when in reality it's blocked with collapsed ice and twisted metal (that is the dead loop). The player puzzles their way out using salvaged equipment from the underground facility to climb up what remains of the damaged elevator shaft.

Not being able to re-traverse a level is a design technique known as a *dead loop*.

In many platform types of games, you may want to keep the player moving in a certain direction, so the ability to navigate back isn't critical; it may be part of the design to prevent the player from moving backward. However, if your game includes towns, forests, rivers, and mountains, you're inviting the player to explore the amazing world you're constructing; allowing them the ability to roam without fear of being stuck is an important feature to keep in mind.

Zandro Chan, creative director at Bedlam Games in Toronto (developer of *Red Harvest*), whose input was crucial for the creation of this chapter, adds this information about traversing games:

> The thing about re-traversal is that the player needs to go somewhere, there needs to be a destination. The re-traversing portion then needs to be filled with gameplay so the player is engaged as he/she continues to play through an area they have already seen. Keeping things fresh in an environment piece that is re-traversable is very difficult to do. The scripting needs to be clever and clean as there will be many layers built upon each other. If a nasty bug exists in one, then it all comes falling down and the game flow will be broken.

**Start by plotting the major events that take place in the level.**

Designing a level for a game includes not only the sights and sounds encountered by the player, but also the gameplay. As we've mentioned before in this book, logic should apply to all you do while working on design. It's often a good tactic to figure out first where major events take place in the level and then work from there. Begin with the core events, and add pieces as you fill in the gameplay to the target timeframe, like peeling an onion in reverse.

**Add places for players to improve skills or equipment.**

If your player needs to slay a boss somewhere on the level, then adding areas where they can improve their skills or obtain necessary equipment while on the lookout for this boss makes the gameplay more enjoyable and helps build anticipation for what is to come.

## How the Narrative Figures into Level Design

Typically, there is a four-point story breakdown:

- ▶ Opening
- ▶ Build-up
- ▶ Conflict
- ▶ Resolution

Those can be considered plot points and marked on the maps showing how the level is being designed.

Figure 7.6 shows a map from *Fröbish,* an adventure game that takes place in an abandoned sanitarium. The player starts at the front door and, after finding clues about how to disable the lock, enters the creepy building.

They encounter a number of clues and odd occurrences in the lobby of the main building. The player chooses which way to go. They can go up the elevator and begin investigating the second floor. They may head into the office area or, after reviewing files they find behind the reception area, head into the Emergency Room.

This is where the player encounters a large puzzle. Solving it leads them to the ambulance bay and a way to open and operate the elevator in that area, which takes them to further adventures in the morgue below.

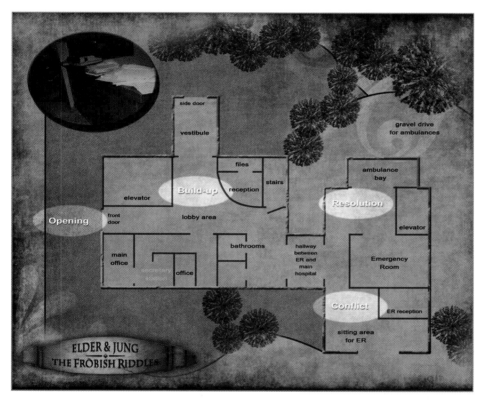

**FIGURE 7.6** The level design for *Frôbish* was created using floor plans for the building where the story takes place. Each floor has many puzzles, scary events, and adventures to experience, but the designer selected these four areas for the story's main plot points to occur—opening, build-up, conflict, then resolution.

# How Large to Make the Level

The designer also needs to consider how many players might inhabit the level at any given time, referring back to the level-design parameters previously established. If the game is designed for one player, allowing exploration with the nonplayer characters (NPCs), then the space can be smaller (taking critical camera-design conditions into account). If this game supports large, multi-player populations, then space needs to be calculated to fit them all in, and the geometry must allow the camera to frame all the players and relevant space for their actions (such as combat).

If 3,000 players can fit in the level at any given time, will the city support that many, or will they be standing on top of each other? How much physical space is required? How will the players see the action? How do they keep track of enemies and friends? If there is a boss fight, how does the boss move? How does the player? How is the shot framed? Again, there is logic here.

As work on the level progresses and areas are set aside for major events to occur (perhaps the start point has been determined along with safe havens and so on), an important aspect of the level design is how to guide the player toward the intended goal.

This can include designing visuals so the player is attracted to something in the distance, such as bright lights or colors. Power-ups or mini-quests can be placed in the level to outline the critical path as well.

> **Make sure your level can fit all the people who need to be in it!**

## MOST POPULAR LEVELS

According to GameSpot (www.gamespot.com), the five most popular level designs for 2011 are in the following games:

- ▶ *Half-Life*
- ▶ *No One Lives Forever*
- ▶ *Thief: The Dark Project*
- ▶ *Clive Barker's Undying*
- ▶ *Deus Ex*

# Level Editors

> **The first game to employ someone as an actual level editor was *Lode Runner*.**

A *level editor* (or designer) is the person who designs the arrangement, look, and feel of a level and determines what the gameplay will be there. The term can also apply to the type of game-development tool (software) used to build, script, and edit assets and events within the level. We're talking about the latter type here.

Numerous types of level-editing tools (software) can be used to build game worlds. Technology is ever-changing, so this book doesn't place much emphasis on this type of software, but we'll explain what a level editor does.

The level editor allows the designer to incorporate art assets from other tools such as Photoshop or 3D packages like Maya and CINEMA 4D. It also allows for the creation of scripted events. *Scripting* is low-level visual programming that lets a level designer create events that happen in the game, from simple actions such as opening a door (with associated sounds) to blowing up an entire neighborhood.

A handful of games made today that are shipped for home computers come with their own built-in level editors. For fans and enthusiasts of games, a huge draw is being able to edit levels or build their own levels in which to continue gameplay. These are often referred to as *mods*. Someone, or a group, can be modding a game by making a unique level that they can share with friends; they can also post it online and invite players through an Internet connection. Many people have done so using Epic's Unreal Engine and Valve's Source Engine, and some of the creations rival the fun and polish of the big-budget games.

## Levels and Their Genres

If the genre of your game is a shooter, then the level design involves catering to genre-specific features such as cover for the player character. In other words, as the player moves through the world, they may need obstacles in the terrain that let them take cover while being shot at or hide while firing at other players or the characters built into the game.

This cover system is an example of how proper level design supports the core mechanics of the shooting feature of the experience. By adding a cover system through the levels, the designer can begin pacing the experience, increasing and reducing player sight lines and thus increasing and decreasing the challenge of the game. The basic action—the intended exchange between a player and their opponent—is fleshed out and replicated throughout the level. Variations of this gameplay exchange are then added so that every fight is slightly different and elicits different strategies from the player.

Although we've looked specifically at the special considerations for a shooter, any genre will have its own special needs that the level designer must keep in mind. Just as a shooter needs areas that provide cover, a platformer needs platform sections to which the avatar can navigate, and so on.

When designing a level in any genre, use the approach we have looked at. Ask these questions:

> ▶ What is the purpose of the level?
>
> ▶ What kind of action do you want the players to experience?
>
> ▶ What needs to be placed in the level to achieve that purpose?
>
> ▶ How does the narrative (the context behind the action) work in relation to the level and its parts?

Add those together with compelling gameplay from the core features, and you'll achieve great level design.

# Spatial Design

As games become more immersive and allow more depth to become visible and steerable, navigation (or *wayfinding*)—physically moving through space—takes on greater importance. The term *spatial design* literally means designing the spaces, or environments, where the gameplay will take players.

Early games like *Colossal Cave Adventure* were played through text, which included written descriptions of the environment, such as this: "You are in a maze of twisty little passages, all alike." When visuals became part of the game design and enhanced technology allowed for bigger and faster games to be developed, that written description of the twisty little passages became a terrain that the player could actually see and traverse.

For the most part, using an input device such as the controller, keyboard, or mouse allows a player to move their avatar through the environment by walking, running, flying, swimming, and so on. The player traverses the worlds, or virtual environments (VEs), by moving directly through the surroundings using visual and audio references that guide them. This method is often referred to as *memory-based navigation* and tends to occur when a player is in a familiar area. At other times, the player may use a map or written directions to find their way. This type of navigation is sometimes referred to as *map-based* and tends to happen when the player needs to travel to someplace new.

With so many games providing full 3D gameplay or 2D environments that display a sense of depth, a top-down map may be provided to help orient the player and guide them through the game space. These top-down maps may scroll as the player moves through environments, particularly in 3D games such as *World of Warcraft*. Other games that have used them effectively are *Populous*, *Sid Meier's Gettysburg!*, and *Seven Cities of Gold*. They're invaluable tools to help guide the player in the right direction and avoid the frustration that can happen from getting lost while en route to a new place or trying to retrace steps.

Many players appreciate maps in games. Maps help provide a sense of order and are critical for those who play strategy games. As the amount and complexity of traversable space increases in games, coming up with map designs has become a significant challenge to designers. As we discovered with the navigation screens that are created for games, for the most part, they tend to have a design and look similar to the game itself.

The *hub-and-spoke* method for creating spatial design has been very popular with designers, so much so that we'll discuss it in more depth in the next section.

Other types of navigation include side scrollers, where the background scrolls back and forth or up and down to provide new playing areas.

Shooters are the most common type of games these days, and they tend to be linear, but most RPGs and strategy-type games use some form of hub and spoke. Most casual/social games stick to a single screen or use an array method that lets the player choose from a variety of screens without a hub. Figure 7.7 provides an example of an array method.

In the game *Fröbish Riddles*, the player can choose a variety of locations to visit by navigating through the scene using visible exits rather than choosing a destination from a central map. Or the player can select another screen from a drop-down menu; this, in a way, substitutes for the hub, but it's not graphical, so the player never changes screens to make a selection.

**FIGURE 7.7** This is an array method for choosing locations to visit. Green highlights indicate doorways the player can choose to navigate to another part of the building.

## Hub-and-Spoke Design

In a hub-and-spoke design (also known as *wagon wheel*), players begin play in a central area of the game and can then choose which direction to go in. They may choose to revisit an area they've already explored or won. They may decide to reenter a section of the game that is in progress or move into an entirely new area.

Linear gameplay encourages players to follow narrow story lines and achieve short, simple goals instead of wandering around the entire world.

The hub and spoke provides an area where the player can get started on a storyline or quest. They can also return there upon completion to get new quests or fuel up and then move on to other spokes.

Many games that use this type of design offer a player new to the game an opportunity to visit only one, or just a few, of the spokes. Once they gain experience or collect necessary items, they can unlock the next sections, or spokes, to enter.

## What Is in the Hub?

The hub is the start point for most games, such as the locker room for a sports game or a town or castle for a questing game. This area often becomes familiar to the player. It's a safe haven of sorts to return to when leveling up characters and looking for new skills to learn, or to acquire better weapons, armor, vehicles, or goods to aid in gameplay.

## What Are the Spokes?

The spokes can be entire levels to be visited and explored or simply areas adjacent to the hub that might house vendors or other benign game elements. The spokes can be travelled to from the hub or directly from each other.

Figure 7.8 is a very basic diagram showing what a hub and spokes can look like. There can be any number of spokes, and hubs can also connect with other hubs, much as airlines designate certain airports across the country as their hubs and fly out to and back from outlying areas.

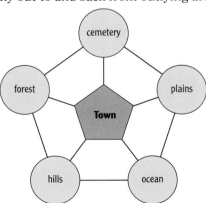

**FIGURE 7.8** Any section, or level, of a game can have one or many hubs and spokes set up. For example, several cities may be safe areas that players can visit and then journey out from.

# The Game Design Document

When you begin to design your game, and the ideas are coming fast and furious, you'll need a method for tracking all the information. In addition, when you work with a team on a game, you'll need a method for communicating information to them about how the game needs to look and what will happen during various parts of the gameplay. This is what the Game Design Document (GDD) is for; it's the team's bible.

As you've seen in this chapter, level design is where you'll begin to map out where events occur, starting points, spawning points, exit points, and so on, so this is a good time to review the GDD.

In Chapter 3, "Core Game Design Concepts," we looked at a general overview of the GDD. As we noted there, the GDD contains specific details about the game's levels.

Bedlam Games, located in Toronto, Canada, and makers of the *Dungeons & Dragons* games, works routinely with this kind of document. You'll find an example of a GDD for *Red Harvest* in Appendix C. At Bedlam, many developers contribute to the GDD but the central authority of the document is the game's Creative Director, Zandro Chan.

In reviewing the excerpt, you'll notice that the GDD contains references to audio, scripted dialogue, lore, and quests along with the amount of time estimated to play the game. For the entire game, the designer's goal was to build a product that would take at least 10 hours to play from beginning to end.

A GDD is a *fluid* document. That means it's a repository of all the elements that go into the game, including art, dialogue, audio, and so on; however, as a game is being built, if certain aspects aren't working or need to be tweaked, you do that through the GDD. Nothing written in it is cast in stone, and the GDD can be altered at any time to reflect changes in design.

## THE ESSENTIALS AND BEYOND

A great deal of information has been presented in this chapter, but you should be starting to understand how a game is designed and then put together. Substantial logic applies to all the work done during the design process; this may seem incongruous for an art form that relies on seemingly random events to make the gameplay fun.

## ADDITIONAL EXERCISE

Create your own level design. Keep it simple, and sketch out just one room from a top-down point of view (POV). Pick one character who needs to be able to get out of the

*(Continues)*

room. Have a place in the room where the character first appears. Add other elements to the room, such as furniture and walls. Plan at least one obstacle the character needs to be able to get around, such as a locked door, furniture that has fallen and blocked the way, or a huge hole in the floor. Place something in the room that must be discovered in order for the character to get past the obstacle.

## REVIEW QUESTIONS

1. What is a level editor? (Choose all that apply.)

   A. The person in charge of designing a level

   B. The system for gauging sales of a game

   C. A dial indicating how fast you can make a character move in a game

   D. Software that is used to compile all of the elements made for the level including visuals and audio

2. True or false. An array method allow players to view screens showing other locations to visit.

3. Hub and spoke, or wagon wheel design refers to

   A. a spatial layout for the world

   B. patterns created on the splash art screens

   C. games that are Westerns

   D. prison games

4. Spatial design refers to all but

   A. depth and dimension of the environment

   B. game levels

   C. the size of the launch icon

   D. VE's, the virtual environment

5. What is the GDD?

   A. Game Doctoring Device

   B. Game Decoration Designs

   C. Game Document Definitions

   D. Game Design Document

# CHAPTER 8

# Sound

*Sounds for games serve* a myriad of roles. Along with creating the signature for a project, music helps to create mood, build tension, introduce mirth, and telegraph conflict. Ambient sounds help construct immersion, and clever audio effects for interfaces communicate a sense of panache, futuristic technology, dark themes, or wacky comedy. The addition of sound, an unseen component in such a visual medium, helps players use their imagination.

Well-designed audio can deeply enhance the gameplay experience, whereas a poor design can damage it. For games that have a long play time, where players may be immersed for 10–20 hours or more, one of the challenges for the audio designers is coming up with enough interesting variation in the sounds to avoid boring repetitions while also keeping file sizes in check.

The art form of designing audio has increased in sophistication as games have improved and developed over the years. Just as movies have used this medium to draw in the audience and help them enjoy a deeper experience, so have games and their designers taken advantage of this rich component to breathe more life into their adventures.

▶ **Organization and planning**

▶ **Music**

▶ **Ambient sound**

▶ **Sound effects**

▶ **Speech**

▶ **Sound-based computer games**

## Organization and Planning

Video games typically have hundreds or thousands of digital files generated during their production. Half the battle is keeping track of all that work as it's planned for, produced, and then catalogued for the production. As with any asset that is planned for inclusion in your game, you should determine the need for each sound, where it will appear in the game, how many variations might be needed, what type of sound it is, and so on.

Sound files can quickly increase the size of the game, so the challenge to the audio designers (and most games have fairly small budgets set aside for audio) is to plan for exactly what sounds are needed.

## Charting Work

The sample chart in Figure 8.1, provided by Brad Beaumont from Soundelux DMG in Hollywood, California, shows how files can be labeled, sorted, and catalogued for your project.

| Generic Adventure Game - SFX Asset List | | | | | | | |
|---|---|---|---|---|---|---|---|
| SFX Category | | | | | | | |
| **Creatures** | **SFX Filename** | **Number of Variations** | **#NAME?** | **Number of Audio Channels** | **Bit Rate** | **Sample Rate** | **File Type** |
| **Monster 1** | Monster1_FS.wav | 4 | Big, heavy footsteps on dirt surface | Mono | 16 bit | 48kHz | WAV |
| | Monster1_Roar.wav | 4 | Loud, deep, throaty roar used when attacking | Mono | 16 bit | 48kHz | WAV |
| | Monster1_Jump.wav | 2 | Quick whoosh used when jumping | Mono | 16 bit | 48kHz | WAV |
| | Monster1_Special_Attack.wav | 2 | Fireball shooting at player | Mono | 16 bit | 48kHz | WAV |
| | Monster1_Death_Cry.wav | 2 | Loud shriek used uon monster's death | Mono | 16 bit | 48kHz | WAV |
| **Monster 2** | Monster2_Splash.wav | 4 | Loud splash used for monster emerging from water | Mono | 16 bit | 48kHz | WAV |
| | Monster2_Roar.wav | 4 | Loud roar used when monster emerges form water | Mono | 16 bit | 48kHz | WAV |
| | Monster2_Swim.wav | 2 | Water lapping sound used for monster swimming | Mono | 16 bit | 48kHz | WAV |
| | Monster2_Special_Attack.wav | 2 | Tidal wave attack towards player | Mono | 16 bit | 48kHz | WAV |
| | Monster2_Death_Gurgle.wav | 2 | Death gurgle as monster slips into water | Mono | 16 bit | 48kHz | WAV |
| **Magic Spells** | **SFX Name** | **Number of Variations** | **SFX Description** | **Number of Audio Channels** | **Bit Rate** | **Sample Rate** | **File Type** |
| **Fireball** | Fireball_Shot.wav | 4 | Fireball shooting from player's hands | Mono | 16 bit | 48kHz | WAV |
| | Fireball_Impact.wav | 4 | Fireball impacting target | Mono | 16 bit | 48kHz | WAV |
| **Iceball** | Iceball_Shot.wav | 4 | Iceball shooting from player's hands | Mono | 16 bit | 48kHz | WAV |
| | Iceball_Impact.wav | 4 | Iceball shattering on target | Mono | 16 bit | 48kHz | WAV |
| **Ambience** | **SFX Name** | **Number of Variations** | **SFX Description** | **Number of Audio Channels** | **Bit Rate** | **Sample Rate** | **File Type** |
| **Forest** | Forest_Air_Loop.wav | 1 | Twenty second loop of light forest air/presence | Quad | 16 bit | 48kHz | WAV |
| | Bird_Chirp.wav | 10 | Single bird callouts/chirps - will be triggered randomly | Mono | 16 bit | 48kHz | WAV |
| | Wind_Thru_Trees.wav | 10 | Single, gentle wind gusts through tree leaves | Stereo | 16 bit | 48kHz | WAV |
| | Tree_Creak.wav | 10 | Single, deep tree creaks | Mono | 16 bit | 48kHz | WAV |
| **Dungeon** | Dungeon_Drone.wav | 1 | Dark, ominous dungeon air presence | Quad | 16 bit | 48kHz | WAV |
| | Ambient_Drips.wav | 10 | Reverberant water drips | Mono | 16 bit | 48kHz | WAV |
| | Rats_Scurry.wav | 10 | Rats squeaking and scurrying past the player | Mono | 16 bit | 48kHz | WAV |
| | Dungeon_Door_Slam.wav | 5 | Ambient doors throughout the dungeon slamming shut | Stereo | 16 bit | 48kHz | WAV |

**FIGURE 8.1** This sample breakdown shows how files are labeled and described along with their technical information.

**When gamers achieve a goal, they usually hear a reward audio, such as a large crescendo, and see a showy, elaborate animation, like fireworks or starbursts filling the screen.**

## What Sounds Will You Need?

As you begin work on the sound design for your game, you should sort out what types of sound you're looking for:

**Music** If your project requires music, will there be a basic background track along with different types of music to telegraph to the player when the game gets intense or calmer, or when there is a reward?

**Dialogue** If there is dialogue, be sure to script the project completely.

**Voice-Overs** Do you need recorded dialogue that plays over a scene to help explain different aspects of the game or introduce a new part of the gameplay?

**Ambient Sounds** What types of ambient sounds will you need? Identify all the environments: forest, city, farm, undersea, outer space, and so on. Then begin breaking down what sounds each location will need.

**Special Effects** These include gun blasts, magic spells, and so on.

**Interface Sound Effects** List each sound you'll need for button clicks and rollovers.

Be as thorough as you can, and list every single thing in the game from beginning to end that will require any type of audio. Yes, your list will be long; but the better you plan for all of the asset development and production in your project, the smoother and more rewarding the final game will be.

As you make your list, also think about how often the gamer will be listening to specific sounds. If you see in your list specific sounds that might be played more frequently than others, consider creating variations that the game engine can play randomly so that hearing the same gun blast or explosion over and over again doesn't become a bore.

# Music

Scores, soundtracks, and music for games started as simple analog waveforms, similar to what had been used for phonograph records and cassettes. One of the first games to use music as part of the gameplay was an arcade tour de force called *Journey*, released by Bally Midway in 1983. The game showcased music by the band Journey and featured a series of mini-games where players could travel to different planets with the band members to search for their missing instruments.

The majority of early games featured seriously simple soundtracks, often generated from synthesizers (*synthesized* means using an algorithm to make sound), that tended to be more annoying than fun. Games now lean toward a fully orchestrated soundtrack similar to what viewers experience in a movie.

Movie makers learned some time ago that music could help complement the story being told. Anyone who has seen the movie *Jaws* should remember quite well the threatening, frightening cello sequence that telegraphs the approach of the shark. The opening title sequences for movies like *Star Wars* could bring audiences to their feet, cheering, as the fully orchestrated score filled the theatre while the opening credits for the film marched boldly into the galaxy.

Game designers strive to create worlds and experiences for gamers that are immersive, challenging, fun, and designed to entice the player to return again

In games as in movies, music helps create the mood and can build anticipation and suspense.

and again. The signature sounds for games, along with stirring scores, have elevated the entire gameplay experience using many of the same techniques devised for scoring feature films.

## Audio Producers and Composers

For the most part, game crews have an audio producer who can act as the supervisor, overseeing the design and development of musical scores or soundtracks, ambient sounds, and special effects audio. Every project is different. You create a prototype first and work with the plans and the producer to continue fine-tuning the vision of the game.

For large games with big scores, much of that work is delegated to professional composers and musicians who are brought on board a project as independent contractors. To get started, the composer will work with the audio producer to get an understanding of the project scope. Music can create such an emotional impact that it's inadequate to simply hand the composer an asset list of scenes or events they need to write for.

The composer needs to see and understand what the world is all about that they're writing for. Is it scary, bleak, intense, damaging, and overwhelming, or light, carefree, and childlike? Using descriptive language to explain the look and feel of the game to express the impact that the project needs is one way to begin communicating with the composer.

> **The composer needs to understand the world being produced for the game in order to create effective music.**

Sometimes there is a script to work from. In addition, providing the composer with concept art, sample animations, animatics, storyboards, and cinematics, or even letting them play what has been developed so far, allows these professionals to immerse themselves in the spirit of the project.

According to composer Garry Schyman (*BioShock 1* and *2* and *Dante's Inferno*), seen on the left in Figure 8.2, one of the techniques used to implement the audio is layering. For example, a section of the game may start with a simple ambient layer of sound or music, that can build in complexity as more audio elements are layered onto it.

The layering can include additional sounds—music or background noises such as crickets, wind, and thunder—or increased instrumentation. In Figure 8.3, Schyman is seen working with a full orchestra as they record his score for the game *Dante's Inferno*.

> **An effective soundtrack for a game tends to be invisible. Its presence enhances but never overtakes the play experience, and effective layering is all but undetectable.**

Each project has unique requirements. According to Schyman, AAA games are like feature films in that they usually have original music recorded with an orchestra, whereas smaller games are like TV shows that can work with music recorded using just a keyboard and software synthesizer. Generally, a AAA game will require 50–150 minutes of music created for the project.

FIGURE 8.2 Noted composer Garry Schyman helps
bring a more cinematic experience to the composition
of music for video games by writing original scores and
working with musicians to record the tracks.

FIGURE 8.3 As with movie scores, music for games can involve an entire
orchestra in a recording session to lay down the tracks.

## AAA GAMES

*AAA* is an industry term for a game that is high quality and produced with a large budget, such as *Halo, World of Warcraft,* or *Gears of War.* The average budget to make a AAA game is about $30 million. These games can take around 18 months to produce, with a crew of approximately 120 people.

A lot of indy games are made with small crews of two or three people doing all the work, with a turnaround time from a few weeks to a few months.

Midsize games employ crews of about 30–65 people and generally take about 9 months to make. Indy game production has grown over the past few years due to increased online distribution systems and the mobile game market.

When music is created for games, the composer will produce what are known as *stems,* or segments, that the audio producer can then program to play during specific moments during gameplay. Some of those tools added to the engine are from third-party software creators with programs such as FMOD (www.fmod.org) and the WaveWorks Interactive Sound Engine (Wwise) (www.audiokinetic.com). These allow the audio producer to tell the game engine when to turn on or turn off specific pieces of audio (the stems).

Stems can also be created as variations. In other words, the composer may create different versions of music that range from subtle to providing a very strong presence. Usually the composer produces high, medium, and low versions. By playing these in loops or layering them, the audio director can build a unique sound experience for each aspect of the game. As soon as stems are delivered for a project, the audio producer will begin to implement them into the game, so that even as a vertical slice is being created, the correct audio is in place. Temp tracks are occasionally used in the vertical slice; however, whenever possible, the more finished audio is always the first choice to see how it works with gameplay. It's best to get the ambient sound down first and then add positional audio for things like waterfalls and streams.

**Audio helps create realism and an immersive environment.**

Ambient sounds are the background noises, the atmospheric audio, that can be heard in a particular scene or location. For example, if you're playing a game where your character is walking through a forest, you may hear crickets, creaking tree boughs, wind rustling the leaves, birds chirping, and other nature sounds. Those ambient sounds, when layered into the game, help create a more immersive environment.

Positional audio plays during gameplay only when players move over or near where a marker is placed to activate the sound. For example, should your character see a waterfall in the distance, you might hear the sound of the rushing water as if it were far away. As you move your character closer to the waterfall, the sound will get louder, helping to add to the illusion of realism.

In addition to creating an immersive environment, audio can add to gameplay. Music and sounds may draw players toward another area in the game. Heightened audio coming from another region may prompt them to explore.

Music can change tempo to create more anticipation during gameplay and raise the player's adrenaline level a bit. It can also slow down significantly to indicate the player is in a safe area.

The music that the composer creates for a project can also be used in marketing campaigns. The use of these original, signature scores is one of the ways the distributor helps to build audience recognition.

A *marker* is a code used to program where in the environment a sound will play.

Music and sounds also give cues that enhance gameplay.

Signature sounds from games are also used in marketing.

## Breaking Down Music Types

The following is a typical list of how music might be broken down for various parts of gameplay. All music in games is triggered by precise cues programmed for the engine to read and act on:

**Scripted Music**   This is the most basic, overriding music in the game. It runs during gameplay and then quits until another command is given.

**Incidental Music**   These tend to be short spurts of music, about 5–15 seconds each, that run randomly in the background to help fill gaps of time if the player is moving in a remote area of the game.

**Location Music**   As the name indicates, these pieces of music are tied to specific locations in a game. As the player enters a city, that city may have a piece of signature music that plays. As noted previously, if the player is approaching a specific area, the location music may trigger to let the player know something important is up ahead and draw them toward that place. Location music can also be cued to notify players if a location is hostile.

**Battle Music**   When players enter into battle during gameplay, the audio tends to consist of three unique segments: an intro, a loop that can play for as long as the battle runs, and an outro sequence when fighting stops.

Just as specific locations may have their own sound signatures, characters sometimes have their own music as well.

Audio and music that change according to what is happening during gameplay are referred to as *adaptive audio*.

# Ambient Sound

Ambient sound systems help to breathe life into projects. These are the gusts of wind heard blowing in the background, falling rain, crickets in the marsh, and the patter of feet from people walking past your character on the street. Because many games are nonlinear, the audio can't necessarily progress in one set path. If the character turns and goes back the way they came, then the audio needs to reflect that. Again, the more overlapping or layered these sounds are, the more immersive a game can become.

To create effective sound for nonlinear games, most audio is created in short loops, about 5–30 seconds long, that can be triggered by the game engine depending on factors such as

▶ Physically where the player is in the world

▶ What the player is doing

▶ Circumstances such as events or other characters the player encounters

In the simplest of games, the ambient soundscape can be described as utilizing a variety of steady loops creating the overall tone of the setting (such as the steady dripping of leaky pipes in a sewer system), as well as one-shots (the occasional rat scurrying by, or a distant pipe creaking). Multiple files of one-shots can be created and played randomly throughout a game, instead of being specifically triggered by locations or events. This randomness also plays an important part in breathing life into the game and avoiding too much repetition, which can become boring in long games.

## Sampling

The sampling rate determines the sound frequency range and is usually viewed as a waveform. This waveform is frequently referred to as its *bandwidth*.

Sampling, referred to in audio production as the *sampling rate*, is the number of samples per second required to digitize a specific sound.

Figure 8.4 shows two sampling rates for the same audio signal. The audio signal is a 1 kilohertz (kHz) sine wave (a fairly common signal used for calibrating audio hardware and software). The screenshots of the different sample rates were taken while these audio files were opened using a program called iZotope RX (www.izotope.com/products/audio/rx/).

The little white square dots that occur along the waveform in each image mark where the audio signal was sampled (to put it in visual terms, it's the same principle of frames per second that is used when discussing film/video: the aperture closing and taking a snapshot of an image in time).

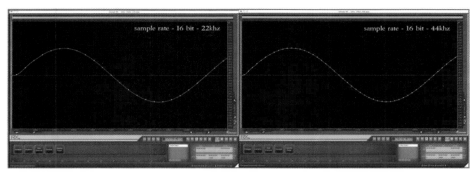

**FIGURE 8.4** The two different images depict the same audio signal captured using two separate sample rates.

When comparing the two images, you can see the 44 kHz sample rate is sampling the waveform twice as many times as the 22 kHz sample rate in the same amount of time, allowing for more fidelity of the original signal.

The sample rate is measured in hertz (Hz) or in thousands of hertz (kilohertz: kHz). The majority of audio for games is recorded at 96 kHz. The chart in Figure 8.4 shows that the higher the sampling rate, the more nuances become available in the sampled sound. When you begin to alter the sampling rate, you're fishing for a unique sound.

The purpose of recording original sound at 96 kHz is to have those sounds at higher sample rates so they can be manipulated at a higher quality in the editing/design process. For example, if you slow the speed of a sound, a recording done with a higher sample rate will yield a much better result due to the fact that a higher-resolution "snapshot" was taken of the audio. Voice-over/dialogue is often recorded at 48 kHz. More often than not, SFX (special effects), dialogue, and music are down-sampled to a combination of different sample rates, usually 48 kHz or lower, to conserve disk space and limit strain on system memory. For many games, those 48 kHz sounds are compressed using a wide variety of licensed and proprietary audio codecs.

The majority of audio for games is recorded at 96 kHz, but generally it's down-sampled to 48 kHz for the final format.

The foley process was first used in film and television and has been adapted for games. Many companies that produce foley sounds do so for all of these industries.

## Foley and Remote Recording

Occasionally, audio designers will go to recording sessions held in a *foley* studio. This type of studio is a controlled environment, and a huge range of sounds can be captured—for example, breaking glass, smashing bricks, or stomping feet on various surfaces such as sand, grass, pavement, gravel, wood, broken china, or glass. If your game has a character who needs to walk through a post-apocalyptic world, recording sounds of someone walking over broken bricks and wood and glass really heightens the illusion of what is happening in this environment and adds to the play experience.

Unlike the foley, which is controlled, other original sounds can be acquired from remote recording sessions, which are specifically geared to capture ambient sounds. Designers travel to places all over the world to record natural or manmade sounds on location for their games. Weapon fire for shooters is often captured this way, by recording the sounds of specific gunfire on ranges.

Some typical remote recording sessions may include

► Missile launches

► Shooting ranges

► Zoos (all types of animals)

► Factories (capturing the ambient sounds of the machines and people working)

► City streets and shopping malls

► Sporting events

Figure 8.5 shows a remote recording session taking place on a ranch, where the sounds of cattle were being recorded.

**FIGURE 8.5** Notice that the microphone used by the remote-recording engineer has a fuzzy covering over it. The purpose of the covering is to help prevent the sound of wind from whistling too much over the mic.

Because audio for games is used in a digital format, it's quite easy to look at massive sound-file libraries to find effects for your game. Recording original audio costs money, so game designers choose carefully when they want to tap a library for sounds and when they want to attempt original recordings. If the designer has made the choice to record original sounds, then something unique, sound-wise, is being sought.

## Original Sounds

Original sounds can be created by blending and manipulating sounds. Brad Beaumont cleverly manipulates and mixes audio to achieve desired results. For one project, Beaumont needed to come up with the sound for a chainsaw wielded by an otherwordly spirit. In Figure 8.6, you see Beaumont working with the computer, blending different tracks to create new sounds.

**FIGURE 8.6** Brad Beaumont from Soundelux, Design Music Group, creates original sound effects for video games.

Even as original sounds are created for unique projects by recording audio or manipulating existing sounds, designers will occasionally play sound backward to obtain entirely new material to work with.

Beaumont started with the basic sound of the chainsaw. To begin altering the sound, searching for the elusive quality that would marry with the chainsaw, Beaumont turned to more organic sounds to blend with the saw's mechanical roaring. After working with a few combinations, he settled on a blending of a real chainsaw and the guttural growling of an adult walrus.

As Beaumont works with the sound, he does so with dual-playback systems. One is very high end, allowing him to hear all the nuances of the sound. The other one is a consumer-grade speaker system. As he listens to the sounds, he searches for the sweet spot in between, where the sound works best. He does so because, as most game designers are aware, home audio systems can vary dramatically.

## Editing Software and File Formats

The majority of editors work with the digital audio workstation Pro Tools, which is a multitrack system. Other favorite systems are Logic from Apple Studios, Sound Forge, GarageBand, and WaveLab.

MP3 audio files get their name from the company that created them, the Moving Picture Experts Group. This file type compresses well and is standard for most home playback systems.

File formats can vary, of course, but most audio for games is delivered as MP3s, which are lossy audio files. A lossy file is compressed, which helps keep overall file sizes down for the game. One of the things a game maker wants to avoid is letting the size of the game get too large, and audio files tend to really add up, size-wise. For example, one second of audio from a compact disc uses about the same amount of space as 15,000 words of ASCII text (that is, about a 60-page book).

Many games also use the Waveform Audio File Format (WAV or WAVE), which is common with more expansive projects. A WAV is native to the PC, and its unique feature is that this format stores sound in what are known as *chunks*. Most WAV files contain only two chunks: the format chunk and the data chunk. WAV files can support compressed data, like MP3s; however, they can also contain uncompressed audio.

Two organizations that focus on audio are the Game Audio Network Guild (GANG, www.audiogang.org) and the Interactive Audio Special Interest Group (IASIG, www.iasig.org).

An excellent website to visit is www.designingsound.org, which provides background information on creating, recording, and manipulating sound. In addition, there are forums where visitors can ask questions of a special guest each month. Another good site to visit for learning resources is www.gamessound.com.

# Sound Effects

Building elaborate scores and immersive ambient sounds is indeed a major component of designing audio for games. When your game is in development and then production, audio work is going on all the time. Along with music and ambient sound, special effects need to be created for explosions, weapons, unique engines (lots of games have fighter planes, spaceships, and cars), and game interfaces.

As navigation is fine-tuned, the designer will want to create unique sounds for button clicks, page turns, inventory opening and closing, and many other events.

## Weapons

Sounds for weapons in games can come from remote recording sessions (traveling to a location where weapons such as guns can be fired, and recording them) or from manipulating existing audio files to get the desired effect. For alien-type weapons, it often works well to record machinery with humming sounds. Many designers mix that highly technical/mechanical sound with organic sounds like animal roars, high winds, or crashing seas to obtain the perfect effect.

## Interfaces

Interfaces for games can be truly expansive, with dozens of interactive elements, or just simple spaces to sign in. In most games, when a player clicks any part of the interface that has been designed to be interactive, they usually experience some type of animated effect along with a unique sound that has been designed to accompany that procedure.

Initially, a simple clicking sound was fairly standard. Clever designers were quick to learn that this was another area where signature audio could be created.

If your game is futuristic with a high-tech-looking interface, that simple click will make the hard work of developing the visuals seem almost pedestrian or even comical. The challenge to the audio designer is to create an audio effect that will complement the graphics.

As with the creation of scores and ambient sounds, the more the designer understands the game, the more effective the sound is. Providing the designer with not only what the interface looks like but also how it functions is critical for successful design. Usually, the designer gets a QuickTime movie showing the look and functionality of the interface; however, whenever possible, they get to play the game themselves to get a sense of the timing and importance of any interactive element.

**For the movie *Star Wars*, audio designer Ben Burt created the unique light-saber laser sound by recording idling interlock motors in an old movie projector combined with television interference.**

# Speech

Dialogue for games, as for any other type of entertainment medium, is planned and scripted. Setting up recording sessions is time consuming and expensive. The better prepared you are for recording, the less likely you are to have to re-record. In most cases, some sections of games need to be re-recorded because of changes in the gameplay or story; but because of the cost and time involved, you want to minimize the need to re-record.

## Dialogue

Often, designers record themselves or others on the team so they have temp tracks to work with. Temp tracks are an important part of game creation, because they give the designer the opportunity to build a section of the game and test the gameplay where that audio is needed before investing time and money in recording final dialogue.

Final dialogue is usually recorded in a controlled environment to avoid picking up background audio that will diminish the performance and quality of the recording. Usually, actors are hired to create the final vocal performances, as seen in Figure 8.7.

**FIGURE 8.7** An ensemble cast of actors in a room set up to record their performances. The walls are draped with soundproofing material to help block out external audio that will spoil the performance.

As I noted previously, games have a history of terrible dialogue. To create a more realistic experience, many games now use writers to create dialogue. The goal is natural language and delivery.

## Cinematics

For audio work on cinematics and some cutscenes, the approach is more linear. These elements are designed and produced much as they would be for film or television. The experience for the gamer is to see a finished, polished, short movie that is scripted from start to end. All dialogue, music, and other sounds are planned to unfold in a controlled way.

# Sound-Based Computer Games

One area that has also been growing, in terms of audio production for games, is sound-based games. These are made for the visually impaired; however, anyone can play and enjoy them.

When approaching the design for a game of this type, the designer should be aware that all information communicated to the player happens aurally with an auditory interface. The majority of games we have looked at in this book have dealt with the creation of visual graphical interfaces. An auditory interface uses recorded dialogue to provide information to the player about how to play the game.

It can become boring to continually listen to a recorded voice saying "turn right, turn left, jump, pick up," and so on. These types of games still need that all-important gameplay to function well; so once the initial instructions are provided to the player, different audio cues along with music and recorded dialogue can be used to clue the player when to turn, jump, pick up, and so on.

To further enhance the gameplay, these audio cues can change during gameplay: for example, if a puzzle is getting more difficult, then those cues can play more quickly or increase in pitch to up the excitement.

These games tend to have large, simple, brightly colored graphics for players who have some visual capabilities. The gameplay is really quite fun. You can find examples at www.audiogames.net. These games encompass a wide variety of gameplay styles, including word, strategy, puzzle, card, educational, racing, role-playing games, adventure, trivia, and arcade.

## THE ESSENTIALS AND BEYOND

Sound has become an integral part of game design, enhancing gameplay without over-powering the experience. The techniques for developing sound for games has paralleled that of films by using multiple techniques and taking advantage of full orchestral sound to record expansive and sweeping scores.

The remarkable difference between the two media is that many games, unlike film, aren't linear, so designers need to work in unique ways to keep the experience fresh and exciting without producing endless mind-numbing loops.

The future for audio development continues to grow as technology embraces more and more of what artificial intelligence (AI) will bring to the table. Improvements with AI can mean the audio will be even more reactive to what is happening during gameplay. For example, if a character picks up a heavy object, then the sound from their footsteps will alter. The field of sound for games will improve and grow as the worlds for the games become larger and technology allows for greater diversity in how sound can be delivered during gameplay.

### ADDITIONAL EXERCISES

1. Sit in your own home, or travel to a mall or restaurant, and close your eyes. Try to identify as many different sounds as you can. Doing this exercise should show you how many sounds are around you on a daily basis that you usually take for granted.

2. Prepare a list of ambient sounds that could be included in your own game design. Select certain sounds that would be heard more than others to create variations.

3. Adapt the list of sounds you created in exercise 2, based on time of day. For example, what sounds are different from day to night: more crickets or owls, or stronger winds? What changes would you need to account for to match weather changes? For example, if there is rain in your game, what materials would that rain strike in your environment: tin roofs, broad leaves on trees, or a windshield? How would rain sound different in those various environments?

### REVIEW QUESTIONS

1. Audio segments created for games are referred to as _____.

   A. Stems                    C. Layers

   B. Chunks                   D. Bytes

2. True or false. A remote recording session is held in a controlled environment.

*(Continues)*

3.  How does layering work?

    A.  Sounds are digitally synthesized.

    B.  Mechanical sounds and organic sounds are blended together.

    C.  Multiple microphones are used in a foley session to capture more sound.

    D.  Audio segments are added one over another to build complexity.

4.  True or false. Location music plays when a player enters a specific region in a game.

5.  What does an audio marker do?

    A.  Provides players with more points whenever a specific piece of music turns on

    B.  Programs the computer to turn on or turn off specific audio files

    C.  Uses a visible kiosk or similar structure in the game to allow the player to generate music

    D.  Uses a unique programming trick where the screen changes color depending on what sounds are playing

# CHAPTER 9

# Job Descriptions, Game Tracking, and Legal Issues

*In this chapter, we'll* review some of the jobs associated with game making, and how they can relate to the production pipeline. Depending on the size of the project and the size of the company or group of game makers involved, the job titles explored here may vary (or combine); however, the descriptions offered here cover the major duties.

When a game goes into production, one of the largest challenges a team has is keeping track of the assets being created and meeting milestones. Nothing is more deadly and demoralizing to a production than to have a team waiting idly for work to come to them in the pipeline due to poor planning or, even worse, losing track of things that have already been done. One of the goals of this chapter is to look at methods for planning and tracking work.

In addition, we'll cover some information regarding copyrighting games and similar related legal issues.

▶ **Job descriptions**

▶ **Pipelines**

▶ **Tracking progress**

▶ **Copyrights and licenses**

## Job Descriptions

Within large companies that do massive projects, crews can be quite extensive, and with these bigger crews, the job descriptions tend to be narrow. The people at smaller companies, such as the majority of the little indie (independent) game makers, often wear many different hats and do a variety of jobs.

Understanding this divide between large and small companies can impact your decisions about what kind of job you want to look for. If you're happy doing one specific job function and sticking with that, then looking at larger companies should appeal to you. However, if you like to do a variety of tasks for a game, then working on your own or seeking a job with a smaller company that looks for multitasking folks could be the way to go. For more information on entry-level jobs and working in the industry, see Appendix B, "Education, Training, and Working in Games."

The following is a partial list of some of the common jobs you'll find in this industry:

- Game developer
- Game designer
- Creative director
- Producer
- Art director
- Leads
- Audio director
- Animation director
- Writer
- Level designer
- System designer
- Interface designer
- World builder
- Q/A (tester)
- Technical director
- Programmer
- Animator
- Modeler
- Rigger

# Game Developer

*Game developer* is a comprehensive, overarching term for the person in charge of almost any aspect of game design and production. If you want to design and then build your own game, you'll be a game developer. Within the industry, though, the developer can also work with others in a group of other developers or specialties associated with design and production in a larger company.

In smaller companies, the developer and designer positions can be covered by one person.

# Game Designer

The designer comes up with ideas and can create art/concepts and playable demos (even the final finished game). They also understand the different platforms such as computer, handheld, console, arcade, mobile, other wireless apps and Internet games, and programming. Therefore, this person needs to remain current with technology and what the demographic the game is targeting looks for in a game. Designers tend to also stay as current as possible with trends in the industry—what kinds of games people like to play and the platforms they like to play them on.

# Creative Director

The role of the creative director is to oversee and assist with developing the overall look and feel of the game during development. This work includes development of the art, animation, and sound, and making any decisions that can affect the gameplay. In addition, as builds are created that can be used to start testing the gameplay, decisions are made about how to possibly redesign weaker aspects of the game, and the creative director is responsible for overseeing that work.

In larger companies, this person may work with a core team of developers, coming up with the art, audio, and other elements that will go into the game. Other companies defer these duties to the lead artists, producers, and programmers.

## SID MEIER, CREATIVE DIRECTOR

Sid Meier, a noted game designer with over 20 years' experience in the industry, was inducted in the Computer Museum of America's Hall of Fame in 2002. Although he is a founder and senior officer for Firaxis, he lists his title as Director of Creative Development.

*(Continues)*

**SID MEIER, CREATIVE DIRECTOR** *(Continued)*

He has piloted several projects to successful completion, such as *Sid Meier's Pirates!*, *Sid Meier's Gettysburg!*, and *Sid Meier's Civilization III!* In 1999, Sid was the second person to receive the honor of being inducted into the Academy of Interactive Arts & Sciences' Hall of Fame for Lifetime Achievement.

# Producer

The job of the producer is essentially overseeing the entire production process. Unlike in other creative industries, such as film and television, the game producer is primarily a project manager responsible for maintaining budgets and timely delivery of milestones and the final product. Again, depending on the size and scope of the project, the tasks that fall to this person can vary. For the most part, their biggest responsibility is seeing that the production stays on schedule and within budget. Successful producers have to be good managers who can have both the big picture and the details in mind at all times—not an easy task.

In a real sense, the producer is the senior or lead manager on a project and coordinates the discipline managers, such as the technical director and art director. Of course, this can vary depending on the team or studio. EA, for example, has producers who oversee budgets and timelines, and others who oversee content production.

> **Most (although not all) successful producers, like Will Wright, began their paths in the game industry as programmers.**

# Art Director

The art director is usually involved in all stages of the project, from working on the early concepts (look) of the game to post-production work with marketing and everything in between. The role of the art director is often extremely critical to the successful look and feel of a game. Art directors have even been known to create the packaging for the game they helped to build.

Often, the art director comes up with guides for the artists that contain specific color palettes, textures, and methods for drawing and painting. This is one of the most critical jobs for which art directors are responsible. They're tasked with creating a style guide for the game that lists all the things just mentioned. The style guide sets the game's overall look and feel.

> **The *style guide*, also called the *art bible*, is the guide that all the artists on a project follow while creating the art assets.**

The art director also serves as a mentor to those on the crew. Mentoring is an often overlooked aspect of the job. However, it can be an enormous part of what this person does, so being able to work well with others and communicate clearly and effectively is a must.

# Leads

There may be a team of artists with a lead creating the art and assets for one level of the game, while another team and its lead are tasked with creating art and assets for other sections of the game, including cinematics, advertising, introductory panels, and so on. The larger a project is, the more likely it is that dozens of people will be brought on board to complete the work; these mini-teams for animation, audio, programming, art, and so on may have their own leads who take direction from the art director to keep everything on track time-wise and style-wise.

# Audio Director

As described in Chapter 8, "Sound," the audio director (or producer) oversees work on the ambient sounds, scores, recorded dialogue, sound effects, and interactive sound elements for the game. Their role is quite large; they come on board at the outset when the concept work is created, because unique audio needs to be created for each original project.

Often, the audio director also works with the programmers to come up with ways to use sounds to help drive the gameplay. Remember that gameplay is paramount. It has to work; and being able to develop the right amount of layered sound to introduce key moments in the game, or devise a fun and unique sound for buttons on the interface, or write the opening score for the game can help create a signature for that project.

# Animation Director

This person needs to have a solid understanding of the principles of animation. They're often selected for a project depending on their specialty in 2D or 3D animation, although in this day and age, most have knowledge and skill in both areas, including motion capture. This person works with a tasks-and-needs analysis for all moving elements in the game and determines the best way to produce them. A *tasks-and-needs analysis* is essentially another way to list assets that are required so they can be examined logically. For example, a tasks-and-needs analysis of a character might look like this:

Needs:

- ▶ walk

- ▶ swim

- ▶ fly

- ▶ cast five different types of spells

Tasks:

- ▶ walk cycle

- ▶ swim cycle

- ▶ fly cycle, including takeoff and landing

- ▶ unique movements to indicate a spell is being cast

- ▶ fire

- ▶ ice

- ▶ stun

- ▶ fear

- ▶ sleep

The tasks and needs analysis is constantly being revised through all phases of game production. More than one type of cycle might need to be created to allow for random movements during gameplay to help keep things fresh. If the character casts spells, then some of those might be removed, added to, or revised.

An animation director's skills and abilities are firmly rooted in the basics of knowing what animation is all about: squash and stretch, holds, cycles, frame rates, and so on. During any production, the animation may require different frame rates. And if the object being animated is created in 3D, the animation director needs to work closely with the modelers to be sure the poly count used to build the model will allow for the type of movement required.

Animation extends to the interface as well as technical animation. The interface may need special effects to show buttons being pushed or menus creatively swapping about.

Technical animation can include weather, the movement of foliage blowing in the breeze, cycles showing water moving on a river, and other secondary animations such as birds flying in the sky or rabbits bouncing about in the background.

Because this person works on sorting out the tasks and needs for each item to be animated, they tend to work closely with any animators on the team—just as the art director works with artists—to mentor and make decisions about reworking the animation if the initial attempt doesn't look or feel quite right.

▶

**The most common 3D models are created with polygons. Other models are made using NURBS, which use Bézier curves and provide more mathematical precision.**

▶

**Technical animation is also called *effects animation*.**

# Writer

Although this position sounds like it might be the first and most important one for any project, it tends to fall in behind game designer and developer. The following are the two biggest tasks for the game writer

**Narrative Writing**   Develop the story/lore of the game

**Dialogue Writing**   Create character dialogue

Sometimes the dialogue is combined with the narrative, but they really are two specific specialties. Large production teams have writers tasked to both items. Small teams usually combine these roles.

Writers may be brought onto a project as well to help with the more technical aspects of the project. Some of these duties include the following:

**Manual Writer**   Write specific instructions to teach gamers how to play the game

**Support of Game Design and Gameplay**   Produce any and all writing related to the game, including press releases and revisions to the Game Design Document (GDD)

**Translator**   Translate the game into other languages. The final text documents from the project are prepared by the game writer and sent to the technical writer for this part of the process.

# Level Designer

The level designer focuses on a specific section of the game to help create its look and scenarios. Often, this means working on the art for a section of the world, such as a town, and then determining where key actions will take place in that location.

Figure 9.1 shows a level design for the game *Vostok* and maps out quite clearly what the locations are and their purpose. The level designer works with these physical locations to assign where specific actions need to take place that are in line with what the story indicates and how to help advance the gameplay.

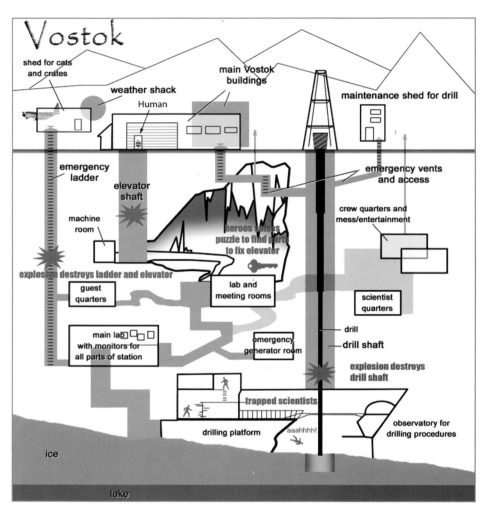

**FIGURE 9.1** In this map, the level designer has determined where key actions need to take place in order to facilitate the gameplay.

## System Designer

The system designer devises mechanics that result in good gameplay. The *mechanics* are the constructs of rules and feedback loops built into the game. Another way to look at how mechanics work is this: a player performs an action in the game, that action causes an effect, and from that effect the player receives feedback. That feedback provides the player with new information or tools, and they're now equipped to perform more actions. This is a highly specialized job.

# Interface Designer

The interface is what allows the player to actually interact with the game. Gorgeous art, terrific animation, and amazing sound can add to a fun gaming experience, but if the player can't interact efficiently with this world you have created, they won't play your game. It's the interface designer's job to create interfaces that allow for a logical interaction with the game world.

## TYPES OF INTERACTIVITY

Because games are player centered, the interface designer must understand what kind of player the game is designed for (the demographic) and what type of game it is (gameplay style). Interaction with a movie or TV show is one-way—from the creator of the program to the viewer. A website adds interactivity by allowing the user to interact with the site and perhaps start a movie or access a catalogue. A game goes further still with interactivity by allowing a player to not only receive information and experiences offered by the game, but also directly affect what happens during the gameplay. In other words, games offer player-to-technology interactivity. Some games such as many of the MMOs offer a social aspect, where players can interact with other players (player-to-player interactivity).

Understanding, therefore, that the player must feel in control of what they're doing and be able to intuitively grasp how the controls work and directly interact with the game makes for great gameplay. In the game *Apparitions,* a variety of screens in the interface allow players to sign in, change their player names, navigate around a haunted hotel to hunt ghosts by using a map, and try to capture evidence of the paranormal. The interface resembles a computer laptop screen because the research team, according to the game narrative, uses a laptop computer to store and analyze the data they collect.

Figure 9.2 shows two screens from an interface designed for the game that let the player record and then review evidence they have captured. Players can also use this screen/menu to remotely place cameras throughout locations in the hotel to try to record video of a ghost and access a tutorial to help them learn how to play the game.

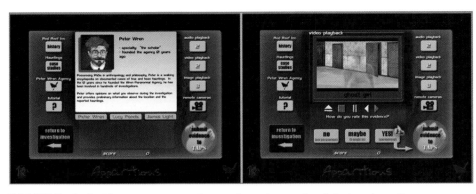

**FIGURE 9.2** These two screens show various phases of an interface from the game *Apparitions*, which resembles a laptop computer and helps players collect and analyze evidence.

Other features on the screens that players can access include these:

**Red Reef Inn**  A brief history of the hotel

**Hauntings**  Access to folders that contain past reports of hauntings at the inn

**Peter Wren Agency**  Biographies of the three members of the paranormal research group: Peter Wren, Lucy Ponds, and James Light

**Tutorial**  Allows the player to see, whenever they want, a tutorial on how to play the game.

**Audio Playback**  Lets the players review any audio evidence they have collected.

**Video Playback**  Lets the players review any video they have collected.

**Image Playback**  Lets the players review any static images they have collected.

**Remote Cameras**  Lets the players access a new menu where they see a map of the hotel and can place up to three cameras in remote locations. Any video evidence the cameras collect can then be reviewed through the Video Playback button.

The other buttons along the bottom of the interface allow the player, at any time, to return to the game or rate the evidence (the three yellow buttons in the middle). Once they feel they have reviewed and judged enough material, they can submit evidence to The Atlantic Paranormal Society (TAPS). TAPS is a real-life group of ghost hunters lead by Jason Hawes and Grant Wilson, and the makers of *Apparitions* worked closely with TAPS in the making of the game.

Many gamers like to have tutorials they can access as a refresher, especially because most games have a tutorial that plays the first time the game is launched.

If you're using real people, places, or events for your games, be sure to investigate whether there might be copyright infringement or other legal issues.

# World Builder

World builders, also called environment artists/modelers, are responsible for creating the look and feel for the worlds the gamer plays in. They create the towns, houses, roads, forests, and so on that may be needed for the project. Typically, those who work in this specialty have a solid understanding of the following areas:

The term *world builder* was adopted by science fiction writers and their fans to describe the worlds they create in their stories.

- ▶ Architecture

- ▶ Landscaping

- ▶ Interior decoration

- ▶ Capabilities of the game engine being used

# Q/A (Tester)

Q/A, QA, or Q&A refers to Quality Assurance. This division is responsible for the very important task of testing the game. Some companies have their own Q/A departments, whereas others use a third-party company because they feel this can be a more objective way to get accurate testing.

The testers begin their task as soon as the first playable version of the game is available and continue right up until the product is released. If a game is sold with mistakes and flaws, months of work and large sums of money spent on making the game can be lost because the game will quickly gain the reputation, through reviewers and gamers, of being flawed and worthless. That kind of disaster is akin to car manufacturers selling an automobile that must be recalled due to faulty parts.

Testing sounds tedious and boring, however, if this important step is not followed through, hard work by a lot of people will be discounted. Even if a game is released with errors and then repaired and rereleased, not many gamers have confidence in the game makers at that point.

# Technical Director

As the name implies, this person works primarily with the technology associated with the production. Like the art or audio director, this individual oversees and manages all things technical, and all the programming leads (supervising various aspects of programming, such as the game engine, gameplay, physics, interface, and so on) report to this individual. This person is the über-technical lead.

The technical director is often referred to as the TD. Their duties can include the following:

▶ Create in-game effects.

▶ Act as a technical liaison between the software engineers and the artists.

▶ Work closely with the art director and lead technical director to research, create, and implement art processes and solutions within the game for final production.

▶ Automate as many processes as possible into tools that can be used by the entire art team.

This job can also be split among different technical directors, depending on their specialties. For example:

**Lighting TDs**  Light and render 3D scenes

**Character TDs**  Rig a character with a skeleton, and create clothing, hair, and deformation controls

**Shader TDs**  Write and adjust shaders to create the appearance of models

Because of the rapid changes in technology, how games are delivered to the players (platforms), and how engines are constantly being revised and updated, this person needs to remain as current as possible with these updates.

A *shader* is a set of instructions applied to a 3D model that tells the computer how the model should be displayed.

# Programmer

Programming is the art of building the language for the game. The language is the way the game talks to the game engine and the playback system. Programmers can work with existing engines or, more likely, create a unique engine for the game they're working on.

Third-party game engines, such as the Unreal engine, can be licensed for use in games. Any programmer working on the game project will need to understand how to work with a system like this. Many small, independent production companies can't afford the large price tag of an engine like Unreal, but game engines come in all sizes and price ranges. Small companies might choose a smaller, more compact engine that can be licensed or purchased for use, such as Torque, or even a freeware engine.

Games may have programming directors, technical directors, and programming leads in charge of whole crews that are working on a game. Technology is ever-changing, which is one reason this book has not focused too much attention on that aspect of game design. Programmers, however, need to have a solid background in computer languages like C++ and work at creating the artificial intelligence for a game along with the simulated physics and many of the graphics for the game.

## Animator

Animators have been working in film and television for years, and when games first started to gain popularity, many people who had worked in feature animated films found their way into this industry. Animators need to have a strong background in the basics of animation, which can include lifelike, believable movement for characters. Some mechanical animations may also fall under the job description of an animator, such as frames per second (fps) and how to do 2D and 3D animation. There is also the specialty of motion capture, which is gaining in popularity within the industry.

## Modeler

A modeler is anyone who creates 3D polygonal models, whether they're characters or environmental pieces. Terms such as *character modeler, prop modeler,* and *environment modeler* are common in game development. On small teams, they're often the same person. Figure 9.3 shows another example of a 3D model of an in-game character for a game from Artery Studios.

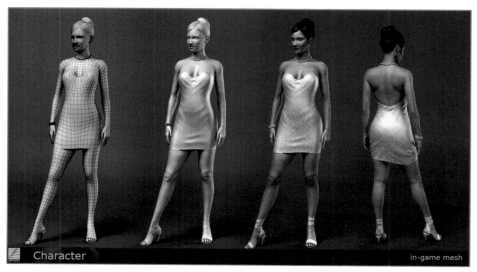

**FIGURE 9.3** An in-game character is one that is animated programmatically from the game engine. Typically, nonplayer characters (NPCs) are animated this way.

## Rigger

For any 3D model that the animator needs to work with, a skeletal system, or *rig*, needs to placed inside the model. A rig is essentially a way of adding controls to the model that the animator can manipulate, in much the same way that a puppeteer uses rods attached to the joints of a puppet to make it move.

Rigging can be used for characters, props, and vehicles (including mounts like horses). Figure 9.4 shows a rig for a human-like character with arms and legs that can be animated to walk, run, jump, and perform all of the types of movements associated with a bipedal figure.

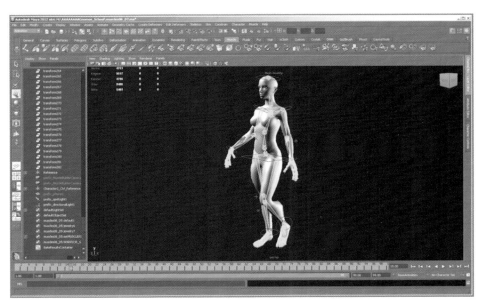

**FIGURE 9.4** A rig, the yellow armature, has been placed inside the model to allow the animator the ability to move it.

## Pipelines

A *pipeline* is the hierarchy of production. Different studios will create their own hierarchy depending on the needs of the project, how much is done in-house, and how much might be done through third-party developers. The pipeline is about putting in place tools, policies, and procedures for how things (content) are created and how they get into the game. A *flowchart* is a visual of the pipeline that explains what parts of the project need to get done before moving on to different groups associated with the project.

Figure 9.5 shows a rudimentary layout for a production chart to visually help explain the order in which things are accomplished during production. Getting organized and laying out the pipeline is actually an extremely constructive part of the process of conceptualizing and then building a game.

| Pre-Production | Production | Alpha | Beta |
|---|---|---|---|
| Story<br>Storyboards<br>Concept Art<br>Maps/level design<br>Audio | Finalize art - refine concept art<br>Modeling - shading, paint/texture, rigging<br>Animation - character, prop, interface and secondary animations<br>Audio - recorded dialogue, scores, ambient sounds<br>Programming - physics, game engine development, AI<br>Testing - test throughout entire production process, as soon as builds are available | All pieces done, and full game ready to play.<br><br>Revise as indicated through testing | Everything complete and ready for final testing |

**FIGURE 9.5** Visual pipelines are good to help identify what departments are needed and when.

Those who are involved in the production can view this visual to see who has work they need to get in order to move forward, and who in turn receives their work.

Managers use these charts to help determine how many people to assign to different parts of the pipeline to help keep the work flowing. An average casual game takes about 9 months to complete, whereas a big AAA title can take 18 months or more. Couple those lengths of time with crews that can range in size from 3 to 300 or more, and the dollars can begin to add up very quickly, so being organized is essential to a successful production.

The chart presented in Figure 9.5 isn't inclusive because each game tends to have unique requirements.

## Production Phases

Typically, the main steps in any production are as follows:

**Preproduction Phase**   The initial game idea is written, and early concept art, animation, storyboards, and vertical slices are created.

**Production Phase**   Each major department begins development in earnest from creation of art assets, to coding and testing every playable piece that is built.

◄

A game enters testing, or the *alpha* phase, when all art (even temp, or temporary pieces) has been completed and all code has been written, allowing a fully playable version.

**Testing Phase**   Testing is closely related to the production phase. This phase begins with alpha and goes through gold:

> **Alpha**   All pieces of the game are done (albeit some may need finessing), and a complete build can take place, prepping the project for testing.
>
> **Beta**   All final pieces of the game are done, and the game is ready to be tested in greater detail. The Q/A department goes over every aspect of the game in great detail, and upon locating *bugs* or errors usually categorizes them as A (top priority), B, or C. Each bug is catalogued, and the game is sent back to the production team for revamping. The higher-priority items are fixed first, but all bugs and their issues are addressed by the production team and corrected before the game is resubmitted for testing.
>
> **Gold**   The game is complete and ready to be shipped. Time to open the champagne!

**Postproduction Phase**   This phase covers all the work for a product that occurs after the game ships, such as additional marketing, trade shows, articles, and advertising. It should be understood, though, that much of the first marketing for a game can begin before the project is complete, to get the audience excited and talking about the upcoming release.

## Builds

During the production phase, the majority of games go through a series of builds. A *build* takes all the art, audio, and coding done at the time and creates a playable version of the game that can be reviewed and tested. A game can go through dozens of builds before hitting the final, finished version that's ready for release.

## Tracking Progress

Pipelines and charts for tracking progress must be flexible. When a tracking chart is created using Excel spreadsheets or Gantt charts, it should include *milestones*, which are the deadlines. These deadlines are taken seriously in the industry. When one is missed, it tends to create a domino effect, causing other divisions in the production to get behind in their work; it can trigger further missed deadlines, and could lead to the cancellation or failure of a project.

The flowchart or production chart is usually created and managed by the producer and the production staff. Some discipline leaders, such as the art or audio director, may create additional flowcharts that show the details of tasks that are specifically related to their departments. Producers use these charts to track and predict the game's progress through production. Missed deadlines can be spotted quickly and then acted on. Failure at this level could lead to the dismissal of the producer.

Not only do these charts set milestones or deadlines for delivery of specific parts of a game project, but they also track progress. For people working on a team, this chart provides a quick view of where the production is, what pieces need to be completed, what is on schedule and budget or behind, and who is handling what phase of the production.

Gone are the days of one person associated with a project carrying all this information in their head: that "go-to" person who could put their hand on any file or tell you who was doing what. This isn't to say that such a person isn't around; however, given the cost and time involved in making games these days, any time wasted trying to track down a file or locate who is doing what is needless and completely unprofessional.

After you create the pipeline and the project goes into production, there are a variety of ways to anticipate milestones and subsequently track progress:

> ▶ Microsoft Project is specifically designed to create very detailed production charts that list milestones and content dependencies.

> ▶ Flowcharts can be easily created using Excel docs (part of the Microsoft Word Office Suite or OpenSource.

> ▶ Google Docs provides an online version. Simply go to www.docs.google.com and create an account. Then share it with anyone on the team who needs to view or edit this chart online. The chart can be updated constantly to reflect changes in the production or exported as an Excel doc for backup.

Most medium to large teams use Project or equivalent software. Small indie teams are more likely to use Excel or Google Docs.

Several companies create flowchart systems that gaming companies license or purchase to use as a tracking system for their games. A lot of these are kept in house; team members can access them using a local area network (LAN), or the company may opt to use an online system. Online systems are widely accepted during productions because game crews can be located all over the globe, and being able to access that pipeline and flowchart is critical.

Flowchart systems are excellent investments for gaming companies because if work is lost, then the entire production may have to shut down while the files are located, and that is a pointless waste of time and money. Any business has a method for tracking work, and gaming is no different, particularly given the amount of money this industry garners every year. Savvy business managers know the value of understanding the pipeline and, more important, tracking the workflow and where the work is at any given time.

# Copyrights and Licenses

Many new game designers tend to be a bit skittish about sharing their ideas, for fear they will be pirated. At some point, if you're going to pitch your idea or seek help from others about getting it made or published, you'll need to share your material.

## Copyrights

Visiting the U.S. Copyright Office website, www.copyright.gov/, to gain information about what can be copyrighted is a solid first step in understanding what copyright will and won't protect. Copyright law gives the creator of a creative effort the exclusive right to control who can make copies or make works derived from that original work.

The government has a fact sheet specifically about games. In part, it says:

> Copyright does not protect the idea for a game, its name or title, or the method or methods for playing it. Nor does copyright protect any idea, system, method, device, or trademark material involved in developing, merchandising, or playing a game. Once a game has been made public, nothing in the copyright law prevents others from developing another game based on similar principles. Copyright protects only the particular manner of an author's expression in literary, artistic, or musical form.

> Material prepared in connection with a game may be subject to copyright if it contains a sufficient amount of literary or pictorial expression. For example, the text matter describing the rules of the game or the pictorial matter appearing on the gameboard or container may be registerable.

▶

**Ideas can't be copyrighted: only the tangible expression of the idea can.**

In addition to providing information about what copyrights do and don't protect, the site also provides information about how to apply for a copyright.

Understanding how copyrights work is also important so you don't infringe on the copyrights of others.

## PMCs

A "poor man's copyright" (PMC) is no substitute for an actual copyright. For a PMC, you write out as much information as you can about your idea; include art, audio, and so on related to the project; seal it in an envelope; and then mail it to yourself. When you receive it, don't open the envelope. The date stamped on the envelope by the U.S. Post Office proves when it was sent.

At the outset, this sounds like a cheap and easy way to protect property; however, PMCs are generally ignored by any court of law and aren't considered a viable method for protecting original material. I don't recommend that any designer attempt to protect their work using this method. Adhere to the guidelines of the U.S. Copyright office, or seek the advice of an attorney.

## Trademarks

A *trademark* is a distinctive sign such as a word, phrase, symbol, or design, or a combination of words, phrases, symbols, or designs, that identifies and distinguishes the product of one party from those of others.

Examples of trademarks can be seen in most AAA titles and lots of indie and casual games. For the most part, trademarks tend to be found in relation to the logo or name of a game, or the name or look of a character. Trademarks can be sought for dialogue too: for example, the manufacturers of *Donkey Kong* sought to trademark a catchphrase from their game: "It's on like *Donkey Kong*."

The phrase has been adopted by pop culture and shows up in movies, television, and music, and when used is meant to intimidate someone (it was made popular on rapper Ice Cube's *Predator* album, released in 1992). Nintendo, which makes *Donkey Kong*, is asserting its right to trademark this phrase, which originated in its game but has been picked up and used in other media; holding a trademark would prevent anyone from using the phrase without Nintendo's specific permission.

## Standards

Manufacturers such as Sony and Microsoft encrypt their final games so that they can only be played on their specific game systems, and you must get the manufacturer's approval before you can begin developing for a particular game system, such as PS3 or Wii. The submission process can be very long and involved, with no guarantee that the manufacturer will approve the game concept or development.

Each game system requires special development kits that are unique to these game systems and can only be provided by the specific manufacturer.

When a game is made to be played on a specific playback system, such as a Wii or a PlayStation, the manufacturer needs to make sure that all the programming built into the game will match what the controllers need to do once the game is installed on that system. For example, games developed for the Xbox gaming system need to always have the B button programmed to allow a player to back out of menus.

The game manufacturer ships a copy of the game to the manufacturers of each playback system for which they have built their game. Those manufacturers test the product extensively before submitting their approval.

## Licenses

Games may require the use of software or hardware that is owned by a separate party but can be licensed for a fee. A good example of this is a game engine.

Certain software packages, such as Photoshop and Maya, require a license for use in the production of games that are created for sale.

Instead, some designers use open-source software, such as Blender, which is free 3D software, or Gimp, which is a free 2D package similar to Photoshop. Although getting the software free seems like a great idea to avoid paying for the software or a licensing fee, if the software doesn't perform properly, there is little or no support to help you troubleshoot problems.

Projects that do license software to be used during the creation of the game can solicit help from these companies when it comes time to market the project. For example, Adobe is the manufacturer of Photoshop and regularly uses examples of actual applications of its software from finished games. Submitting work you created with your licensed software to the software company can help provide solid promotion and endorsements for the game if it uses your examples in the promotion of the company's products.

> Developers who don't license this software in the proper way prior to shipping a final product could face strict legal action.

## THE ESSENTIALS AND BEYOND

Throughout this book, you have had a chance to review some of the major steps involved in game design, and in this chapter we looked at job descriptions and methods for planning and tracking progress. Coming up with the idea for a game can be fun, but that is usually the easiest part of the process. Logically sorting out how to go about making the game can be an enormous challenge.

There is a logical process to everything that goes into developing and making a game. Identify the necessary steps, and sort out how to complete each one. Break the huge process of game production into pieces, and patterns will emerge. Don't hesitate to keep revising your pipeline and tracking system as needed. It will get done.

### ADDITIONAL EXERCISES

1. Designing a pipeline is a worthwhile exercise for any potential designer. Review a concept you have, and break down the steps required to produce the final product based on the information you've read in this book. Determine what would be involved in preproduction. Then, from that, write down the production steps.

2. Visit www.copyright.gov/, and review the copyright information and procedures for video games. Carefully read the steps outlined to see when and where a copyright can actually be applied.

### REVIEW QUESTIONS

1. What does a level designer do?

   A. Focuses on smaller sections of the whole game to design the layout and the events that occur there

   C. Calculates how many levels characters can reach depending on their specs

   B. Determines ways to allow a character to level during gameplay

   D. Determines how many levels multistory structures have in a game

2. True or false. A PMC, or "poor man's copyright," is a recommended method for copyrighting a game idea.

3. What are standards?

   A. The level of quality the designer is aiming for

   C. Matching programmed elements in any game with the specific type of playback system they are designed for

   B. Moral or ethical requirements for the game

   D. Hiring practices for anyone entering the production pipeline

   *(Continues)*

**THE ESSENTIALS AND BEYOND** *(Continued)*

4.  True or false. The programmer always creates the engine for any game they are working on.

5.  The primary roles of the producer cover all of the following except _____.

    A.  Helps the project meet critical deadlines

    B.  Works with the managers to make decisions about what parts of the production to change or cut in order to meet critical deadlines

    C.  Helps the project stay on budget

    D.  Creates the concept art for the project

# CHAPTER 10

# Distribution and Marketing

*Distribution for games has* expanded from the early forms of arcades to home computer systems to extremely successful console systems. Games run on numerous platforms.

Add to that the ever-increasing handheld markets, with laptops that have extensive battery life (great for long flights) and higher-powered cell phones that play hundreds of games with better, faster graphics and larger display screens, and the gaming industry currently has many different platforms for which to create games.

Gaming has grown so dramatically, surpassing even the sales of feature films, that marketing for them has also increased. Not only do the manufacturers of games recognize the massive revenue coming in from sales, but advertisers have also embraced this medium as a genuine avenue for advertising other products.

Clever marketing people have looked at all the methods people can use to access and play games. They have explored and exploited numerous schemes for getting their products in front of consumers, both to sell the games themselves and to use them to help market other products. As technology continues to provide more methods for distributing games, advertising is expected to keep pace with that growth.

▶ **Platforms**

▶ **Online**

▶ **Using games for marketing**

▶ **Marketing of games**

## Platforms

In a nutshell, a *platform* is the electronic system used to play a game. Home computers like the Mac and PC are platforms, and dedicated consoles like the Wii and Xbox are platforms that play games. There are numerous online avenues and, of course, the expanding markets for mobile and handheld devices.

Many game companies build their games for more than one platform, to capitalize on the different markets available for sales and reaching their demographic.

The following is a list of some of the more common platforms used for playing games:

► PC

► Console

► Handheld

► Mobile

► Arcade

Games created for many platforms can be played online. We'll talk about online games after we look at these common platforms.

## PC

**PC**, short for personal computer, is generally accepted as the term for any home computer system, whether it's a Mac or Windows.

Games that are distributed for the PC market indicate in their specs whether they're playable on the Mac and/or Windows. Crossing platforms (being able to have software work on either Windows or the Mac OS) is becoming more common; however, fewer games are built for or retooled for use on the Mac, simply because more gamers own PCs (Windows). Also, most development systems for consoles, handhelds, and mobile systems are Windows-based.

Games for the PC market can be downloaded directly onto the computer, played online, or installed using a CD or DVD.

The biggest challenge in PC development is piracy. That's the main reason most companies cite when discussing why they aren't developing games for the PC, and also why casual games are turning more to ad-based and micro-transaction/social games.

## Micro-Transactions

A *micro-transaction* occurs when a player buys, with actual real-world currency, some type of in-game bonus. These can be special items like new potions or spells. This type of business model can be lucrative for game makers. These transactions tend to be quite small—about a dollar or so (hence the term micro-transaction); but if a game is popular (even a few thousand players), the micro-transactions can add up. They give players access to new, fun items that add to the gameplay but don't cost a great deal of money to buy.

The downside is that some players feel nickel-and-dimed, so game makers need to choose wisely about introducing micro-transactions into their games. Otherwise, they may turn players away.

An excellent example of how this approach to marketing and making a profit through micro-transactions works can be seen with the company Zynga, which makes *FarmVille*. Yes, Zynga has ads associated with the game; however, the company generates the majority of its revenue by selling virtual goods to players (seeds, livestock, and so on). Players use those virtual goods as currency in the game when they play with each other. Zynga has earned over a billion dollars using this system.

## Property Rights Issues

Another issue is the debate over intellectual freedom versus intellectual property rights, especially where the Internet is concerned. Copyright, which was designed to protect intellectual property, can sometimes interfere with free speech. Game makers that post their games online can acquire a copyright. Others may play a game and build one very similar to it, and that is legal.

## Development for the Home Computer Market

It's worth noting that the speed at which faster computers come out has made developers lazy. Twenty years ago, developers spent a lot of development time optimizing the product's code and resources to make it run as efficiently as possible on the computers available at the time. That is hardly a concern anymore, except for the most high-end games. Many developers would rather give up the portion of the market that doesn't have the newest high-end computers than spend additional development time optimizing their products.

Similar changes have happened with file sizes. The best resource-compression routines were developed during the time of the floppy disk. Work of that type slacked off following the advent of CDs. Eventually we started running out of room on CDs, and online digital delivery became more popular, so compression has become more interesting again; but part of the response has been to increase bandwidth rather than improve compression routines.

Performance-wise, PC development depends on the minimum or recommended system requirements needed to run the game. Or, another way to say this is that PC development depends on the minimum system requirements you feel will run the game without taking away from the gameplay experience. For most indie developers, it's not an issue, because they aren't doing super-high-end graphics; a basic machine these days will run their games fine. For bigger companies, generally, a cross-platform game made to run on Xbox/PlayStation will run on a PC without much trouble; you just have to improve the interface to work with a keyboard and mouse (although several don't—the game makers just let the PC gamers complain about the poor controls).

## GAME-MAKING SOFTWARE PACKAGES

For those interested in creating a game for the PC, a number of software packages are available, such as GameMaker, which has versions for Windows, Mac, and HTML (www.yoyogames.com/make). Programs like GameMaker allow new designers the freedom to use drag-and-drop features to build their games without needing to write complicated code.

GameMaker is for creating 3D games. To experiment with making a 2D game, Game Editor (www.game-editor.com/Main_Page) is an open-source, cross-platform game creator that lets the user create their own games, not only for the Mac and the PC but for mobile applications as well. If you visit the site, there are sample games that users of the program have created.

It is a good idea to play the games made with these packages to get an idea of what can be accomplished with graphics, sound, and animation and to see how the gameplay works.

Other packages to look at include these:

**MUGEN**   Makes 2D fight games

**RPG Toolkit; RPG 95, 2000, 2003, and XP; Hephaestus** Make role-playing games

**Adventure Game Studios (AGS)**   Free software that can be downloaded and used. Users need to have some knowledge of coding

The program Flash is also used extensively by novice/amateur game makers. Professionals also regularly use this more complex system to create not only graphics but also animation and coding.

There are plenty of online sites that offer tutorials on how Flash-based games are made, including the following:

▶ www.flash-game-design.com

▶ www.dezinerfolio.com

▶ www.pelfusion.com

There are thousands of Flash-based games that have been made and success-fully marketed. Flash is an excellent program for the first time game maker in that you can make an entire game with just one to three people. The production time for these can be short, especially if you work through some of the tutorials found on the websites listed in this section.

Projects made using Flash can be played on PCs, along with web, mobile, and handheld systems. Flash creates 2D games. If 3D development holds your inter-est as a first-time game maker or indie developer, Unity may be the package you will want to explore.

## Unity

Unity is another terrific development tool to look at which is quite popular with developers for the home computer market. Games made with Unity are also playable on mobile devices, the web, and social gaming. Downloading the soft-ware is free from their official site: www.unity3d.com.

One of the nice features of this package is that you can publish the 3D content made with this software to the web with the Adobe Flash Player. When you visit the site, pay special attention the "gallery" location because you can view trail-ers of products made with Unity and play several demos.

Playing the demos, again, is an important step in understanding the abilities of the engine, the creativity involved, and how well the gameplay works. You can also download demo projects that come with content that you can create games with.

At the site Activetuts+ (http://www.unitymagic.com/shop/en/unity-tutorials/ and http://www.digitaltutors.com/training/unity-tutorials) you can find more examples of projects made with Unity and work through some good tutorials on creating games with this software.

## Consoles

Console systems are a huge aspect of the gaming industry. A great deal of money has been spent designing and building them, and substantial dollars have been invested in creating games specific to them.

Examples of console systems include the following:

▶ Microsoft Xbox

▶ Sony PlayStation

▶ Nintendo Wii

▶ Nintendo GameCube

▶ Sega Genesis

The first successful console to use car-tridges that plugged in new games was the Atari 2600. Released in 1977, it has a library of nine games.

These systems generally attach directly to a TV monitor or a computer monitor or have their own projection systems. Every console has a microprocessor, a graphics system, and a controller. The controller is specific to the design of the console and allows the player to interact with the game.

The Wii (Wireless Interactive Interface), originally called Revolution, has a unique controller that is motion-sensitive. As the gamer moves the controller, they're able to mimic movements such as casting a fishing pole, wielding a drumstick, and even slapping with a flyswatter.

The controller is extremely fast and accurate, and it allows gamers to enjoy interacting with the game and mimic the movements needed to play. For example, in a sword-fighting game, players lunge and twist with the controller as if it were a blade, and enjoy some astounding gameplay results.

Figure 10.1 is an image of a Wii controller. These units are small, lightweight, and extremely easy to operate, which is essential, especially when the gameplay is fast-paced.

**FIGURE 10.1** This handheld controller for the Nintendo Wii features a wing shape that is ergonomically designed for ease in holding the unit and operating the buttons with fingers and thumbs.

Other controllers, like the wing-shaped one for the Sony PlayStation, are designed to be held comfortably in the hands. The PlayStation controller has 14 buttons that the player can customize. There are also controllers that use joysticks, trackballs, footpads, and paddles, among other devices.

# Handheld

This section focuses on handheld devices designed specifically for gaming, such as the Game Boy.

Games for handheld devices may come preloaded or can be installed by inserting cartridges or accessing the Web.

The Nintendo DS and Sony PlayStation Portable (PSP) are excellent examples of handheld devices. These devices can play all of the gameplay styles discussed in this book, including adventure, arcade, board and card games, sports-related games, RPGs, and strategy. Not only are all gameplay types represented on handheld games, but the variety of games available is extensive.

Figure 10.2 shows the Sony PSP portable handheld unit that can be purchased with Sony's game *God of War* already loaded. The unit has a portable charger, so it can be powered up from any outlet. It also comes loaded with what is known as *firmware*. Firmware and software are similar; the only difference is that *firmware* (which is a combination of software and hardware, also referred to as the *system software*) is the term used for software that comes preloaded onto a device and has been written onto read-only memory (ROM).

Mobile phones can fall into the handheld category, but they're better classified as mobile platforms (discussed next).

The first handheld game was *Auto Race*, released by Mattel. The first to use interchangeable cartridges was Milton Bradley's *MicroVision*.

**FIGURE 10.2** PSP units are highly portable, lightweight, and durable. The version shown here is the Deep Red unit.

These units can connect wirelessly to the Internet, and in addition to games, they're able to play movies (in the MP4 or AVI format) and music and display images.

Handheld devices appeal to people who travel a great deal or who simply like their portability. Handhelds (and mobile devices) also appeal to consumers because of the other features they come with, such as the ability to access email, online conferencing, Internet access, and many applications that let users manage their calendars.

As on mobile devices, the screens are somewhat small, so game makers need to handle real estate carefully by using simple graphics and large type.

# Mobile

Smartphones, such as the iPhone, Android, and Blackberry, are great examples of mobile devices. They're usually equipped to access the Internet, so online play is available; and many mobiles have games installed on them when purchased.

Mobile devices are approaching the functionality of laptops. Most fall under the overarching term *mobile Internet device (MID)*. Some of the companies that create these are Acer, Asus, Casio, Dell, E-TEN, Fujitsu, and Group Sense PDA.

Some games are made specifically for these mobile devices (as you saw in Chapter 2, "Gameplay Styles," with the work Mobile Pie does); however, adapting games to mobile devices has been a challenge for designers because of the tiny amount of real estate available.

Designers have to find a way to set up the unit so a gamer can interface comfortably with the game. Initially, games for mobile phones were fairly low-end in terms of graphics, animation, and speed of gameplay, simply because the phones didn't have the computing power to run anything else. *Minesweeper,* shown in Figure 10.3, was one of the popular earlier games these mobile devices could play.

> ▶
> The amount of space that is visible in any game (what you see on the monitor) is referred to as *real estate*.

**FIGURE 10.3** Early versions of *Minesweeper* were quite simple visually.

Figure 10.4 shows the look of a newer version of *Minesweeper.*

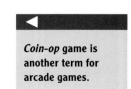

**FIGURE 10.4** Along with improved graphics, this modern, revamped version of *Minesweeper* includes special-effects animation and audio that run when the mines explode.

As computing power increased along with the quality and speed of graphic displays, applications for improved phones were in demand. Flash-based games were a popular method for providing games for this increasing market.

The interface uses the touchpad on the phone. The Android HTC Desire smartphone has added to that interaction by providing a slight buzzing sensation as the player uses the touchpad interface, thereby giving the player more of a feeling of being involved with the game.

Critics of the games being designed for mobile applications feel that the products being offered are too repetitive and lazy in their design. As mobile device designs continue to improve, with lightweight cases, larger full-color displays, and faster computer speed, the challenge for game makers will be to come up with gameplay that is more challenging and compelling.

## Arcade

Arcade games saw their golden era in the 1970s and 1980s with great games such as Galaga, Asteroids, Defender, and Centipede.

*Coin-op* game is another term for arcade games.

---

### Classics Still Popular

Many game aficionados actively seek out, purchase, and renovate older arcade games. They play them, too!

---

Many arcade games today are redemption games. These types of games are often found in restaurants that cater to young children, such as Chuck E. Cheese's. A good example of a redemption game is the claw type. The player inserts money and then operates a mini-claw that looks like a tiny construction crane, trying to pick up a toy inside a closed glass box.

There are modern arcade games that are highly popular, and what sets them apart from games played in the home are their elaborate controllers. Rhythm games, for example, have footpads for the gamer to dance on; the focus of these games is not so much the story or the gameplay, but the performance of the gamer using the device. This aspect allows these types of games to thrive in arcades, which are, ostensibly, social environs.

# Online

Online gaming is one of the areas that has shown the most growth and diversity, which makes sense, given the increase in broadband use by consumers. Even users in remote areas that don't have access to cable systems for high-speed Internet can subscribe to online services through a satellite hookup (HughesNet is a good example). Online can be considered a subset of the PC, console, handheld, and mobile platforms, because any of those platforms can access games using this route.

Online games fall into three basic categories:

- ▶ Massively multiplayer online games (MMOGs)
- ▶ Social games
- ▶ Portals

## MMOGs

The leading contender in this category is Blizzard's *World of Warcraft (WoW)*, with millions of subscribers and billions in earned revenue. This game can be downloaded for free. After playing the free trial offer, gamers pay an initial cost plus a monthly subscription fee to continue playing.

The majority of MMOGs have the same type of business model: the initial game is free to download and play for a short time; then, if the gamer wants the full version, they're given an access code to unlock the rest of the game after making payment.

Some companies provide what is known as a *demo version* to play. Because these are such massive games, downloading a full version just to try it for a short time is prohibitive; therefore, many companies offer a pared-down version that provides enough of the actual gameplay experience to let the potential gamer decide whether they want to buy the full version without taking a huge amount of time to download or using up an inordinate amount of computer space.

There are several varieties of these massive online games, including MMORPG (role-playing games), MMOFPS (first-person shooters), and strategy and racing games, among others.

MMOGs tend to be highly social, and players interact with others a great deal. Because most of these games include a social feature that lets players talk to each other in-game, not all games are appropriate for all ages. *WoW* provides a language filter that essentially bleeps out foul language, and the company tries to be sure players don't select offensive names; however, the game isn't monitored closely enough for very young players. *Club Penguin*, currently owned by the Disney Corporation, is a MMORPG designed for children. In this virtual world, gamers assume the role of a penguin and live in a small town filled with igloos and other penguins. The game is highly social and filled with all sorts of mini-games. It has numerous safety features in place, so younger gamers can interact in a virtual community that is highly monitored for foul language, inappropriate comments, and so on.

As we have discussed previously in this book, when a game designer begins to work on a new project, special consideration needs to be given to the target audience—the demographic. In the case of online social games, players are likely to encounter other people; therefore, your demographic becomes part of the gameplay. Predators seek out these social forums to prey on young people or try to bilk other players out of their money and gather personal information with scams of all types, especially spy software like keylogging programs. Hackers use programs such as keyloggers to infiltrate users' computers and monitor what they're typing (like passwords), along with sites they may be visiting (such as an online bank).

Designers of MMOGs need to provide strongly written disclaimers for their games and build in filters to prevent predators from accessing personal information or targeting other players in the game. These disclaimers should be written, or at least reviewed by, the company's legal department or a lawyer.

## Social Games

A *social game* is one that can be accessed and played through an online social network like Facebook. Some companies, such as Social Express Inc., which is owned by Viacom, develop social games for MTV, Nickelodeon, and other brands. Nickelodeon provides an entire website called *The Big Help*, which offers excellent information—especially for young or new gamers—on how to protect your privacy while learning how to enjoy social gaming.

The company Zynga has made great strides in covering the social games market with its game *FarmVille*. This social game is accessed through Facebook and has attracted an enormous audience of players—over 80 million at the time this book was written. One of the reasons Zynga has been so successful with this venue revolves around the variety of ways the company uses the medium successfully through online advertising and sales of virtual goods.

> **AppData is an independent data-collection and -analysis firm that tracks usage of sites online and can help identify trends.**

*FarmVille* is free to play, but Zynga makes money through advertising and selling separate assets to players. According to AppData, *FarmVille* attracts approximately 7,400,000 daily users (see Figure 10.5).

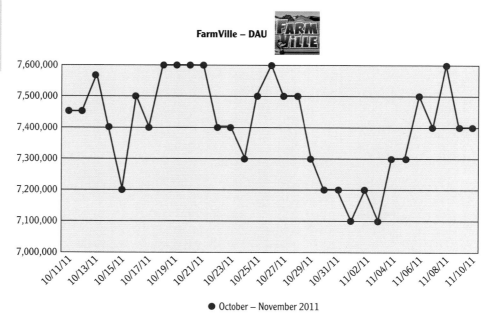

**FIGURE 10.5** This graph is adapted from data presented online by AppData, which charts daily use of the game *FarmVille*. DAU means daily active users.

Social games are growing in popularity, due mostly to the increased use of social sites like Facebook, Twitter, LinkedIn, MySpace, Ning, Google+, Badoo, and Friendster.

Disney, which maintains a large online presence through its websites, is pushing forward with more social gaming for its subscribers. One of its acquisitions, Playdom, has created the game *Gnome Town*, where players can assume the role of a gnome and save animals in an enchanted forest.

Other social online games include *BittyBay*, *BoomBang*, *Second Life*, *IMVU*, *A Mystical Land*, *Warbears*, *World of Cars Online*, *Virtual Family Kingdom*, and *Stardoll*. Figure 10.6 shows a screenshot from the game *Virtual Family Kingdom*. Unlike other social-gaming sites, this one doesn't present ads to players; the focus is on interaction and gaming for any age group.

**FIGURE 10.6** *Virtual Family Kingdom* offers several areas where gamers can play and compete with each other for points on a leader board.

The interest in social games remains strong. Many game designers approach this type of gameplay as a casual form of an MMOG, where gamers can interact with each other, play online for a short amount of time, and not have to immerse themselves in elaborate or deep lore.

# Portals

A *portal* is an online site that allows gamers to either download and sample games with a try-before-you-buy strategy (shareware) or pay a subscription fee to play any games available through the portal. There are also sites that offer free games (freeware) and tend to earn their revenue through ads on the sites.

Big Fish Games is a portal site that offers a new game every day. Its model is simple:

1. Download the game for free.

2. Play for an hour for free.

3. If you like the game, buy it. After the purchase is complete, Big Fish provides an unlock code.

Portal sites offer an enormous variety of primarily casual games, such as match-three, hidden-object, card, board, time-management, strategy, adventure, and puzzle games. The games they offer for sale are, for the most part, developed and created by independent game companies that make a profit of about 30 percent per sale.

This may seem like a big chunk of money going back to the portal, but these sites handle all the sales and marketing, which can be a huge strain for a small company to manage. For little indie companies, portals like Big Fish, PopCap Games, and Newgrounds are a good way to market their products, particularly because many of these portals have millions of visitors/subscribers.

Simply visit the sites, and review the posted submission policies. These sites make their businesses work by acquiring new games, so their submission methods are fairly straightforward and simple to read.

## BIG FISH GAMES SUBMISSION GUIDELINES FOR PC GAMES

Different sites have different guidelines, and the guidelines may change. At the time of writing, the Big Fish Games submission guidelines were as follows. Check the website for the most current guidelines.

### SUBMIT A DOWNLOADABLE PC OR MAC GAME

**Do you have a new downloadable game?**

Then please send us the following:

▶ A short description of your game

▶ 2 representative screenshots of your game

*(Continues)*

## BIG FISH GAMES SUBMISSION GUIDELINES FOR PC GAMES *(Continued)*

▶ The genre your game fits into (if one exists)

▶ And most importantly, a link to download your game and try it

Our dedicated team will review your submission as quickly as possible and get back to you with options for how we can work together.

Remember, your game doesn't have to be completely finished to show it to us. We see games at all stages of development. We're happy to give you feedback or answer questions that will help you move the game towards completion.

Contact us with your game or any questions at:

gamesubmissions@bigfishgames.com

If you have a game that you wish to submit to a portal for review, again, their business is to be straightforward in their dealings with developers, and they go to great lengths to avoid theft or plagiarism. If a portal damages relationships with developers, word of that quickly gets posted to the Internet and can cause developers to keep away.

Before you submit a game, review the site you're interested in, research posts about that site, and check the quality of the games posted there. Read the site's submission policies. Make sure you maintain ownership of your game. Pay special attention to the payment percentages and timeframes for making payments (some sites don't pay until nearly three months or longer have gone by). The usual timeframe that is reasonable for payment is within 30 days of your game being posted. If a company wants more than 90 days, or specifies a cap of more than $100 earned before payment can be made, you should probably avoid that site. Also be sure that payments can be made with the correct currency for whatever country you're living in.

Other portals, like Pogo, offer a huge variety of games as well; however, their business model is somewhat different. They offer many of their games, including those where prizes can be won, on a subscription basis. Pogo also offers some free games on ad-supported sites.

Quite a few online portals are meccas for gamblers. These sites allow players to use credit cards or PayPal to play for actual money awards. Many of the games are typically found in casinos, including poker, blackjack, and slot machines. For the most part, online sites that offer games where real money is used for betting purposes don't use games submitted by individual designers or small companies. They tend to do business with established companies like Video Game Technologies (VGT, vgt.net), which specializes in these types of games.

# Using Games for Marketing

Because of the huge popularity of games, they're a great vehicle for reaching a large audience. Marketers have found various ways to use games for advertising, and these marketing schemes can be implemented in different ways.

## Product Placement

Product placement is one significant way games are used to market other products. In film and television, where this method was first used, a specific product that actors can interact with is placed in a scene. For example, a particular brand of potato chips or soda might be seen in the shot, with the label clearly visible. The manufacturer pays a product-placement fee, and if the movie or TV is a hit, their product receives a massive amount of exposure and endorsement.

Product placement is also a marketing technique used in games. According to the independent survey company Nielsen, Gatorade was able to increase dollars spent on their product by 24 percent with their product placement in Entertainment Arts (EA) sports games.

"Nielsen's study is a milestone for interactive entertainment," said Elizabeth Harz, Senior Vice President of Global Media Sales at EA. "For the first time, advertisers are able to link the value of their in-game marketing or sponsorship to actual sales. Now brands can feel confident adding gaming as a core media channel for their advertising."

Nielsen's study was focused on households that purchased at least one of EA's sports games: *NHL (R) 09, NHL 10, NBA LIVE 07, NBA LIVE 08, NBA LIVE 09,* or *NBA Homecourt.* Without a doubt, product placement in games can boost revenue for the company buying that ad space.

Figure 10.7 shows a screenshot from the Electronic Arts game *NBA Inside Drive 2004* with an ad for Air Canada prominently displayed in the arena.

According to Gerardo Guzman, Director, Media Product Leadership for Nielsen, "Video games are a deeply engaging consumer experience. Bringing our industry accepted ad effectiveness understanding to video games is another way to help marketers understand how consumers respond to advertising across different environments. This should help optimize the impact of and derive a return on media investments. In this case the story is simple—dollars put into video game product placement result in more retail dollars."

The game *Alan Wake* features prominently placed products from Verizon, Duracell, and Energizer.

The character Lara Croft from *Tomb Raider* often rides a Ducati motorcycle, which is a savvy use of product placement in a game.

**FIGURE 10.7** This ad for Air Canada appears in the EA game *NBA Inside Drive 2004*. It scrolls the same way an ad would in an actual arena.

## In-Game Ads

The majority of all the money spent for product placement and advergames is spent on in-game ads. There are two types of in-game advertising:

**Dynamic** Updated every time the game is played, dynamic ads can be specific to a location and time zone. For example, if the game is being played in France, the language automatically adjusts to French. Dynamic ads are served to video-game consoles in real time from the Internet. An example of such an ad can

Early forms of in-game advertising, such as the McDonald's sign seen in EA's *Battlefield*, were branded as spyware, but people still played games that contained them.

be found in *Swat 4*, developed by Irrational Games and published by Vivendi Universal: a poster for the movie *Tripping the Rift* hangs on a wall in the game.

**Static**   Static ads are embedded directly into the game. The downside is that such ads can never change after the game is released.

Some examples of in-game advertising include McDonald's one-day use of gardens in Zynga's *FarmVille*. Players could plant a garden using just mustard seeds and tomatoes. The end result was a garden with the McDonald's logo growing in the center, as shown in Figure 10.8.

**FIGURE   10.8**  Using seeds for tomatoes and mustard, gamers playing FarmVille were able to grow a McDonald's logo.

## Advergames

Advergames tend to be fun little casual games created with assets that relate directly to the advertisers that pay for their production. They're a combination of game and advertisement.

Cheetos, Laffy Taffy, Cheerios, Froot Loops, and Sweet Tarts all have advergames, as do movies such as *Pirates of the Caribbean* and organizations like the United States Army.

Essentially, there are three types of advergames:

▶ A game may be created and then showcased on the official site for the company it represents. This form of game entices players to the site. Cheerios, made by General Mills, has a few on its site, including *Honey Defender* (www.honeydefender.com) and *Buzz's Honey Bust.*

▶ A game may be made and then marketed on more traditional game sites; however, the theme of the game is directly related to the message or product it was intended for. A good example is *America's Army,* which was designed to increase recruitment www.americasarmy.com/).

▶ The third type involves in-game advertising, or product placement, discussed more in the next section.

Companies such as Advergames (www.advergames.com) and Giant Bomb (www.giantbomb.com) offer a huge assortment of advergames you can study and play. Raw Computing (www.rawcomputing.co.uk/advergames.html) offers instructions on how to create an advergame; check them out to see how simple these games are to make.

Many third-party, independent game developers are routinely hired to produce advergames for their clients for a variety of platforms. One such company is Skyworks (www.skyworks.com). Skyworks specializes in creating advergames for the iPhone and iPad for clients including Sony, Ford, and ESPN. Star Mountain Studios has a fun Flash-based advergame called *Genie Joe and the Axeman,* made with Joe Perry from Aerosmith, which promotes Perry's hot-sauce company (www.starmountainstudios.com/FreeGames/GJandA.html).

Another company that specializes in making advergames is Game and Buzz Factory (www.game-buzz-factory.com/games.php). The company's products are playable on many platforms in a wide variety of advergame categories, including sweepstakes and point-of-sale games.

Ads may be shown to gamers at different places in a game. Any time an ad appears in a game, it's known as an *in-game ad.* Ads can affect the flow of gameplay, so it's important for designers to understand where an ad may appear: *pregame ads* are shown just before the game loads, *postgame ads* run after the game ends, and *interstitial ads* can pop up at any point during regular gameplay.

# Sponsorship

This type of advertising allows a sponsor to invest dollars in the development or production of a game, or sponsor an event related to the game in exchange for owning a substantial amount (even 100 percent) of the territory in and around the game. *Owning the territory* means that no other advertisers can use the project for advertising unless authorized by the sponsor.

# Marketing of Games

Marketing of games has grown in diversity. TV and print ads remain popular avenues; however, the industry has also embraced forms of advertising that take advantage of other media.

Side industries can benefit from successful games through *merchandising*: creating and selling items related to the brand, such as clothing, books, and toys.

## Viral Marketing

Viral marketing is based on how infectious an ad (or the game itself) is. If the ad is well-made enough, people will pass it along for others to see. Offline, this phenomenon is known as *word of mouth*.

Most viral marketing shows up as YouTube videos or blog posts. If a game has *gone viral*, it means information about it is flooding the Internet. Comments can be negative or positive. Many game makers try to get the ball rolling with a positive viral campaign by posting positive videos or blog posts to see if the thread will be picked up. This is a bit of a shot in the dark; however, if the product is good, then the ads or the game may go viral.

## Web Presence

Pretty much any game produced and marketed today has some type of presence on the Internet through an official site dedicated to the game or via other online avenues like portals and fan sites. These sites help build communities that blog about the game, share tips for playing the game, and create mods (modifications) that they share with each other.

These types of online communities tend to be supported by the game makers by offering discounts on products, sweepstakes, and news about events related to the game. The more these communities talk about the game and/or create mods to share, the more interest is developed and maintained, which is in itself a type of marketing.

## Marketing to the Demographic

Involving marketing input while a game is still in production is more and more common these days. Marketing expertise can help influence the look of the characters, environments, and even gameplay, to help ensure that the product being marketed will correctly appeal to the demographic(s) it's targeting.

For the game designer, this involvement can be a mixed blessing. The marketing input provides ideas for placing ads (including how they look or can be interactive); however, some designers feel this input dilutes their game design with material that has nothing to do with the gameplay.

## Reviews and Endorsements

Game makers can use reviews to make better games. By reading reviews about games that are similar to ones they're making, they can learn about aspects of the design that were well received and, more important, those that were not. If your goal, for example, is to make a HOG, hundreds of them are online along with comments about them. By using reviews of similar games that are already being played, game designers can improve their chances of garnering good reviews when their game is released and played.

You can seek endorsements by submitting a game to established reviewers. If they're reputable and offer solid feedback on the game, they can help provide much-needed exposure. Online sites like www.gamespot.com regularly review games.

Game reviewers can also provide substantial marketing power. If their feedback is negative, those reviews can help the designer revamp the game and release it with the improvements. However, once negative feedback about a game hits the Internet, there isn't much that can be done to fix the resulting damage.

## Beta Testing

After a game has gone through exhaustive testing internally, beta tests by players not associated with the game's production can provide substantial objective feedback that goes above and beyond testing for bugs. Beta testing helps game makers avoid releasing a game that might fail.

Beta testers do occasionally find bugs; however, their importance lies more in verifying the gameplay and whether it's fun and compelling. For some of the larger games that come from bigger companies such as Blizzard, EA, and LucasArts, companies seek beta testers from the gaming community and reviewers to play the game and provide truly objective feedback.

Almost all beta testers sign a nondisclosure agreement (NDA), stating they won't disclose anything about the game. Still, they often leak information about the product. The game companies know this and frequently capitalize on it. The downside, of course, is that in beta testing, a game that isn't ready, a negative loop may get started.

## Conferences

The Game Developers Conference (GDC) meets annually in San Francisco and is the oldest confab for game developers, designers, programmers, artists, producers, marketers, and so on.

Conferences used to be an opportunity for game makers to meet and discuss trends in the industry, present new technology, and view each other's games, but they have changed remarkably over the years. Most of them are now enormous, media-driven extravaganzas. Game makers still meet and discuss all the things mentioned, but they take advantage of the marketing potential by inviting media to cover the events.

The media blitz at a conference includes live streaming of video on the Internet, reviewers playing and then writing about new games or technology on their blogs, and local and national news coverage.

The Electronic Entertainment Expo (E3), www.e3expo.com, is a media *tour de force* at which new games and sequels to past hits are introduced. This enormous symposium fills entire convention centers in very large cities. Fans travel from literally all over the world to attend this event, so they can experience firsthand new games and new technology and occasionally meet their favorite designers.

Figure 10.9 shows an image of the exterior of the huge convention center in downtown Los Angeles, California, where E3 was held in 2011.

**FIGURE 10.9** E3 is a *tour de force* media event where game companies introduce new products.

The gigantic Comic-Con, held each year in San Diego, is another avenue for marketing new games. Comic-Con was initially a mecca for comics enthusiasts to meet and talk about comics, trade them, look for vintage ones from sellers, and so on. Over the years, it has evolved into more of a media event, and video-game makers, recognizing that comics enthusiasts also fall into their marketing demographics, flock there to market games.

Savvy marketers continue to research how their demographics talk to each other, share information about their favorites (for example, via viral marketing), and use that information to get their products in front of these potential gamers. Game companies spend millions during these shows and conferences to showcase new and upcoming games. The purpose is to attract distributors and consumers, and to get the attention of the media. Building hype is a big thing.

## THE ESSENTIALS AND BEYOND

An enormous challenge for any game maker is distributing and marketing their games effectively. The marketplace for games is global, but reaching the target audience for a game and making the sale can often prove more challenging than making the game in the first place.

To be fair, there are more gaming companies and more products competing with each other; however, the sheer number of gamers willing to spend time and money on games indicate that sales are happening and continuing to grow.

### ADDITIONAL EXERCISES

1.  Choose three different gameplay styles, and research comments posted online about those types of games. Look for the ways the comments are written. Are there similarities in how the information is presented? Of the similarities you uncover, do you notice trends in the positive and negative statements? List any must-do/include items along with any must-avoid items.

2.  Pick one game that comes from a fairly large company such as EA or LucasArts (larger companies are more likely to have multiple reviews). Do an online search for any reviews of those games. Try to find at least three. Of those three, are there similarities in what the reviewers were writing about? Try to play the game you're researching. Do you agree with what the reviewers wrote?

3.  Visit one of the advergame sites listed in this chapter, or do an Internet search to find others, and play a few of those games. After playing them, did you feel as though you wanted to buy or at least investigate the products in the advergames? Do you think this is a good advertising vehicle? How would you design an advergame for your own project?

*(Continues)*

## THE ESSENTIALS AND BEYOND  *(Continued)*

### REVIEW QUESTIONS

1. A platform is _____.

   A. A specific level in a game

   B. A type of social game

   C. The system the game is designed to be played on

   D. A type of advergame

2. True or false. A portal is a forum for game fans to meet their favorite designers in person.

3. What is product placement?

   A. Giving out video games for free at conventions

   B. Cleverly placing video games at key locations in conventions

   C. A type of game offered by advertisers where the winners redeem points for actual products

   D. Placing products directly in the game where the player can see and sometimes interact with them

4. True or false. Beta testing involves testing the game with testers who can objectively provide feedback about gameplay.

5. What is an advergame?

   A. Adversaries battling each other

   B. A game that showcases the product being advertised

   C. A game that requires two or more people to play together

   D. A game that is text-based

# Answers to Review Questions

## Chapter 1

1.  **C.** *The Royal Game of Ur*, discovered by Sir Leonard Woolley in the ancient city of Ur, Sumer (modern-day Iraq) in 1920, is considered to be the oldest game in recorded history.

2.  **False.** *Galaxy Game* was created at Stanford University by Bill Pitts and Hugh Tuck in 1971. This arcade game (a coin-operated game) was built using a DEC PDP-11/20, and only one was made.

3.  **B.** The title holder for the first digital game is often debated, but NIM can arguably be considered the first. Created in 1951 by Ferranti, it debuted at the Festival of Britain, and a computer (the Nimrod) was built just to play the game. *Spacewar!* is generally considered to be the first example of a *shooter*.

4.  **C.** Many of the precursors to board games that we are familiar with, such as *Snakes and Ladders*, were created to teach the players moral values of good deeds versus bad. *Snakes and Ladders* has its origins in India approximately 400 years ago, and one of its early names was *paramapada sopanam*—the ladder to salvation.

5.  **False.** The game is analog.

6.  **A.** *Travellers' Tour Through the United States* is recognized as being the first board game published in the United States. It was published in New York City by F. Lockwood, a bookseller. The year was 1822, during a time in the United States when culture was shifting away from a primarily agrarian society to a more urban lifestyle that provided more leisure time and a rise in income for many Americans.

# Chapter 2

1.  **B.** *Colossal Cave Adventure*, which is based on Mammoth Cave in Kentucky, was the first adventure game. *Civilization* is a simulation game, *World of Warcraft* is an action/adventure/RPG massive multiplayer game, and *Wolfenstein 3D* is classified as being a first-person shooter.

2.  **True.** Immersive games tend to have multiple things moving and many overlapping sounds during play, giving the gamer the opportunity to feel that the world is more real.

3.  **D.** A strategy game is generally played between two or more players who take turns implementing their strategy during gameplay.

4.  **False.** The system is voluntary. However, many retail stores only stock games that are rated.

5.  **C.** *Presence* references how humans can extend their perceptions beyond the physical limitations of their sensory organs. When playing an immersive game, the player temporarily perceives two realities (environments): the one in which they live and the one that they perceive through the digital medium of the game.

# Chapter 3

1.  **C.** The success or failure of a game hinges on the gameplay. Regardless of how amazing the characters, environments, and quests may be, if the gameplay isn't fun and intriguing, the project will suffer.

2.  **True.** Designers who need to work with people or animals should mimic correct movement as much as possible. Understanding anatomy helps the artist know what muscles groups are moving and why. Should your task be to create something otherworldly, it's incredibly helpful to know anatomy so you're aware of the size and shape of muscles that perform specific functions in humans and animals. For example, if you need to put wings on a creature, then look at winged animals and see how the muscle structure works so you can adapt that to your own design.

3.  **B.** Lore is the backstory for the game and is generally required for immersive RPG, action/adventure, and adventure games. The lore explains the origins of characters, places, and conflicts that can drive the game.

4.  **True.** Flowcharts are wonderful tools that you can use to help organize when and where events occur in games.

5.    **C.** When you create an environment, there is the visual component of how it looks; however, the game uses animation and the engine to show how the player moves through the world. Some elements in the environment can affect movement, such as constant wind, severe weather, time warps slowing movement, and so on.

# Chapter 4

1.    **D.** All of these are excellent reasons why a designer will want to come up with a variety of designs to review during the initial concept art phase.

2.    **False.** Although the finished game may indeed look and feel just like the vertical slice, the "slice" is meant to show, during very early phases of design and production, how the gameplay works. It can do that using temp art pieces, animation, and audio.

3.    **C.** Demographic refers to who the audience is. This can mean age group, sex, race, or cultural values. Understanding the demographic when designing games helps pinpoint what things may be more successful based on other things that demographic tends to like.

4.    **True.** A way-cool character is fun to look at. But if the gameplay is not fun, no one will play the game, and the character will soon be forgotten.

5.    **C.** Concept-vis is not a type of previs. Essentially, all types of previsualization deal with concept work.

# Chapter 5

1.    **C.** The isometric type of axonometric projection shows three faces to any object, like a building, that are all the same size.

2.    **False.** The demographic for a game is the audience it is designed for.

3.    **False.** Most games played are categorized as E for everyone by the ESRB rating system as reported by the ESA.

4.    **B.** Games are designed using either first-person or third-person POV.

5.    **True.** These kinds of backgrounds allow for infinite scrolling.

# Chapter 6

1. **False.** QA refers to a specific department in a gaming company—Quality Assurance and Software Testing. Because the success of a game relies so heavily on feedback from game testing, many companies farm that work out to third-party companies that provide intense, highly structured testing scenarios.

2. **B.** The HUD is the visual component on the screen that allows a player to see the state of the character or environment and can include health, points, time, and so on. The term comes from the heads-up display created by the military, which displays critical data about an aircraft directly on the pilot's faceplate or windshield so the pilot can keep their head up and not have to look down to read dials in the cockpit.

3. **False.** A diegetic interface is part of the gameplay. It's often shown as the dials on the dashboard of a car. The game *Dead Space* uses a diegetic interface: marks on the avatar's space suit show the health of the avatar.

4. **True.** An argument exists among game designers as to which approach to designing games is better: linear or nonlinear games. Statistics in sales and feedback from gamers indicates there are likes and dislikes with both styles, so it is likely both styles will continue to exist.

5. **A.** The EULA is an agreement, provided by the game company to the purchasers of their game, that outlines the user's rights and permissions as granted by the designer. The purchaser must agree to it in order to gain access to the game.

# Chapter 7

1. **A, D.** This term is used to describe the job of the person who designs a level and the software that is used to compile all of the pieces made for a level. Many games today come with level editors built right into them so players can make their "mods" or custom levels to play in based on the components provided with the game like characters, architectural and landscape elements and sound.

2. **True.** The array method shows a snapshot, moving footage or a graphic that represents another location in the game the player can jump to. This is another type of navigation in a game different from using a map.

3. **A.** In this type of game design, the spatial layout provides a central hub that tends to be a bit friendlier for the player, a place they leave from and return to without fear. The larger challenges tend to be out on the spokes.

4. **C.** A launch icon is a shortcut a gamer can click to launch their game.

5.    **D.** Everything that is designed for a game is written down in the game design document. It is used to organize the gameplay and to communicate to others on the team what needs to be created for each part of the game. The GDD contains the name of the game, the genre (gameplay style), information on the demographic, and detailed information on the purpose and play of the game. All of the information in the GDD is fluid and can be tweaked as the game is actually built.

# Chapter 8

1.    **A.** Composers brought onto a project to write and record original music create variations of the music that are delivered in sections called stems. The audio producer decides how to add them to the game. Stems can also be variations of the same piece of music so the producer can build up the music for a scene or have it playing quietly in the background.

2.    **False.** Remote recording sessions happen on location. Unlike generating audio in a controlled environment, the goal is to record live noises, primarily for ambient sounds.

3.    **D.** Layering is a method where simple or complex music or ambient sounds are combined to add complexity and richer sound for the game.

4.    **True.** Location music is one way designers can add a signature sound to a specific region of the game. For example, only while in the capital city do players hear the music written specifically to complement gameplay in that area.

5.    **B.** As a player moves through a game world, they may hear sounds in the distance that become louder as they get closer to where the marker was placed in the environment. The marker serves as a programming switch to turn music on or off or adjust volume.

# Chapter 9

1.    **A.** Level design is very involved and gives the designer the ability to focus on gameplay by deciding how an area will be physically laid out and what events will occur there based on the needs of the story.

2.    **False.** This method, although widely used, generally is not accepted in a court of law, should an accusation of copyright infringement go to trial.

3.    **C.** If a game is designed for a PC (home computer system), the designer can pretty much use any keys or mouse controls they desire. If, however, the game needs to play on a commercial system such as an Xbox, Wii, or PlayStation, then the controls need to match the company's requirements for their controllers.

4.   **False.** Although one of the things programmers do for games is build the engine, commercial engines are available for sale or licensing, and there is also freeware that can be used.

5.   **D.** The role of the producer is primarily to help keep a project on time and on budget and make critical decisions if it gets derailed. Some producers work on the art or other aspects of production; however, concept work is not generally considered part of the job.

# Chapter 10

1.   **C.** Platforms are the systems that play games. A game must be designed specifically for a platform, whether PC, console, handheld, mobile, arcade, or online. A game may be played on a variety of platforms, but a separate version must be created to run on each platform.

2.   **False.** A portal is a website where gamers can download shareware or freeware games to play or become members, for a fee, to play the games in the portal's catalogue.

3.   **D.** Product placement, popularized in film and television, where actual products appear in shots, has successfully migrated into video games.

4.   **True.** Successful games are tested throughout their entire production process. A beta tester is someone who was not involved in the game and has no ties to the production company and can thereby provide objective feedback regarding gameplay.

5.   **B.** Advergames are small, casual games that are fun and easy to play and that showcase, in the game, the product they are advertising. You can view more advergames here: www.adverblog.com/category/advergames/.

# Education, Training, and Working in Games

*If you're interested in* getting a foothold in gaming, attending a school that specializes in teaching game-art courses, modeling, programming, or animation can be helpful, although a degree isn't necessary to gain entry into careers in this arena. Many people learn on the job—what are known as *journeyman skills*—and can start in entry-level positions or internships.

Job or internship seekers need to prepare a variety of materials to showcase themselves and their skills and find ways to interact with people in the field. This appendix discusses some of the materials that should be prepared and offers suggestions on ways to network and get training.

## Education

People seeking entry-level jobs with a degree or certificate in game-related fields may have a better chance of getting a position doing modeling, animation, level design, and interface design due to their specific training with schools that have curriculum geared to teach those skills. Anyone can apply for any advertised position in a gaming company, but in this competitive business, having experience and education is a plus.

Some schools you may wish to look at include the following:

▶ Carnegie Mellon University: www.etc.cmu.edu

▶ Art Institutes (offers online courses as well): www.artinstitutes.edu

▶ DigiPen: www.digipen.edu

▶ Full Sail University: www.fullsail.edu

▶ University of Southern California (has an extensive interactive media division): http://interactive.usc.edu

- ▶ University of Utah: www.eae.utah.edu

- ▶ Michigan State University (has an extensive Serious Games design division): www.seriousgames.msu.edu

- ▶ Worcester Polytechnic Institute: www.wpi.edu

- ▶ Drexel University (offers online courses): www.drexel.com

- ▶ Champlain College: www.champlain.edu

- ▶ Rochester Institute of Technology: www.rit.edu

- ▶ Becker College: www.becker.edu

Some of these schools, as noted in the list, offer online courses. Many more schools, even at the time this book was being written, are developing curriculum and portals for online courses. Investigate the websites, and do research on your own, to locate schools that can provide solid curriculum for the areas in gaming that interest you. Also be sure to find out about the hiring success of their graduates.

Attaining a degree from one of these schools is time-consuming and can be quite expensive. Ask lots and lots of questions when looking at any of these institutions. Find out about job placement services, and ask to look at a list of graduates who have been successful at pursuing their career goals.

Many of the schools listed are career focused, or offer career-oriented programs and classes. If your interests are serious, then you may be more inclined to investigate these kinds of schools. They tend to have instructors who are currently working in the industry and maintain up-to-date technology and instruction so that graduating students will have an optimum chance of landing their dream job.

In addition, most schools today, particularly career-focused ones, have a placement service that assists students with getting an internship or, more important, a job. For example, schools may develop relationships with companies that are willing to hire students right out of school for entry-level positions.

# Getting Started in the Field

You may start your career in the gaming industry with an internship or with an entry-level job. Although related experience can help, these positions usually don't require it. As noted previously, if you're enrolled, your school may support you in finding a job or an internship.

You can do research on your own, too. Gaming companies often have information about jobs on their websites. Quite a few other websites host information about available jobs for entry-level work, including these:

▶ Game Industry Grunts: www.gameindustrygrunts.com

▶ Get In Media jobs in the entertainment industry: www.getinmedia.com

▶ GameJobs: www.gamejobs.com

Two websites that contain excellent information about internships are www.gamasutra.com and www.gamecareerguide.com. *Game Developer*, an online magazine, also offers useful information regarding jobs and internships: www.gdmag.com.

Other sites to review for information about jobs and internships and the state of industry are these:

▶ Game Developers Conference (GDC): www.gdconf.com

▶ Association for Computing Machinery: www.acm.org

▶ Special Interest Group on Computer Graphics and Interactive Techniques (SIGGRAPH): www.siggraph.org

▶ Game Developers: www.gamedev.net

▶ Game Artist Forums: www.game-artist.net

## OPEN-SOURCE PROJECTS

Open-source sites are another resource for job seekers. Often, small teams of people working with Open GL are making independent projects and looking for crew members. OpenGL (Open Graphics Library) is a royalty-free application programming interface (API) provided by the Khronos Group. Open-source sites include these:

▶ Crystal Space: www.crystalspace3d.org

▶ OpenGL: www.opengl.org

It's good to review what the best-selling games are (successful companies are more likely to have jobs available) and also what the average salaries are in the industry. The following site contains some of that information: http://www.gamecareerguide.com/features/980/game_developer_salary_survey_.php.

## Entry-Level Jobs

Entry-level positions include the following:

**Testing (Part of the Q/A Team)**   Many companies accepting applications for jobs or internships in the testing department require the applicant to submit their review for a game or games they have played. Do some research on how reviews are written. One of the best sites to find reviews is www.gamasutra.com.

**Customer Service**   Entering into this area lets you learn some of the behind-the-scenes aspects of how gaming companies are run. Primary duties include interacting with customers who have purchased products (you'll need to learn about how the game is run, and help troubleshoot problems from FAQs prepared by the game makers) and passing along to the production team information about issues customers are having so they can be addressed.

**Clerical**   Pretty much any department in a company has clerical duties, and accepting a position here lets you interact with the producers, art directors, animators, and so on. Primarily, these jobs involve filing assets related to games, double-checking that naming conventions and formats are correct, and managing office supplies.

**Junior Programmer**   In order to enter into game programming, you're expected to have knowledge of computer game languages (basic C++ and Visual Basic are good examples) and a demo portfolio (information about preparing demos is covered later, in the "Applying for Jobs and Internships" section of this appendix).

**Assistant Producer**   Also known as a junior producer, this person typically facilitates communication between teams, helps the producer keep schedules to ensure timely delivery of assets during different phases of a game's production, and assists with the day-to-day running of the project. It's typical, especially on large projects, for an assistant producer to be assigned to one area of the game to monitor production and communicate information between the producer and team leaders.

## Internships

Internships are another way to enter and gain experience in the field. Internships are sometimes paid, although most are non-paid but allow the intern the opportunity to learn on the job and network with seasoned professionals. If you're a student at a school that offers game art courses, then it would be in your best interest to find out if you can also get course credit for your internship. Many schools offer such opportunities.

Locating an internship in a gaming company is an excellent way to get career experience in the industry. Keep in mind that you'll be competing with people who are in school or recent graduates with a game art, animation, or programming degree. If you aren't in school or don't have a degree at this time, that shouldn't stop you from applying. There are plenty of opportunities to apply for internships, and once you get one, you can learn a tremendous amount about career pursuits and how the business works.

When you apply for an internship, demonstrating that you're enthusiastic about the opportunity is a plus. If a specific area of gaming interests you, career-wise, then indicate that. But if you aren't sure what area you're aiming for, it's fine to be open to learning different parts of the business. Exposure from your internship will help you understand how various jobs are accomplished and what areas you may wish to pursue as a career.

In other words, if you're offered an interview for an internship, and you indicate that you're so determined to do one thing and one thing only, then the company interviewing you may believe you aren't interested in learning about other parts of the business where the company needs an intern. The company then may not want you on board. Being flexible is in your best interest.

# Applying for Jobs and Internships

The bulk of your efforts in applying to any company will consist of assembling a body of work that demonstrates your skills. If you don't have any yet (and even if you do), you should prepare a clear, concise resume and cover letter to accompany any demos or paperwork you submit that explains your career goals.

Research the company or companies you apply to so that you can understand their products, what kinds of jobs they offer, what training they expect or offer (entry-level positions sometimes offer training, especially with proprietary products the company uses), and how successful they have been. Startup companies often promise the moon and want to rush you on board, and everything may sound great, but they tend to be risky. More established companies, although harder to get into, are well worth the effort of preparing application materials.

There are two highly important items you'll need to create and update regularly as you apply for jobs: your portfolio and your resume.

You should consider including these three formats in your portfolio:

- ▶ Flatbook (printed pages in a bound book, and often referred to as a portfolio
- ▶ Digital reel
- ▶ Website

Many companies request web portfolios or samples online, websites, or blogs. The flatbook is becoming less important, and the demo reel can be embedded in a website; however, the information covered in this appendix can apply to work that can be showcased on the website. Sometimes the flatbook is a nice take-along to show a potential employer work in more detail. Professional online forums are also a good place to display work and get feedback from game pros.

Be aware that many companies that allow you to submit work for a job or internship application have specific requirements regarding what they want to see. Check their websites, look at the Jobs or Careers section, and see if requirements are listed. Adhere to those guidelines; otherwise, you can pretty much count on your submission being discarded.

Send *only* the materials accepted by the company you're applying for, in the correct formats. The following is a list of things most companies look for in a submission:

- ▶ Submit your movie reels on a DVD, with a cover that shows your name, contact information, and specialty. If the company you're applying to doesn't specify a format, a QuickTime movie usually works well and allows the viewer to easily toggle through frame by frame if they choose.

- ▶ Running time for reels should be about 1–4 minutes. Music is good, but not necessary, and it shouldn't be offensive or overwhelming.

- ▶ Put your most recent, best work at the beginning of the reel.

- ▶ Include a printed breakdown explaining what you did in any particular shot (this is especially important if you're submitting work done by a crew, and others contributed) along with the type of software used.

- ▶ Portfolios (printed samples) should be submitted in a folder or inexpensive binder that doesn't need to be returned.

Following instructions is, believe it or not, one of the hardest things for people to do. Read the directions a few times if necessary. Make sure you're submitting all required materials and that they're in the appropriate format. Remember, different companies have their own specific guidelines. Make sure you understand them before applying. Don't send more than what they ask for.

When you're preparing work to showcase your skills, make an attempt to demonstrate abilities with both 2D and 3D.

Once you have a job, keep following directions. One of the top reasons people are dismissed from jobs shortly after they're hired is that they can't follow instructions.

## The Flatbook (Portfolio)

When preparing a flatbook for submission, you'll want to include 5–12 pages of your best work that show solid art skills, include a variety of media, and are extremely neat, orderly, and well presented. Again, any work you prepare for your flatbook can be optimized and placed on your website. Here are some general guidelines:

▶ Create a title page that states your name, phone number (extremely important), email address, specialty (modeling, environments, rigging, and so on), and website address.

▶ Avoid titles or copy of any kind other than credits for professional work on pages that display the work.

▶ Avoid patterned or brightly colored backgrounds, borders, scroll work, drop shadows, and other page adornments. None of those things will make your work look better.

▶ Let the art be the star of the page.

▶ Design clean, neat, orderly, easy-to-view pages.

▶ Combine similar images onto a page in an uncluttered fashion.

▶ Always include your contact information on every page. You can place the contact information wherever you like, but don't let it compete with the artwork. Be sure the phone number is highly visible. Avoid using fonts that are too flourishy. Keep it simple, clean, and easy to read.

▶ Keep a white border at the page edges, so your printer won't cut things off (this is known as the *safezone*): ½" for the top and sides, and ⅝" at the bottom. Having a bit more white space at the bottom helps weight the page better.

Figure B.1 shows a sample page showcasing environments created for games. A good rule of thumb is that bigger images on a page work better than many small images.

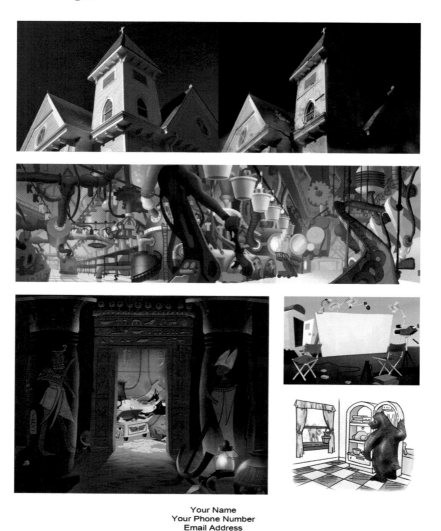

Your Name
Your Phone Number
Email Address
Website

**FIGURE B.1** Sample flatbook page showcasing environments created for games

It's fine to use both portrait and landscape layouts (vertical and horizontal), but group them together so the person reviewing your work isn't constantly having to turn the book.

# Flatbooks Are Rarely Returned

When you submit a flatbook for job or internship applications, there is a very good chance you won't get it back. Many people apply to game companies, and unless you go to extraordinary lengths to provide shipping or offer to come pick up your flatbook, getting it back isn't always possible. Be savvy about your methods for putting together a good-looking flatbook without spending a fortune.

Printing color pages on a home computer system is totally acceptable. Choose a good quality paper. Avoid using bond, and instead try using a glossy, bright white paper that is photo quality (or close to it). Something like that will show off your work the best.

If you don't have a printer at your disposal, plenty of printing companies (FedEx Office, for example) provide this service at a reasonable cost. If you choose a commercial printing company, request a sample printed page first to check how the artwork looks.

# Binding Flatbook Materials

Once you get your pages printed, how do you submit the work?

Again, review the submission policies and recommendations for any company you're applying to. If the company doesn't specify how it wishes to receive printed material, then we suggest printing your pages (like the example shown in Figure B.1) as a standard U.S. paper size—8.5″ × 11″—and placing them into a folio or binder.

Many binder brands on the market are inexpensive and lightweight (remember, you probably need to mail it). We're partial to the folios available from Staples (although many similar stores let you physically buy the item or order online).

Shop for a presentation folio that has pages (10 pages usually works well because you can insert your printed pages back to back) and also a pocket for your DVD (on which you burn your reel) and a business card. Often, you can neatly place your printed resume and cover letter in the folio as well.

Your folio should be clean and neat. Aim for a sturdy, professional-looking presentation, but don't spend more than a few dollars on it. Remember, you may not get it back!

If you buy a folio that contains pages you don't use, cut out the extra pages before you ship. The only things you should ever include in a flatbook are pages with work. Don't send empty pages.

## Types of Flatbooks

The following is a list of types of flatbooks you can prepare, depending on your interests and the type of job or internship you're applying for:

**Art**   Avoid copying other artists' work. In other words, don't include your drawing of Spiderman or copies of *World of Warcraft* characters. Do your best to show original work. Art directors who want to hire artists or interns are looking for the basics: perspective, anatomy, life drawing, gesture drawing, environments/landscapes, and portraiture—good, solid drawing skills.

▶ Showcase only your best work, and place the best of that on the first page (never the last).

▶ Don't use pieces in progress.

▶ Avoid titles unless absolutely necessary.

▶ If you're showcasing 3D models, then show your process, how many polygons were used, and how well you constructed the topology.

▶ When showcasing 3D character or creature models, pose them. Avoid leaving them in the T-pose, and be sure to have them textured and lit. It's also a good idea to place a character in a background, similar to where you might see them in a game, although that isn't totally necessary—it's just a good way to help set your work apart.

If the art you're showing was professional work (and that can include work you've done on production teams in school or with friends creating your own game), then add a title explaining the name of the project, what kind of project it was, and what medium you used is standard.

**Modeling**   An enormous amount of 3D work is done for games these days, and most companies are always on the lookout for good artists with 3D skill sets.

▶ Choose your best work for the first piece.

▶ Pose models, but avoid leaving figures in the T-pose.

▶ Show your process. This is extremely important. Figure B.2 shows how you can set a model up from mesh to finish, textured, painted model. Unless you're applying for a texture-painting job, it isn't necessary to include the map used for adding the texture and paint to the figure.

Character                                                                retopologized low-poly mesh

(Image courtesy of Artery Studios)

**FIGURE B.2**  Setup from mesh to textured, painted model

> ► Include a good variety of models. For character creation, have at least one realistic figure. Include bipedal figures and quadrupeds. Many games being made now use 3D models and have very realistic characters, including *Gears of War, Grand Theft Auto*, and *Splinter Cell*.

**Interfaces**    Because every game has an interface, and the look and feel of the game needs to be reflected in this functional piece of art, studios are often looking for artists whose work shows a strong range of style. Create new pieces to show, but also consider redesigning an existing interface that will match the look and feel of the game and clearly show ease of function—in other words, can the player find things they need to interact with on your sample interfaces?

> ► Show a variety of interface examples.

> ► Include images, or callouts from the full screen, showing rollover and click states.

> ► If you're showing an interface for an original project, include a short description of the gameplay style, genre, and platform (the platform is important because the interface for a tiny screen on a handheld should be larger and easier to see than a game played with a larger monitor).

# Reel Types (Digital)

As with your flatbook, anything that goes into your reel needs to be your strongest work. Reel lengths should be about 1–4 minutes. Anything more than 4 minutes is a bit long. If your strengths aren't evident in the first few seconds, it's unlikely that anyone will watch to the end. Here are some things you should consider when creating your reel:

► Always include a title card at the beginning and end of the reel (hold it for 3–5 seconds).

► Usually, light gray type on black works well for titles. Keep it simple and easy to read.

► Include your name, phone number, and specialty (animation, modeling, environments, and so on).

► If you're showing cycles, repeat them two to three times.

► If you're showcasing performance animation, try to include one or two that showcase lipsync and/or characters interacting with each other.

► Having music to play with your reel is usually a good idea; however, avoid music that is too loud or distracting.

► End by showing the title card again.

# Types of Animation Reels

Animators are always in demand for video games. People who apply to gaming companies for work in this area come not only from gaming backgrounds but also from animation for television, feature films, shorts, and web design. You should show specific types of experience in a reel.

**Character Animation**    If you're looking to do character animation in the industry, then you should showcase performance animation. Avoid walk or run cycles because those are extremely rudimentary and considered student projects (this includes bouncing ball and jumping flour sack exercises). Some of the more interesting cycles you may want to consider include dying, fighting, and idles. If you're showcasing animation with a humanoid, then show realistic movement, along with more fantastic actions like over-the-top fighting or casting spells. It's also in your best interest to showcase a quadruped character.

**Technical Animation**   This animation shows buttons being pushed on an inter-face, or unique ways to present reward animations or things moving on the toolbar when you access them. This type of animation can also include weather, cloth, hair, and fuzzy objects, so being able to work with particles is extremely important. When you showcase particle work, include the process. In other words, show the dynamic simulations you created along with a short movie demonstrating what the animation looks like.

# Types of Modeling Reels

As mentioned previously, modelers tend to be in demand for gaming proj-ects. Even 2D games need 3D modelers to help develop characters, props, and environments.

For any 3D model being showcased in a reel, show your process, including the concept drawings and the mesh. All models must have textures; those that don't generally aren't considered.

Some of the types of modeling reels are as follows:

**Character**   Show at least one realistic human, bipedal characters, and quadru-peds. Avoid showcasing a model by rotating it. If you're showing figures, then pose them or have them animate slightly to indicate clearly that the models work and won't break when moved.

**Props**   Weapons, carts, airplanes, cars—generally large, complex objects dem-onstrate skill better than small handheld ones.

**Environments**   Some of the modeling that is done for games is derived directly from an engine (like Unreal), but many games have large crews of 3D modelers devoted to creating environments. Prepare a range of examples, from highly architectural structures to organic shapes like rocks or trees. Move the camera through the environment at about the eye level of a character, to indicate what a player might experience if playing in a world of your creation. Show your pro-cess, and be sure to texture and light the images.

**Rigging**   A number of different rigs can be created for 3D models. Riggers have a unique skill set, in that they need to be able to build the rigs and also interact with the animators (or animation director). The animators, after all, are the ones who need to operate the rig, so the rigger will need to communicate with them and learn what kinds of movements the character needs to make. When showcasing rigs, show the controls, and provide some movement of the figure to show how the rig works and that you're able to avoid interpolation of the figure.

# Web Portfolios

As you work on your reel and flatbook, you should invest time in creating a website for yourself as well. Having a website allows you to instantly update your work and contact information. It also gives you an easy way to let others see your work. You can share a link through a network like LinkedIn or post the link on sites such as www.conceptart.org. Often, the first exposure prospective video game employees have is through their websites.

Review this appendix's information regarding what kinds of work you should include in a reel and a flatbook, and use those same guidelines to determine what you'll showcase on a website. Although you can add other features to a website, such as fun, splashy music and animations, keep in mind that your work needs to be the star. Adding too many animations that don't relate to what your work is about is distracting. Keep the design clean and neat and the navigation extremely clear and easy to use. If someone can't find their way around your site, they will quickly pass it by.

Setting up a website doesn't need to be expensive; for the most part, unless it's your choice to hire a designer, you can do it on your own. Keep in mind that creating the site is just half the task. Once the design is ready, it must be published to the Web. To do that, you'll need to purchase a URL (the website address), also known as the *domain name*, and pay for publishing the site (most companies offer to do that for a year at a time). The following is a short list of companies that offer these services:

- ▶ www.vistaprint.com

- ▶ www.webs.com

- ▶ www.thesitewizard.com (this service also provides an excellent FAQ on how to make a site)

- ▶ www.netidnow.com

When you get your website set up, be sure to test it to make sure the address works and everything can be viewed. Also check the limitations of the site you're making—in other words, can you make changes to the site after you've published it? Some services don't allow that; or, if they do, they charge a substantial fee. One of the reasons you have a website to showcase your work is so you can update it frequently, so make sure you read all the restrictions that might apply.

Here are a couple of websites that artists use to showcase their work. Do your research! Look at other websites, especially from artists who are involved in careers that interest you:

- ▶ www.maritimecathedral.com: Work from animator Richard Sternberg

- ▶ www.paisleyshark.com: Work from environment artist Briar Lee Mitchell

- ▶ http://reels.creativecow.net/c/Animation: Work from a wide variety of animators

- ▶ www.cgsociety.org: Also showcases a wide variety of reels

- ▶ www.deviantart.com: Another wide variety of reels

# Copyright

Frequently, students ask if they should copyright material that goes into a reel or flatbook for a job/internship submission or what they showcase on a website. If the work is yours, you don't need to obtain a copyright for a reel or flatbook; but if you feel compelled to do so, keep it simple and avoid distracting from the work. For work on your website that is yours, include a line of copy somewhere on the site that simply but clearly states that the work is copyright protected.

If you're showcasing work from other sources on your reel, in your flatbook, or on your website (for example, from a job you did or from a project you worked on with others), then indicate who owns the work. For example, if you place an image on your reel from a game you made for Company X, add a short line of copy, discreetly but clearly written, that indicates the work is owned by Company X.

# Materials for Other Positions

You may have other interests in the industry, such as writing, producing, audio, or programming. In those areas, you'll still want to prepare work to present that indicates your interests and level of skill:

**Writer**   The following things are useful to include with your resume and application if your interests lie in writing for games:

- ▶ Game Design Document (GDD): Prepare a short but well written, abridged version of a GDD.

- ▶ Narrative: Write a sample quest line (preparing a flowchart with it is a useful task, to more clearly demonstrate how the quest line works)

- ▶ Add some art for a character, and write a description of the character's abilities and traits.

**Level Designer**   As we discussed in Chapter 7, "Designing Levels and the Game Design Document," for this type of application you should come up with a visual of some sort that represents the environment and then design the events that will occur and where they're located.

Keep the map and events simple and clear, and demonstrate that you know how to avoid clustering too many occurrences together. Prepare a range of styles, and also show where the hookups can be and how they work logically. (A *hookup* is where one level connects to another.)

**Producer** Quite a few internships and entry-level jobs are available for assistant producers (and clerical positions, which can provide similar on-the-job learning). Good organizational skills are prized here, and the ability to run programs such as Microsoft Word, Excel, and MS Project and use Gantt charts is a huge plus. Excel can create Gantt charts, but some excellent ones are available online (for example, www.ganttchart.com).

Prepare a short example of how you would chart progress for a game. Be prepared to demonstrate how you can revise the chart if certain areas of production become bogged down. Understanding budgets is also a good skill set to demonstrate.

More than anything, demonstrating that you're reliable and detail-oriented is critical to landing a position.

**Audio** As reviewed in Chapter 8, "Sound," understanding what types of audio are used in games and how they're created is where you should start with your application. If your interest is in creating scores, then prepare two or three samples that demonstrate a range of emotional impact. Create a scary one, a happy one, a military one, and so on.

A fun method for demonstrating audio skills is to capture some action from a game you like and redesign the audio.

## CREATING AN AUDIO REEL

To capture action to create your reel, there are a variety of capturing programs you can use for free. Some of them offer trial versions with watermarks, which is fine. After all, you're interested in showcasing the audio, not the video.

Some of these capturing programs are as follows:

- ► Fraps: www.fraps.com
- ► Camtasia Studio: www.camtasia.com
- ► LiteCam: www.innoheim.com/litecam.php
- ► RipTiger: www.riptiger.com

*(Continues)*

**CREATING AN AUDIO REEL** *(Continued)*

Capture a segment of two or three different types of games, like a casual game, a MMO, and an RPG. Have characters or objects (such as the gun in a Snood game) to use for your demo. In your reel, run the actual video first, and then run two or three examples of how you would redesign the audio for a different feel to the gameplay. For example, if you show a segment of gameplay from a shooter, then create your audio with different shooting sounds from cartoony to hardcore. Make sure your timing is as correct as possible.

Another interesting approach to designing audio demo reels is to use a short piece of footage from a feature film. For example, take one of the more intense scenes from *Jaws* and run the original audio first, and then run a version where you completely change the feel of the scene by creating your own soundtrack, including music track, dialogue, and sound effects.

You're demonstrating your ability to affect the mood of the gameplay or scene, which is the job of any audio designer in the industry. By providing a few variations, you're again demonstrating exactly what any working audio designer would do: provide variations for the producer of the project to select from that complement the gameplay.

**Programming**   This type of work is highly specialized, and most people seeking jobs in this area need to have an understanding of C/C++ and PC programming skills. Examples of how characters interact (such as fighting sequences), explosions, deformations, and cloth and other particle movements are excellent to include. Even if you're interested in a specialization, such as physics, gameplay, or special effects, it's good to show examples of different types of programming to demonstrate your range of skills.

In addition, showing programming skills for interfaces such as the menu, sign-in screen, loading screen, and high-score table is beneficial.

When you prepare any type of demo for a prospective company, understand that your job is to realize someone else's vision. If you work for a company, you'll be called upon to come up with original ideas from time to time; however, your main job description will entail working with a team to create a game that is driven by someone other than you.

## Resume and Cover Letter

Applications for internships require you to fill out the usual paperwork for the job. Don't worry if your resume doesn't have game industry experience on it. That is one of the reasons you're seeking the internship or entry-level position.

Your resume should contain your contact information at the top and then clearly and concisely state your goals. For example, if you want to do 3D character modeling in the game industry, list that first.

Below that, by year (starting with the most recent year), list your education and work experiences. Don't worry if the jobs you post on your resume aren't directly related to the game industry. If you're on the starting line, that is to be expected. Entry-level or intern applicants often have little or no experience in gaming. If that is the case, then you should prepare your resume to indicate that you're responsible and can work with others.

Along with your resume, you should write a cover letter to accompany any materials being submitted. Tailor your cover letter for each application. Your cover letter is where you can go into more depth about your enthusiasm, but keep it professional, to the point, and relevant for a particular company. Demonstrate that you understand the company and its products.

# Networking

Networking is an important activity when you're seeking your first job in the gaming industry. In fact, most people who have been working in game art for some time will probably tell you they got their start through someone they knew.

How does that happen? There are many steps you can take to make connections with people in the industry:

**Join Professional Organizations**    Become a member of groups like the International Game Developers Association (IGDA), and take advantage of opportunities they have for those interested in entering the industry. For example, you can enter competitions, attend special events, and accept invitations to hear guest speakers.

There are a variety of websites where you can network with others and gain experience through tutorials:

> ▶ GameConnection: www.game-connection.com

> ▶ LinkedIn: www.linkedin.com

- ▶ Video Game Professionals: www.videogameprofessionals.org

- ▶ Game Mentor Online: http://archives.igda.org/women/gmo.html

**Attend Events**    Conferences and expos give you a chance to speak with people in the industry and attend the mixers and job fairs that are usually held at these events. Industry events include the following:

- ▶ GDC: www.gdconf.com

- ▶ SIGGRAPH: www.siggraph.org

- ▶ Electronic Entertainment Expo (E3): www.e3expo.com

- ▶ IGDA conference: www.igda.org

**Participate in Online Communities**    Online forums like ConceptArt (www.conceptart.org) allow you to get feedback from other people who view your work and also post links to your work for a prospective employer.

Other sites that support discussion about the industry are these:

- ▶ GameArtist: www.game-artist.net

- ▶ Polycount: www.polycount.com/forum

- ▶ GameArtisans: www.gameartisans.org/forums/index.php

**Read and Respond to Blogs**    Quite a few people working in the industry, both game makers and reviewers, maintain blogs about the state of business. Here are some blogs you may want to check out:

- ▶ Top Indie Game Development Blogs: www.gameartisans.org/forums/index.php

- ▶ GameDevBlog: www.gamedevblog.com

- ▶ Developer Blogs: www.1UP.com

**Make Mods**    Making a mod (short for *modification*) means building a level or levels using the environments and characters from an existing game. In doing so, it's also common to adjust the look and abilities of characters and structure new environments for them to play in. Many of the larger game companies maintain sites you can visit with complete instructions on how to mod. These companies usually enjoy supporting the creation of mods because it allows fans to further explore the games, and maintains interest in their products. Creating mods can be fun—and a good tool for people trying to break into the gaming industry.

The following is a list of some of those sites (the ability to make mods tends to be free):

▶ Valve (*Portal, Half-Life, Counterstrike*): www.developer.valvesoftware .com/wiki/Making_a_Mid.com

▶ Unreal (game engine): www.udk.com and www.wiki.beyondunreal.com

▶ Mod DB (contains blogs, tutorials, and links to other sources for creation of mods): www.moddb.com

**Work with Recruiters**    There are companies and individuals that help people land jobs in the industry. For the most part, they tend to shy away from those who are just getting started. Recruiters are generally used by people applying for upper-level positions and aren't the best source if you're seeking an entry-level job or internship. But if you've tried other options with no success, you can contact them to see if their services might be useful. Two recruiters are Mary-Margaret Network (www.mary-margaret.com) and Interactive Selection (www .interactiveselection.com).

The bottom line is that you're interested in working for the gaming industry, either for a company, for yourself, or with a small group of friends or like-minded designers, to create original games. Review every option you can to reach your goals.

The game industry is lucrative and employs tens of thousands of people, but it's in flux. Technology has a huge impact on how games are played and produced, so stay current, continue to read as much as possible, network as much as you can, and play as many games as you can.

# Game Design Document

*Bedlam Games, located in* Toronto, Canada, and makers of the Dungeons & Dragons games, work routinely with Game Design Documents. The following is an excerpt from their GDD for the game *Red Harvest*. The excerpt was prepared by their creative director, Zando Chan.

Notice that the GDD contains references to audio, scripted dialogue, lore, level design (map and metrics, which are the dimensions of the space), concept art for the characters, description of the actions, and information about the interfaces including the importance of a timer.

Keep in mind that what you are reading is part of an actual GDD that many different artists, programmers, animators, etc. worked from to build the game. As you read, imagine what role you might adopt for such a project. Pay special attention to the information provided for whatever role you might take on, and determine then, how you have complete instructions on what to create, but plenty of room to develop your part of the project based on the skills and experience you would bring to the team.

## *Red Harvest* Overview

Your bus has crashed in the town of Crestwood and you are the only survivor. *Red Harvest* is a third-person true survival-horror game with innovative new mechanics that redefine the genre to heart-pounding effect. With demonic enemies attacking from every direction, you must make your way through the town in order to survive. Use fortification to buy precious time for your escape. Discover weapon improvisation using everyday objects found throughout the town and do whatever it takes to outlast your enemies. This unique blend of action and horror creates a new player experience that induces primal fear and tension in players, simultaneously empowering them with tools to confront challenges in a close, visceral way. *Red Harvest* is a world of nightmares and terror that will test your limits in order to survive.

# Player Characters

There are two playable characters in the game. Player one plays as Sam Wells, a blues musician, and player two plays as Job, an electrician.

Over the course of the game story, each of the protagonists faces nightmarish creatures and their own dark secrets.

## Sam Wells (Player Character 1)

**Height:** 6′
**Weight:** 181 lbs
**Age:** 44
**Complexion:** Caucasian
**Hair:** Silver, long
**Build:** Tall, thin, and wiry
**Nationality:** U.S.A.
**Background:**
Sam Wells is a 46-year-old blues master. He has been playing the blues guitar from the day his mother bought him a cherry-red Stratocaster for his sixth birthday. He's average height, scruffy-haired, flecks of grey blending with a permanent stubble. Never caught without his leather boots and guitar, he has lived most of his life as an enigma, a wandering traveler with no family and no connections. Finding session gigs wherever he can, he travels by bus to wherever he feels like going. He is revealed to be suffering from signs of schizophrenia, as a coping mechanism for the horrors he witnesses during *Red Harvest*.

## Job Waters (Player Character 2)

Height: 6′
Weight: 170 lbs
Age: 32
Complexion: Caucasian
Hair: Black
Build: Thin
Nationality: U.S.A.

Background:
Job is an electrician of average height, clean-shaven, with jet-black hair and fairly athletic. Job is an obsessive-compulsive perfectionist suffering schizophrenia who has been in and out of hospitals since he was a child. He developed night tremors and imaginary personas that dissipated once he was on the proper medication. Ultimately, Job is a figment of Sam's imagination, a result of Sam's schizophrenia.

# Narrative

## The Story of *Red Harvest*

*Red Harvest* is a story of panic and survival.

Sam Wells, a 46-year-old blues musician, boards a bus on an otherwise average mid-afternoon. He settles into his seat, falls asleep, and sets out on what appears to be an uneventful journey.

Sam awakes to find the bus has pulled over to the side of the road with its hazards blinking. Every passenger has vanished, save one: Job Waters, an electrician who seems to know less about what has happened to them than Sam does.

The two stranded passengers set out for a journey into the town of Crestwood, only to discover it is overrun with an endless array of disturbing creatures who wish nothing more than to add Sam and Job to the long list of missing townspeople. There is little choice but to run and attempt to fortify within any space available and with whatever dilapidated pieces of scrap are left for them. Weapons are scarce, food nonexistent, and each moment of life becomes more precious by the second. A breakneck tension takes an uncompromising hold on the events and refuses to let go. An uneasy feeling permeates the minds of the two survivors; there seems to be more to this forsaken spot of the earth than previously thought.

Their journey takes them through the various overrun hallmarks of the town: a farmhouse, a church, a warehouse and finally, the Crestwood police station, located on the downtown strip. Here they discover a seething nest, steadily spawning creatures to attack the town. Sam and Job take it upon themselves to raze the downtown core and thus, the nest, by lighting fortifications on fire. Successful, they escape to the bus station, steal a bus and leave the town hoping their nightmare is over. Sam, exhausted, collapses into a bus seat and falls asleep. He wakes only to discover he is in the exact same situation as he was when he arrived in Crestwood. The bus is pulled over, the hazards are blinking, and Job is nowhere to be seen. Unsure of whether Job was real or imagined, Sam breaks down under the pressure as a horde of new creatures descends upon the bus.

## *Red Harvest* Matinees

The *Red Harvest* matinees are comprised of motion comics that will serve as narrative devices used in the game. They include an introduction establishing the setting and characters, interstitials between the levels, and a conclusion to end the story.

### Opening intro (loads into Level 1, Farm)

1. Sam Wells is at a busy bus terminal in the city. The afternoon sun is bright and the city is loud: other cars, passengers, all make a

bustling combination of noise fighting for attention. There are several mechanics working on one bus. Sam sees a billboard that reads, "Learn a Trade, Find a Job" with an electrician posing beside it.

**2.** Sam lines up to put his luggage away and rudely reminds the porter to be careful with his guitar.

**3.** Sam boards the bus and looks around at the other passengers (this is where we show that Job is not on the bus). Disgusted by the noise and confusion, he puts his hat over his head and falls asleep, his eyes closing to black.

**4.** Sam jolts up only to find that the bus is empty. It is pitch black outside and the only sound that can be heard is the ticking of the hazard lights of the bus. Looking outside, Sam can see the road to one side and a dense forest on the other.

**5.** Sam starts to get up and walk off the bus and finds another passenger sleeping. He wakes the man up, an electrician named Job, who is equally confused, and the two get off the bus together.

**6.** Coming quickly to the conclusion that not much can be done at the bus, the two start walking to a farmhouse up the road in search of help and answers.

## Script

**EXT. BUS STATION—DAY**
We open to a billboard with a tagline that reads, "LEARN A TRADE, FIND A JOB" with an older, mid-50s bald man wearing a welder's mask underneath.

It stands above a crowded bus station, mid-afternoon. The sun is shining and the sky is clear. There are several buses, each with their own exclusive lines of people waiting to board.
**SFX:** Noise pollution: traffic, murmurs of conversation, city rumble.
SAM WELLS, 46, a scruffy blues guitar master, stands in line beside his bus, guitar case at his feet.

Sam watches the bus next to him. The bus is broken down with several mechanics examining it. They wear coveralls and are looking into the steaming, open engine. The potential passengers are already frustrated with the service.

A scrawny porter, no older than 20, grabs Sam's guitar to load it into the cargo carrier.

Wells suddenly GRABS the kid's arm.

SAM

That guitar is worth more than your weight in gold, kid.

Sam lets go of the stunned porter and boards the bus.

**CUT TO:**

**INT. BUS**

Sam gives his ticket to the driver and we follow his gaze as he scans the seats. The average mixture of students, new parents, lost fathers, all bundled together for the next 8 hours.

Sam finds his seat and sits down. The bus pulls away.

Sam's eyes close as he speaks, fading us to pulses of black.

**CUT TO:**

**INT. BUS—NIGHT**

Sam startles himself awake. The bus has stopped; the sun is gone, replaced by a cool night blue interrupted by the flash of the bus's hazard lights.

**SFX:** Hazards clicking (prominent), night country noises, i.e., crickets, ambience.

Sam is confused; he checks his surroundings, the bus looks completely empty. He gets up and walks to the front exit. He sees a young man dressed in coveralls sleeping with his head leaning against the window. Sam wakes the man, who is startled and confused.

SAM

Hey, you, what's going on?

JOB

(Startled, as if daydreaming, calm)
Oh, I'm not—I have no idea. Where...where is everyone?

Sam gives him a puzzled look. Sam isn't sure what to make of this kid.

                    SAM
Well, don't you think we should find out what the hell is goin' on?

                    JOB
Yeah, yes. Yes, we should.

**CUT TO:**

**EXT. HIGHWAY**

Sam and Job step off the bus. It is pulled over to the side of the road, hazards still blinking. On one side of the road is dense forest, on the other, a farmhouse in the distance.

                    SAM
So I doze off, and everyone's gone. No driver, no note, no nothing. Did you see where they went?

                    JOB
No, I don't know.

                    SAM
Were you asleep?

                    JOB
I think so.

                    SAM
You think so? How can you think so?

                    JOB
There's a farm up that hill, maybe they went there.

Sam stares at the silhouette of the lonely farmhouse ahead.

                    SAM
Let's get going then.

                    JOB
Yeah, sure, okay. Let's get going.

Sam gives Job an annoyed look as they walk towards the farmhouse.

# Levels

While chapters are sequential and linear, the challenges the protagonists have to face (and survive) in each chapter are not always linear, and can often be approached in any order. In this way, each chapter acts like a hub, with the players having to work together in order to survive and progress in any way they can.

Time management is a key to the players' survival. Distancing themselves from enemies and fortifying or barricading entryways will give them more time to solve gating devices. Levels are designed around balancing the resources of time, health, and weaponry. For instance, scenarios are presented in which the player can sacrifice some of his physical health in order to preserve time.

Interior environments will contain fortification points at doors, door frames, and windows. Fortifying these points prevents groups of enemies from entering a room through multiple entry points all at once. The player can shut and lock doors and windows, use found items to create a fortification, and move objects in front of doorways to form barricades.

The target playpath for the game is 90 minutes of gameplay spread out across multiple levels and gameplay modes. Each level will take approximately 15 minutes to complete.

## Level Design Metrics

| Fortification Point | Size (Unreal Units) | Notes |
| --- | --- | --- |
| Window | 144 wide × 128 high × 104 from the floor | This is the standard size for all fortifiable/vaultable interior windows. |
| Door Frame | 128 wide × 224 high | This is the standard size for all fortifiable interior door frames. |
| Vaultable Object | 216 wide × 104 from the floor | This is the standard size for all vaultable interactive objects. |
| Rollable Object | 136 wide× 120 from the floor × 256 deep | This is the standard size for all vaultable objects that the character rolls over. |

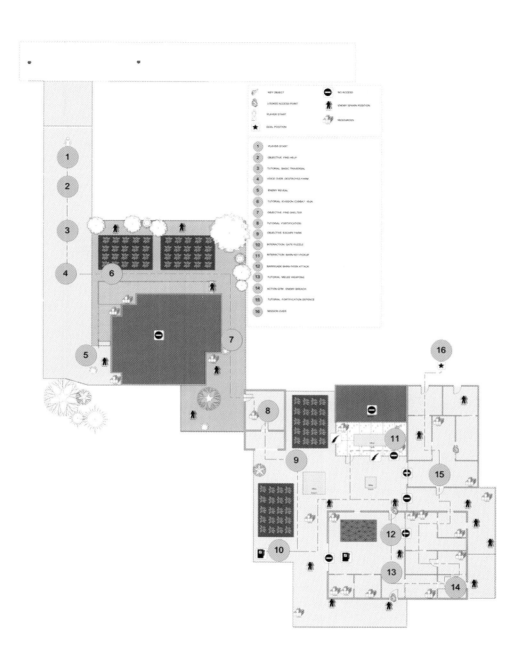

# Level 1—Farm

## Farm Walkthrough

1. Player wanders through a deserted farm field with a lone light source illuminating the barn next to the heavily damaged farmhouse.

2. Objective conveyed to player on HUD—Find help.

3. Basic traversal tutorial conveyed to player on HUD.

4. Player voice-over reacts to sight of smashed farmhouse.

5. Enemy Intro Matinee—A drone enemy jumps out of house and charges at the player.

6. Run and Evasion Combat tutorials conveyed to player on HUD.

7. While player evades multiple enemies around the farmhouse and goes to a shed, objective to find refuge in the shed is conveyed to player on HUD.

8. Player enters the shed behind the farmhouse and is presented with Fortification Tutorial via HUD. Player finds multiple resource piles in shed and fortifies the entrance, shaking the pursuit of the enemy creatures.

9. Player enters farm working area. He is presented with a new objective via the HUD—escape the farm.

10. He sees a few barn-like buildings and a key on the wall of a shed protected by an electric fence. Player must retrieve the key from behind the fence, but in order to do so must shut off the power to the farm at the electrical box across the yard. Touching the fence while it is electrified will deliver damage to the player character.

11. Once power to the fence is shut down, player retrieves the key and is ambushed by a large number of enemy creatures.

12. Player must retreat into the barn and begin to fortify the exits and entrances.

13. Inside the barn, player finds a melee weapon pickup. He is presented with the Weapon Combat Tutorial via the HUD.

14. Player must fight at multiple entry points to slow the decay of the fortifications and replenish when possible. At this point, near the back of the barn, an action QTM Event occurs in which an enemy lieutenant reaches through the window and attempts to grasp the player.

15. Player must use the weapon to break a fortification point blocking his path to the back of the barn. Player leaves barn and enters stable. Player reinforces fortification point and a Drone Enemy sticks its head through a gap in the fortification. Player is presented with the Fortification Defense Tutorial via the HUD.

16. Player must fight off limited horde numbers and escape through the back of the stable into a blood-soaked cornfield.

# Interface—HUD

## HUD Design

This section describes the appearance, layout, and functionality of the in-game HUD for *Red Harvest*.

### Overview

The HUD for *Red Harvest* keeps the screen traffic to a minimum, keeping most of the screen real estate free to show the action.

► The player's primary status cluster is visible at all times.

► Additional information, such as timers, ammo counts, and context-sensitive messaging, are only displayed at times in which they are relevant.

## HUD Elements

| HUD Element | Functionality |
| --- | --- |
| Health Meter | The health meter represents the amount of damage the player character can sustain before dying. |
| | The meter diminishes from right to left as damage is inflicted upon the player character. |
| | Once the player's health reaches a value of zero, the meter is fully depleted and the player character falls prone. |
| | In single player games, falling prone is as good as dead, and the game is over. In multiplayer games, prone characters can be revived by their partners and recover a limited amount of health in the process. |

| HUD Element | Functionality |
|---|---|
| Rage Meter | The rage meter represents the player character's anger and emotion level, and is used to enable the fatality mechanic. |
| | The meter increases from left to right as the player's rage grows. |
| | Rage increases by static amounts with successful attacks and shoves based on weapon type, but depletes again at a fixed, but slower, rate. |
| | Once the meter has reached its full capacity, the player can enter rage mode by holding the Special Attack Button. During rage mode, the player can initiate a fatality attack using the Special Attack Button. |
| | While the player is in rage mode, the edges of the screen flare with a deep red colour and the rage meter continues depleting at a steady rate. Once depleted, the screen returns to normal display. |
| Inventory and Ammo Gauge | The inventory and ammo gauge displays in the bottom right corner of the screen. |
| | This gauge is context-sensitive with the item or weapon in the player's hands and will reflect this with an appropriate icon and a number indicating the number of units in the player's inventory (i.e., shotgun shells, fortifying planks) |
| Message System | Messages that need to be communicated to the player (e.g., tutorial text) is displayed in the bottom centre of the screen. |

| HUD Element | Functionality |
|---|---|
| Ranged Weapon Aiming Reticule | When armed with a ranged weapon, holding the RT Trigger / R2 Trigger will bring up a targeting reticule. |
| | The reticule is represented by a red X onscreen that indicates where the player's shot will be directed. |
| Timer | The timer is displayed in the upper right side of the screen only during times when it is required. It represents time in minutes and seconds in a mm:ss format. |
| | In instances where the player is required to hold out for a period of time, the timer starts at the maximum value and counts downward to 0:00, at which time it fades away after a brief pause. |
| | During Time Trial mode, the timer starts at a value of 0:00 and counts upward in real time until the player completes the level. |

# INDEX

Note to the reader: Throughout this index **boldfaced** page numbers indicate primary discussions of a topic. *Italicized* page numbers indicate illustrations.